E.A.R.L.

Ever Always Real Life

T0159663

E.A.R.L.

Ever Always Real Life

The Autobiography of
D M X

AS TOLD TO **SMOKEY D. FONTAINE**

DEY ST.
AN IMPRINT OF
WILLIAM MORROW *PUBLISHERS*

*Some of the names of individuals in this book have been changed to protect the innocent,
and several characters and scenes are composites.*

PHOTOGRAPHY AND IMAGE CREDITS
Photographs on pages 7, 8, 12, 15, 16, 17, 18, 19, 23, 24, 25, 28, 46, 57, 58, 66, and 103
courtesy of Arnett Simmons. Photographs on pages 16 (bottom), 22, 36, 44, 70, 113, 142, 143,
227, 243, and 290 courtesy of Smokey D. Fontaine. Photographs on pages 21, 33, 35, 42, 50,
91, 103, 114, and 211 courtesy of Ennis Addison. Images and photographs on pages 140, 145,
165, 179, 186, 199, and 233 courtesy of Superior. Images and photographs on pages 124, 133,
188, and 189 courtesy of Jack MacNasty. Photograph on page 101 courtesy of Shayla
Simmons. Photograph on page 106 courtesy of Collins Middleton. Photograph on page 160
courtesy of Autumn Martin.

All insert photographs courtesy of Jonathan Mannion, with the exception of the dog morph
photograph by Nitin Vadukul and the black-and-white family photograph by Anthony Cutajar.

Grateful acknowledgment is made for permission to reprint from "Silver Shadow" by David
Lewis and Wayne Lewis. Copyright 1984 (ASCAP) Almo Music Corp., o/b/o itself and
Jodaway Music. All rights reserved. Used by permission.

First paperback edition published 2003.

Designed by Adrian Leichter

The Library of Congress has catalogued the hardcover edition as follows:

DMX.
E.A.R.L.: the autobiography of DMX / as told to Smokey D. Fontaine.—1st ed.
p. cm.
Includes biographical references.
ISBN 0-06-018826-X (hc: alk. paper)
1. DMX. 2. Rap musicians—United States—Biography.
I. Title: EARL. II. Fontaine, Smokey D. III. Title.
ML420.D11 A3 2002
782.421649"092—dc21
[B]
2002068502

ISBN 0-06-093403-4 (pbk.)

21 22 23 ❖/LSC 30 29 28 27

Contents

Prologue

*To live is to suffer, but to survive, well, that's to find the
meaning in the suffering[1]*

If I don't know where I'm coming from, where would I go?[2]

ALL YOU SEE IS DUST, A THICK CLOUD OF REDDISH-BROWN
dust that follows him everywhere he goes. There is a trail out there in
the brush, a path through this jagged Arizona landscape that was cut
just for this purpose, but he chooses not to take it, preferring instead
to use his four-wheel all-terrain vehicle to forge a more entertaining
course up and over whatever rocks or giant cactus plants that may
stand in his way. The bike is supposed to be capable of off-roading at
over sixty miles an hour, but Earl Simmons is capable of anything.

"I'm having the time of my life right now," he says.

The whine of his engine almost drowns out his words, but the smile
says it all. Here's a man who's enjoying his life.

"Hi, Boo Boo!" he yells down the end of a miniature black cell
phone. "Boo Boo, I just wish you could see how beautiful the sky is
today."

The love of his life and wife of four years is home in New York
expecting their third child.

"But you know your man Patrick is out here looking like TJ again,"
he says, playfully changing the subject to his security guard's habit of
wearing tight jeans. "*And* he has his boots tied all the way up. . . ."

Earl will continue to ride well into the evening, until he's reminded
that a home-cooked dinner should be ready for him at the house that
he's rented and soon the local bars will be filling up with new people
he can win money from playing pool, but whatever time he chooses to
finish, odds are that his other most loyal companion will be waiting for
him.

"Phoenix!" he calls out to the black-and-white pit bull jumping
around hysterically in the back of the security truck. "What's up, girl?

Did you miss me?" The three-month-old puppy can't contain any of her enthusiasm for her new owner.

He play-fights with the dog for a minute and then puts her into the passenger seat of his convertible 2001 Mercedes-Benz. Earl's red Timberland boots, which were brand new before this ride, are covered in dust and sand, as are his matching sweatpants and white tank top, but he doesn't care. He reclasps the silver dog chain that he wears around his neck and without waiting for his bodyguards to pack up the equipment, jumps in his car, punches the accelerator, and quickly pulls onto the highway.

For Earl Simmons, the artist known to the world as DMX, this is a good day.

Or is it?

Seven miles up the highway I see Earl's car pulled off to the side of the road. The engine is still running and the door is flung open, but Earl has gone somewhere else. The flashing hazard lights do little to warn anyone of the trouble on his mind. There is nothing in the direction that he's walking, just a desert sky filled with the red and orange colors of sunset, and when I catch up to him, I realize that's all he's looking at.

"Do you ever have nightmares?" he asks. "I mean I have nightmares every night, dog. Every fucking night I have people rocking me to sleep in my dream, whispering, 'We love you DMX!' then they pull out burners and *pop pop!*"

The gunshots hang heavy in the air.

"This shit is crazy. When am I ever going to be able to just relax and be me?"

It's a question I've heard him ask before. A question he has yet to find an answer to, but a thirty-one-year ride can often kick up many troublesome thoughts, especially when under the questions, hiding there in the dark, there is the lingering idea that there's a price to be paid.

"There are just so many thoughts inside my head all the time."

A few weeks earlier, Earl Simmons agreed to tell the story of his life. It was a bold decision based on two ideas that have framed much of his music. First, that the only way to survive a lifetime of suffering was to uncover the meaning behind that suffering, and then, simply, if you don't know where you're coming from, where would you go? It's easier said than done.

> Places that I have been, things that I have seen
> What you call a nightmare, are what I have as dreams[3]

"Now that I have to replay everything, it gets hard to talk because the feelings come back and it's like I go through it again. Sometimes it makes me not want to say anything at all because I could fuck around and remember too much . . . "

The thought makes him pause, but then, slowly, purposefully, he keeps going.

"But I also know the more you think, the more you want to know, and I'm always going to ask questions. Who are you? What are you here for? It means something to ask yourself those things because it forces you to look inside the deepest, darkest corners of your life. There is a lockbox there, but if you ever allow yourself to open it, you will realize so much."

The sky has now turned purple, gray.

"So where should we start?" I ask, feeling for the recorder in my pocket.

"I don't know, dog. You're just going to have to catch it without catching it."

> Let me go my way, but walk with me
> See what I see, watch me, then talk with me[4]

This is the oral history of DMX.

PART I

ME AS A BABY

1

First Memories

My name is Earl Simmons. I was born December 18, 1970, in Mount Vernon, New York, the first and only child of Arnett Simmons and Joe Barker. I've always hated my first name because it always sounded so corny to me and no, I don't have any middle names. Why my mother couldn't give me the names of some of the other men she dated, I don't know. There were certainly enough of them around.

My mother found out she was pregnant with me when she was nineteen. It was bad because she already had a two-year-old, Bonita, and hadn't planned on having another baby. So she moved into this home for unwed mothers in Mount Vernon and asked her sister to take Bonita off her hands for a while because her "nerves were shot." My sister ended up staying with her until way after I was born while my mother tried to get her life together.

When I was one, my mother's mom died and even though she didn't grow up with her, my mother lost the only other person she felt she could look to for help. Laverne wouldn't take *both* of her kids, so my mother was forced to realize that she had to find a place of her own. Yonkers had more low-income housing than Mount Vernon, so that's where we went.

We lived in a small, dark, one-bedroom apartment in a building called the Roker. My mother was on public assistance and it was really hard for her to take care of us and pay all the bills and the rent at the same time. I was also sick a lot as a child. I inherited a bunch of allergies from her and bronchial asthma from my father. My shit used to be real bad. I remember many scary nights waking up not being able to breathe. My mother used to have to take me to the emergency room and they would often end up keeping me overnight. Sometimes my asthma got so bad they would keep me for a whole week and they never could find the right thing to do. One night I had to go back to the hospital *three* different times because the drugs they were sending me home with kept making me sick. Then the doctors would give me breathing treatments. I had to lie down in this crib-like bed that had a white net over it and they would pump in this medicated air. You couldn't move or get out and I remember being trapped in there having to just breathe in and out for hours. In the spring and summer I was under that net almost every week. I never knew if it helped or not. One time I had such a bad asthma attack my sister told me that my heart stopped beating and the paramedics had to take me out of my house in one of those sit-up stretchers because I almost died. I don't remember that, but I *do* remember the day I got hit by a car.

I was playing by myself in the street and found a dime. I was so excited; it was all silver and shiny. I immediately wanted to go to the store but the problem was that I knew I had to cross Riverdale Avenue to get there, and that was a pretty major trip for a kid my age.

But after a few seconds, I summoned up my courage and with a little burst of speed, made it across and got to buy what I wanted: a lollipop and a superball. You know those balls that bounce all crazy and go in different directions? *Yeah! I'm the man* . . .

It was on the way back that I caught it. The impact was so hard, I got knocked halfway up the street, all the way under a parked car. But for some reason, even though I was badly hurt, I didn't feel nothing. All I was thinking about was how my mother was going to whip my ass because I wasn't supposed to be outside.

When I tried to get up, this white lady with a clipboard was standing over me; she must have been checking parking meters or something.

"Stay down! Stay down!" she kept yelling.

ME AND MY SISTER BONITA

Then other people walked by and *they* started screaming. I can imagine how folks must have felt to see a little boy pushed under a car like that. Everyone crowded around and then somebody gave me a jacket to put under my head and I just lay on the street until the ambulance came.

Luckily, I didn't break anything, so I got better in a few weeks, but what hurt the most was when I found out later that I could have gotten some money from the accident. See, not only had the driver run a red light, but he was also drunk. A month after the accident an insurance company man had come to my house talking about a settlement and my mother turned down ten thousand dollars!

"Thank you, but we don't need your money, sir," my mother told him. "My family is Jehovah's Witness and our faith teaches us to be self-sufficient."

Huh? That was the loot that was supposed to be mine when I got older, the money I could have been straight with! Half of the kids in the ghetto get a little bit of money when they reach a certain age for something that happened to them when they were younger. Why not me? And if the insurance company was offering ten thousand dollars, my mother could have held out and got a lot more, too. Hitting a child, drunk driving, *and* running a red light? I didn't understand why Jehovah's Witness would have wanted to mess with my money, but the man obviously didn't wait for my mother to change her mind.

Before that I actually *liked* Jehovah's Witness as a kid. Ladies that my mother would get to baby-sit my sister and me would always take us to the different churches they went to, so I had experience with many kinds of religions growing up, but my mother said she liked the structure of Jehovah's Witness for us kids and I always enjoyed it when she took us to the local Kingdom Hall for service. I remember the little gold books of Bible stories they gave out and I used to read *The Watchtower* magazine a lot. In service they often asked questions about the reading and I remember one time I got up enough courage to raise my hand to answer one. The hall was mostly filled with adults that day, but the leader acknowledged me.

"Yes. The young brother right there," he said, walking up to me with the microphone. I don't remember the question, but whatever it was, I got it right.

"Excellent, young man. Excellent!"

That felt good. I used to like knowing the answer to shit.

But every few months my mother would take us to one of the conferences they used to have in this big stadium in upstate New York and I didn't like that as much because I used to get embarrassed when everyone else got to buy food from the concession stands and my sister and I had to eat the bag lunch we brought from home. Kids looked at us when we pulled out the sandwich with the bologna. That was like bringing lunch to school in a bag. It meant we were poor.

I did used to like the traveling part of those trips, though.

I can see clearly now, the rain is gone . . .

One family we sometimes rode with had a van. We would sit in front of their house before we left and open the van's doors so we could hear music off the radio.

. . . it's gonna be a bright, bright, sunshiny day[5]

It's crazy how different songs can bring you back to a certain memory. The Spinners' "I'll Be Around" reminds me of those days. My mom used to play that in the house on this old eight-track cassette deck that had these big gray buttons. I remember the tapes only had four songs on each side and I wanted to hear the Pointer Sisters or Chaka Khan all the time.

My mother sang. People actually used to say she sounded like Chaka. At one point she tried to start a singing career and joined this group. It was her, this woman Eileen, and these two other guys. They rehearsed at a club called Browneyes right down the street from the Roker. When my mother couldn't afford a baby-sitter she used to bring my sister and me with her and we would just sit up on the speaker. I remember the music was so fucking loud! She was with the group for over a year, but after they did a talent show at the Apollo, someone asked them to go on tour and that's when my mother dropped out. She told her partners that they'd have to find another singer because she didn't like the idea of shuttling her kids back and forth on the road. She never said anything to me about it, but I bet she probably regrets that decision to this day.

My moms used to be real nice looking. She had a pretty face, sexy smile, and a real attractive shape. And, yeah, she had that walk, too. When we were outside, dudes in the street used to always turn their heads to watch her go by. I used to hate that. I couldn't have been more than four years old when, on the way to nursery school, I started to hear guys on the corner hollering at her, "Hey, pretty lady. What's happening?"

My mother never answered them. She never even looked their way.

"Aaaah, you so hateful, you so hateful!" they used to yell.

I didn't know what the word "hateful" meant but I knew it was bad. I didn't want anybody to talk to my mother like that and after the third or fourth time I heard them say that to her, I suddenly got the urge to kill each and every one of them. Every time we walked by them I became more and more confident that I could do it. *I could kill a grown man.* All I had to do was jump on his back, choke him, and he'd be dead—obviously not understanding that he would have fucked me up at four years old, but I was sure I could do it. A couple of times I actually did turn around with the mean face on.

"Don't call my mother hateful!"

"Come on, boy, and shut your mouth," my mother would scold me. Then the guys would laugh and we'd keep walking. My mother never thought I meant anything by it, but I was dead serious. *She* was the one always explaining to me how I needed to take care of things. *She* was the one that told me I was the man of the house, so why wouldn't I have believed that it was my job to protect her?

I should have realized then that my mother was going to be on some bullshit. See, if I was the man of the house, I sure had a lot of company. And whenever my mother's boyfriends would come over, I always had to go to the store in the morning for bread, eggs, and cornflakes. It was always bread, eggs, and cornflakes. The guys would have rarely been there for more than that night, but I guess they needed their breakfast. Of course, I never got what I wanted to eat.

"I want the cereal with the sugar in it already because we don't have sugar upstairs!"

But my mother didn't hear me, and the guys didn't give a fuck. They got their pussy already.

I remember my sister's father, Charlie Mack. He always wore this blue mechanic's uniform. That meant that he had a little bit of money, because growing up in the projects you knew that anyone you saw with a uniform on had a good job.

Another dude was called Cookie. Can you imagine a nigga named Cookie? But he was all right. When he came over he made the best homemade bread. It tasted so good I wished I paid better attention to how he made it because he only ever used the ingredients that we had in the cabinets already. One Saturday morning before breakfast, Cookie actually walked with me to the store and I remember thinking how rich he was because he had money to pay for the food so I didn't have to use our food stamps. That was big. He scored even more points when he actually stayed the whole weekend. I thought maybe he really liked us. Then my hopes were dashed a few weeks later when I saw him outside on my way home. I was really happy to see him, thinking I could go over and ask him when he was coming to our apartment again to make some more bread. But when I walked over with this big smile on my face, he turned around and looked at me like he didn't even know me!

I couldn't believe it. I had watched TV with this guy all day. We had hung out, gone to the store. To see a man that you thought you knew, that you thought liked you . . . then he doesn't even speak to you on the street? That hurt. If I was older, I probably would have tried to kill him, too.

Looking back, I don't think my mother was too prepared to have kids. After me, she had two other sons, but they both died at birth. I was the only boy that she had and I've always thought how unlucky I was because, man, *did I catch it*. My mother beat me for every man that did her wrong, for every man that fucked her and left her. And I know she beat me because I reminded her of my father.

"You ain't shit, you're just like your father," she would say to me over and over again. See, my mother and father were never close, that's why she didn't give me his last name. They met at Yonkers High School a year or two before I was born and, by the time I happened, whatever relationship they had, had been dead for a while.

My father was a pretty cool cat in high school. He always had a lot of girlfriends. He was the kind of guy who got attention by doing something corny like wearing a suit to school, and he was a good artist. That's probably why him and my mother got together: He was the man and she was a dime. But despite what must have looked like a winning combination to anyone in the neighborhood, they never clicked beyond just having sex. He was only eighteen himself at the time and he didn't want my mother to have me. After I was born, he never thought about living in the house with us. He never called me on my birthday or helped raise me at all. That made it hard on my mother and she must have taken her frustration out on me because no matter what I did, I was always wrong. Bonita was the perfect child and I was the problem. My mother took a few judo classes, too, so she was good with her hands, and whenever she got tired of beating me, she would just call another nigga over to whup my ass.

When I was five, the guy I was named after hit me with an extension cord. His name was Earl Scott. He was the only one in the house with us at the time, and me and my sister were bored so I dripped hot candle wax on him while he was sleeping. When he got up, he just went crazy and started swinging on us. (My mother did get mad at that one, but that was only because he hit Bonita with the cord as well and her eye got real red and swollen.)

Another guy, Richie, was the mailman and you better believe he delivered more than mail. My stomach would get butterflies every time he came over because I knew he loved to administer the ass whippings. He would come in the house and my mother and him would go right in the bedroom. After they'd do whatever, then she would fill him in on everything my sister and I had done wrong— even shit that happened two weeks before.

I always asked my sister, "Why she got to tell him everything like that?" and when he came out with the belt, I knew it was on.

"Stand up. Stand up the both of you." I hated the sound of his voice. "Now bend over."

He gave out a certain amount of hits per offense. It was like military style.

"Bonita, for not finishing the dishes, you get two hits. Earl, because you slammed the door and have been acting up, you get five . . ."

Bam! Bam!

If you moved, he'd start from one again.

Bam! Bam! Bam!

It was the worst.

Bonita always started crying watching me get mine after her. But my mother always gave my sister a hug and told her to go to the bedroom. I remember my mother sending me away after Richie finished with me, too. I just don't remember the hug part.

2

Our Side of the World

IN 1975, WHEN I WAS FOUR YEARS OLD, MY MOTHER finally found a nice place of her own in building 80 of the School Street apartment complex. The project would soon become one of the most dangerous and neglected areas in all of Yonkers, but for us, coming from the cramped and lonely space of the Roker, moving to School Street was a definite step up.

Building 80, like the rest of School Street, was all black and Hispanic. Yonkers was filled with white people, but you would never know it if you didn't go to their side of the world. There was only one white person in our building and of course he was married to a black lady. He was the maintenance man responsible

THE FAMILY

for everything from our heat and hot water (which was often cold) to the elevators (always broken) and the stairways (that were covered in piss, broken glass, and tobacco spit). An all-black and Hispanic building having to call a white person to get any kind of service was fucked up, but that's just how things were in the 'hood.

The bugged-out thing about Yonkers, New York, though, was that the ghetto was in the best area of the city. Living in buildings that sit on or close to the waterfront, directly across from the New Jersey Palisades, most of the poor folks in Y-O had a much better view across the Hudson River than the rich people in Yonkers did that lived mostly further to the east. I don't know how that happened, but life for us was still crazy.

There were six sets of projects on this side of Yonkers and they were all different: School Street and Slow Bomb ("Schlobaum Houses") were your typical high-rise units. Then there were the more country-looking low-rise projects like Mulford Gardens and Cottage. The better-kept buildings of Ravine stretched a long way and didn't feel like projects because of their unobstructed view of the river, and while Warburton Avenue, where my grandmother ended up, was not one specific place, the part of the

SCHOOL STREET PROJECTS

block that led all the way down to South Broadway was considered its own 'hood. (And there weren't just black 'hoods to deal with; in Yonkers you could find Puerto-Rican 'hoods, Mexican 'hoods, Arabic 'hoods, even Italian 'hoods.)

In the middle of all of that mess was Getty Square, the only "downtown" area Yonkers had, which, until about midnight when things got grimier, was filled with the normal hustle and bustle of any big shopping area.

I've always thought there was a black cloud over Yonkers. A big curse that attached itself to anyone who grew up there, because some-how any ghetto I've seen anywhere in the world reminds me of a place in Y-O. Anytime I travel I always go looking for a feel for the community, a sense of the people, and I end up saying, "Oh, this looks like Mulford," or "This reminds me of Ravine." And even though Yonkers is one of the biggest cities in New York State, growing up everybody knew everybody. There were a lot of big families with even bigger extended families and we were all interconnected. Nothing could go down on one side of town without someone knowing about it on the other before the day was out.

FIRST GRADE

It was the same in the house. My favorite thing about living in School Street was that I could hear everything that was going on in the neighbors' apartments. There were ten families to a floor and because of how all the heat and hot water systems were connected, it was hard for anyone to keep their business to themselves.

A girl named Yeta lived below me on the tenth floor. I could hear her getting her ass whipped all the time. I'd be chilling in my bedroom and then out of the blue I'd hear, "Ahhh! I told ya, I told ya," coming through the pipes as loud as if it was happening in my own room. It was the funniest thing in the world. (Mothers tend to repeat themselves a lot when they're whipping ass. "Didn't I say . . . didn't I say . . . didn't I say?!" they scream without ever completing the sentence. *Well, what the fuck did you say, lady?*) But when I teased Yeta about it the next morning, her and her friends would always remind me of my "Oh, Momma, no, Momma, no!" cries they heard when *I* was getting it.

"Yeah, but you got fucked up last night, too!" they'd tell me.

The apartment was my mom's first real place of her own, the first place she really cared about living in, and once we were there, she began the slow process of getting herself off public assistance to try to build a better life. The first thing she did was get a new couch. It was so much more comfortable than the ugly maroon futon we had to sit on in the Roker. It was a big, green fluffy thing and whenever she had a camera she always told me to sit on it so she could take a picture.

Breakfast was my favorite meal at home and I used to love pancakes, especially when my mother cut them up in even squares

UGLY MAROON COUCH IN THE ROKER   BIGGER COUCH IN SCHOOL STREET

for me. I liked them so much I didn't even mind when she put corn in the batter so that they'd be extra filling and hold us down till dinner. I tried to make them myself, too, but my mother said I never cooked them all the way through. If she didn't let me make pancakes, sometimes she would give me money to go to the store to buy honey buns instead. I would heat them up in the oven and serve them with butter. First we would say grace, then my sister and I would climb in the bed with her and we'd all eat together.

My mother always loved it when I got up to make her some tea.

"Baby, fix me a cup of tea," I'd say in this high-pitched voice, imitating Eddie Murphy's *Delirious* routine. She'd laugh. It was like the best of times.

Even though I had my own room in School Street, it never really felt like that because somehow I would always end up having to sleep on the floor in the living room. That was mostly because of my mother's younger brother, Robert.

Uncle Pinky we called him, and he was a smooth brother when he was young. He was the only one in the family I remember who ever had a car. It was a metallic blue Cadillac Coupe de Ville and one time he took me for a ride downtown in it. But he was never a hustler. In the early seventies, hustling wasn't big money and Pinky was more the fixing type anyway. He liked to work on cars or stoves or TVs. Any-

thing you needed done, Pinky could do it. He was the local handyman. It was hard work, but it always kept a few dollars in his pocket and my uncle stayed with a job.

But if he always had a job, then the other thing he always had was a new baby mother. Uncle Pinky was always bringing women around my mother's house.

"Hey, Earl, I want you to meet my old lady . . . " he'd say before asking my mom if him

and his girl could stay for a few days. First I would have to meet the girl, then I would have to meet all my new cousins. There was Li'l Robert. Then Li'l Li'l Robert. I have a cousin named Damien. None of his chicks ever agreed to sleep on the couch, though, and that's how they ended up in my bedroom and I ended up on the living room floor.

For a time, I didn't give a fuck. It was more like an adventure.

UNCLE PINKY

Yeah, now I got the run of the house all night. The kitchen was right off the living room and with new people in the house I could eat what I wanted and blame it on them. I just had to make sure everyone saw me go to the fridge *before* they went to sleep.

"I'm so full, Momma, I think I'm just going to go to bed," I would announce real loud. In the morning when my mother noticed that the last two slices of bread were gone, then I hit her with, "You know *I* didn't do it,

Momma, because you remember I was full when I went to bed, right?" If my face was serious enough, I would get away with it, thinking about that extra cheese sandwich I had in the bottom of my stomach.

But when Pinky's few days turned into a month and I was *still* on the living room floor? Then it got annoying because then I had to deal with the mice and the roaches. I didn't mind the roaches, I really didn't. They would walk on you, but just normally keep going because they were always boogying somewhere, and if you realized one was on you, you could just knock him off like it was nothing. Roaches never really mean to fuck with you. Occasionally, you'd get a stupid one that would stay around, but that's probably because you had some crumbs in the blanket or something and he was hungry. But mice always liked to run around you, and they made *a lot of fucking noise*. I could never get to sleep with them about. (Sometimes during those nights on the floor, I actually saw roaches that were as big as mice! They were dark brown and had wings. They bit, too. But their bites didn't itch, so I didn't care. If you bite me and I itch, you're a pain in the ass. If you bite me and I don't itch, what the hell? Forget about it.)

People often said Uncle Pinky and me looked alike and as a kid I really admired him. It didn't hurt his image with me that he was always getting pussy, constantly fucking in my room. There was no lock on my bedroom door, so in the morning I would walk in there and see him and his girl laid up, legs hanging out all crazy.

Oh . . . You guys were doing something!

I just couldn't figure out why the room smelled like cornflakes—*soggy cornflakes*. You know when you leave your bowl on the table for like three hours and the flakes get all stuck to the sides? That's what pussy used to smell like to me.

"I know what you guys are doing," I can remember thinking when I caught him in the room for the third time, "that's the soggy cornflake thing!"

Needless to say, it didn't take long for me to be right up under him. I wanted to do everything he did, go everywhere he went.

There was a problem, though, a major problem. My mother would never let my sister or me go outside. It was one of her rules when we moved to School Street. She said that because we lived up so high, if something went down while we were playing outside, it would take her too long to get down to see what was going on, so we had to stay in the house—*all afternoon*. Even though Bonita was two years older than I was, it didn't matter. Unless we were running an errand or going to the store, neither of us was ever allowed to leave the apartment.

That made me so mad because they had built a new park around the corner from our building and I couldn't even go to it. *But all the other kids were there.* The only way my sister and I could go was if my mother took us herself and that didn't happen very often.

So first I would just constantly joke and run around inside the house or try to play games with anyone who came over, but I didn't get away with that for too long.

BUILDING 80

"What are you doing, Earl? Stop that! Go sit down somewhere."

Realizing I had to find ways to entertain myself, then I started playing with those little green plastic army men all the time. I would line them up and have them fight each other in imaginary wars. Then I took it further. I figured out if I got one of those thin, clear plastic bags from the supermarket that they used for fruit and tied the handles together with string, I could make a parachute for them. Being eleven floors up, if I dropped the little guy out the window and got enough air under the bag, he would float like a charm. (With practice, I found out that it worked better if you cut the plastic bag in half before you tied it to him.) I was so into it, one time I spent a whole week making paratroopers and paper airplanes. Then I matched them up and sent the whole squadron out of the window one by one. That was fun.

But toy cars were my favorite. I could play with them for hours. It didn't matter if they were the small Matchbox collectibles or the larger ones that you could put your foot in and push yourself around.

(School Street's hallways were pretty slippery and I always ended up busting my ass in those.) And I especially loved anything that had a remote control. I had this one remote control pickup truck that I figured out a way to fasten other model cars to and it would still run. I remember I attached a *Dukes of Hazzard* General Lee body to it and it sat right on the top. It looked so hot. I loved that pickup truck because the steering wheel would actually turn and I could maneuver it all around the house.

Sometimes Pinky would leave one of his women alone for a minute and play with me and my cars. That was cool. Until, of course, my mother would say it was getting too late to play over other people's heads. Sometimes he'd try to argue with his sister, telling her it was only six o'clock and still light outside, but it rarely worked. Our game was over.

The fact that Pinky stuck up for me added to the love that I felt for him. He was probably the only man around I had any respect for, but no matter what he did, he would never be my father.

The only time I saw my father was when he took me to New York City with him to sell his paintings. See, my pops was an artist. He painted watercolors of street scenes and sold them at local fairs or malls. Art was his passion and

MY HALLWAY

22

he spent his entire life working on it. He was so committed to his craft that even during the times he wasn't making any money, he always refused to do anything else. One time, instead of getting another job, my father chose to go homeless and live in Central Park for a few weeks because he refused to do anything else besides paint. That was just what he loved to do.

When we went down-town I remember there was always a whole line of people up against a black gate. Each of them had different blankets set up on the sidewalk where they would sell their books, or toys, or different kinds of gadgets. It was always a warm day, too, most likely spring or summertime, and I remember always eating a bag of fresh roasted peanuts—probably

ME AND MY FATHER

because that was all he could afford to get me to eat. When we got there my father would introduce me to his artist friends like, "Yeah, this is my boy." I really enjoyed it because the people would actually seem happy to meet me. "Oh wow, man," they would say, and then shake my hand and smile. I felt glad that I was a part of something. It was different than what I was used to at home, it was like the real world, the part of the world I never got to see, and I never wanted to leave.

Being with my father was what got me started drawing. By the time I was six, the walls of my room were covered with pictures I had made. I used to look at the characters in *Mad* magazine and just copy them into my notebook. I used pencil or this set of colored drawing pens that my aunt Vern had given me. I never used tracing paper. If I was going to do it, I had to do it for real. I got really good with faces and my sister used to always ask me to draw her. She would just sit across from me in the living room and I would get busy.

When I got older, I started doing more stuff. One time I made this stencil of a woman's profile out of wood. I gave her earrings shaped like the African continent and this red, black, and green scarf. The scarf was checkered and it took me forever to fill it all in because you had to burn the design into the wood before you painted it.

I think I only went downtown twice with my father, but those trips really meant a lot to me. He was my father and even though I didn't know him, I liked spending that time with him. He was good for just popping up out of the blue, though. One time he arrived at the door to our apartment in School Street and told my mother that he was there to walk me to school.

That was my first day of kindergarten, September 1976.

I WAS A PRETTY GOOD ARTIST.

3

From Bright to Bored

Which would you rather have: ten you found
   or five you earned?
Became a man at six 'cause at five you learned
To take nothing for granted except death
Man of the house 'cause you the last nigga left[6]

THERE ARE TWO WORDS THAT COME TO MIND WHENEVER I
think of my time spent in elementary school. The first one was *bright*.

"Your son is extremely bright," I would hear teachers tell my
mother during their parent-teacher conferences. Or I would see

"Very Bright" written in the comments section of my report card. I didn't know what the term meant, let alone that it was something positive. What do you mean "bright"? Is there a lightbulb over my head like in the cartoons?

The second word I heard used to describe me was "manipulative."

"Earl is very manipulative, Mrs. Simmons."

I figured that one wasn't so good.

As a kid, I loved to read. I was just so into words. I loved to read all of the Dr. Seuss books and books like *Where the Wild Things Are* that had all those funny-looking monsters with the giant heads. I was into any books that had to do with dinosaurs.

For most of my time in elementary school, the principal put me in this advanced reading class that had only six or seven kids. In the morning I would go to my regular class but then every day at a certain time another teacher would take me and a group of kids into the old music room where we would do more advanced work. I was in advanced classes. Bonita was in special ed.

I remember my third-grade teacher, Mrs. Smith, one of those black, no-nonsense types. She was short, kept her hair in a bun, and wore the tight face that said *no bullshit*. She would always pull me and some of the other kids aside and be like, "Listen boys, you got it harder 'cause you black and I'm not going to let you make a fool of yourselves in front of this class." You could tell she cared about you by those talks.

"Earl, I know your momma raised you better than that," she would tell me whenever I was messing around. She was the only teacher I ever had that did that and I always did good in her class.

Ever since I first learned how to read I was a big spelling nut and every Tuesday Mrs. Smith would have a spelling bee. If you won the spelling bee, not only would your name go up on the bulletin board, but she would buy you a wedge sandwich around the corner from Landy's Deli. Now every kid in Yonkers knew about Landy's wedges. You were the shit if you came to school with food from there. It was like having a pair of Pro-Keds sneakers on, or something, because the sandwiches were so damn good. The bread was always soft and the tomatoes were sliced real thin. They added just the right amount of oil and vinegar.

While some of the kids had the money to buy their lunch from there anyway and others always had money to buy extra things in the lunchroom, I had nothing. All I had was one big lunch ticket that they'd punch holes in every day that meant all I could eat was the exact food the school gave out. No cookies, no ice cream, no chocolate milk. If I was lucky, my mother would give me some crackers to bring from home, but all she would ever buy would be the nasty, unsalted kind. I hated those. So the spelling bee was big. It was the chance for me to be the best in the class *and* eat like the kids who had money. Every week I sat in my room and memorized each and every one of those words. It was hard, but I liked to do it and once I learned a word, I never forgot it.

Because I spent all week studying and knew all of the words by heart, week after week none of the other kids could beat me. It got to the point where every Tuesday I would go to school looking forward to a Landy's wedge and after a few months my spelling got so good I could spell almost *anything*. I remember I used to know how to spell "Empire State Building." I thought it was one whole word, but I knew all the right letters.

"Momma, can I tell you something?"

When my mother had company, I used to try to wait for a good time to go into the living room.

"What is it, Earl?"

"Momma, I can spell 'Empire State Building!'"

When my mother heard me call her, she'd stop whatever it was she was talking about for a second, but never really turned her head all the way around to look at me.

"Oh, that's nice, baby. Now go to your room, okay, because grown folks are talking."

"But Momma, I can sp—"

"Go to your room, Earl!"

It was like she couldn't be bothered, like I was always interrupting her. I just wanted to tell her what I knew, to show her how I was doing good in school. What the hell was wrong with that? It was like my moms didn't give a fuck and I guess that's why she never made me feel like I was worth anything. But I couldn't understand that. I couldn't understand that because I was good. *I was a good motherfucking kid* . . .

· · · · ·

As the third grade went on, I started getting bored. The challenge of the spelling bees came only once a week and the other days I just got tired of doing what felt like the same work over and over again. Nothing in school inspired me and after I learned all of the material and finished all of the assignments they gave me, I didn't have anything else to do.

One afternoon Mrs. Smith pulled me aside to ask me why I seemed so unmotivated, but I told her that I was doing everything that she gave me to do. If I'm still going to get 100 percent, why should I do any more than I have to? If it only takes me 60 percent effort to get 100 percent results, why should I do 80? It was like when I finished taking a test ahead of everybody else she wanted me to just sit there with my hands folded and my pencil down. I wasn't supposed to do anything, I wasn't supposed to look at nobody, but there was another half an hour left.

Oh no. I can't just sit here. Especially after I'd just taken a test and my mind was thirsty? I had to do something. So first I'd wait about ten more minutes to see if anyone else would finish so that I'd have a partner. Then, if no one was done, I'd just say fuck it . . . it's spitball time.

Splat. I'd hit a kid in the front of the class on the back of the neck. As soon as he'd turn around, I'd put my head down like I was sleeping.

Splat. Splat. I'd hit him again and then he'd get mad and tell Mrs. Smith but she wouldn't know who hit him. Then as soon as she turned around again, I'd sneak an eraser off the blackboard and throw it across the room.

"EARL!"

"What's up? It wasn't me, Mrs. Smith."

After I started throwing erasers, it wasn't long before I quickly became the wildest nigga in school. I used to just zap out, do the things that made other kids say "Oh, shit!" when they weren't supposed to say "Oh shit!" Then I would stab them with a pencil. That really made them curse.

Mrs. Smith would punish me by keeping me after school. Three or four times a week I would have to stay in her class an extra half an hour for detention. But that didn't bother me. I didn't want to be home anyway, and I found out that after school was a great time to steal.

See, most of my classmates' parents didn't allow their children to have toys. But the rich kids would buy them anyway so they could show them off in the cafeteria.

"Look what I got . . . the new red Matchbox!"

Since their parents would find the cars if they brought them home, they'd leave them in their desks at school, so during detention, when the teacher would go to the office or step out to have a cigarette, I would just raid their desks and grab all of the toys I could find. The next day, the kids would know it was me that took them because I was the only one who had to stay after, but they couldn't say anything because they weren't supposed to have them in the first place—and I'd probably spit on 'em for snitching.

After a while, some of the smarter kids thought they could hide their goods after school without me noticing. *But I saw you. I saw you try to hide that Matchbox in your desk behind your notebook. Now all I got to do is wait you out. I bet you go home before me, punk, and when you leave, your car is mine!*

It was like I was a step ahead of everyone around me. Teachers, too. One time I actually had the main office believing that I had moved, that I had a different address and phone number so that they could never find my mother to tell her what I was doing. When my mother finally came to the school wondering why she hadn't got any letters from them in a while, they told her, "Well, Earl looked so sincere . . ."

I understand why School 18 had no idea what to do with me. To them there were just supposed to be good, smart kids and bad, dumb ones, but I wasn't either of those. One year I remember they tried to leave me back because of my bad behavior, but they couldn't do it when my mother reminded them that I was the top student in my class. When they kept arguing with her about it she had me IQ-tested and when my scores came back higher than some kids that were two and three years older than me, they had to promote me.

But the smarter I got, the more bored I got. And the more bored I got, the more trouble I caused. Then no one cared how smart I was. It was a fucked-up cycle and through it all, I just felt that I wasn't being heard. I wasn't being allowed to fly.

One day I didn't go home after school. Me and this kid named Baron had detention together and afterwards he invited me over to his house. He had a pretty sister, so first we hung out with her, then we went to the supermarket, stole some gum, and stayed outside to play. After a few hours running around we found this big car tire in this garage near his house. It was already after dark and I had never been out this late by myself before but we were having so much fun rolling the tire up and down up this little hill, watching it crash into things, I didn't want to stop. It was a school night. I had a pocket full of gum . . . a tire . . . freedom. *Fuck the world, man!*

Then we saw the flashing lights of a police car. There weren't any street lights where we were playing, so the blue and red colors lit up everything. I thought the police were coming to mess with us for the tire until I saw my mother in the backseat.

"Oh, shit, *we're in trouble!*"

My mother was scared to death. She had been looking for me since four o'clock and had made the cops drive her around all of Yonkers. When they passed this street, she caught a glimpse of a little boy playing with a tire and just knew it was me.

"Let me outta here, let me outta here!" she started screaming. "That's my baby."

The cops got out first.

"Do you know how much you scared your mother, Earl?"

I shook my head.

Then they asked me if I wanted to go home and I shook my head again. I could see the belt curled up in my mother's lap.

As soon as he saw the cops, Baron had run back around the corner to his house. I wished I was him.

The cops saw how upset my mother was so they tried to calm her down before they told me to get in the car, but when I got in the backseat, instead of being scared of her, I just saw how upset she looked. She was shaking. Her eyes were red from crying. *Oh shit, my mother does care about me.*

When we got home, my uncle Pinky was sitting on the couch.

"Don't whip him, 'Nett," he said to her after she told him what had happened. "Just talk to him."

And that's what she did. My mother brought me into the kitchen and sat me in front of the stove. We always kept our oven door open to help heat the apartment and I can remember feeling the hot air hitting me on my back.

"I'm just so glad to see that you're okay, baby. You had me so scared, Earl . . . So I'm not going to do anything to you this time, okay? I'm just happy to see you."

Then she paused and stared me right in my face.

"But if you *ever* do that again, I'm gonna . . ."

Two days later, I did it again.

I was in that new park I always wanted to go to around the corner from our building. It was about 7 P.M. Stupid me for being there.

As a child, anytime I did something wrong, I used to feel like I had to go to the bathroom. I don't know what it was, but when I knew I was in trouble I had to pee bad as a motherfucker. I guess I was just nervous. That day I almost peed all over my pants. First my mother beat me in the park; then she beat me all the way home, making me stop on each corner so she could get all of her hits in.

When we got home she got the stick.

"You're a big man now, right? You wanna stay out late like this?"

She was standing over me in the hallway, hitting me in my chest.

"You're a big man now, right?"

"No, Momma, no!"

"You out this late, you must be doing something. So where's my money? Huh?"

"No, Momma. I'm not doing nothing!"

"Yes, you are. Yes you are, because you're a big man now. Where's my money, Earl?"

She stopped when the stick caught me in the face.

I used to stay getting beatings. Extension cords, hangers, brooms. My sister used to always cry, yell at my mother to stop, but Mom never did. After a while it became normal. If that's all you know as a kid, you get used to it. It's just your life.

I stayed wanting to play outside, though. Everybody else got to play outside. *Why do I have to go straight home, upstairs, in the fucking house? Fuck you. I wanna do what the rest of the kids get to do. Let me live, lady.*

"But we ain't like everybody else!"

My mother always swore we were better than somebody. The funny thing was, in the neighborhood, *I* was the kid who was the problem.

"I don't want you with that boy . . . " my mother always told me.

Yeah, okay. His mother don't want him with me either. So we're even.

My mother didn't understand that parents got scared of kids they never saw outside, because that's what they used to do with crazy kids: keep them in the house. As a parent, after a whole year of not seeing a kid outside that you know lives in the building, it's only natural to get nervous.

"Make sure you don't play with that Earl, something ain't right with him," I used to hear parents tell their kids all the time, or my friends used to come up to me and tell me, "My momma said I can't play with you no more." After a while, only the homeless kids around School Street could fuck with me, or the kids with the parents who were high, or didn't give a fuck.

By this time, my father had disappeared, too, so I couldn't complain to him about my mother's rules. At first he would call to say he was taking me to New York and then never show up. Then he just stopped calling altogether. I had a feeling something was going on. My mother said it was because he met another woman, a white woman who lived on Woodworth Street. My moms was never what my father wanted and living with my mom, I knew the feeling was mutual so I couldn't have expected them to be together, but I took my father's leaving real hard.

4

The Hollaway House

LIFE FOR ME WAS VERY DIFFERENT AT 19 LAMARTINE Terrace. That's because the house belonged to Mary Ella Hollaway, my grandmother. My father was one of her eleven kids (eight boys and three girls) and was the first to add another baby to the family, so I was her first grandson.

MY GRANDMOTHER'S HOUSE ON LAMARTINE

Since everyone else lived in the projects or tiny apartments, Grandma's house was the home base for my father's side of the family and I knew that anytime I could make it over there, four or five of my aunts and uncles would be there, too. Needless to say, I wanted to take the bus to Grandma's as much as I could. Most of my aunts (Rhonda, Raquela) and uncles (Jarvis, Buckeye) were much older than I was, but two of my uncles—Collins (we called him Collie or BJ) and Kisley (better known as Buzzy)—were a little younger than me so the three of us became like brothers. Part of the reason I loved going over to my grandmother's house was that I knew I could hang out with them, and *we were allowed outside to play.* I also lived without fear of constant whippings. Since I was my grandmother's baby, she rarely punished me and since she also had bad asthma like I did, whenever I had trouble breathing, Grandma would take care of me and even let me sleep in her bed when I wanted to. She worked as a nurse in the New Rochelle Hospital and whenever I thought I was getting an attack she used to watch over me all night. Grandma was disappointed that her son wasn't taking better care of me, but that didn't matter. Grandma always took care of her baby.

My grandmother didn't like my mother very much. She didn't like the way she was raising me, didn't like all the beatings. I used to hear the two of them arguing about me on the telephone. My grandmother felt my mother should be doing more, felt that if she just paid attention and went up to School 18 more often to check on me, I wouldn't have so many problems. My mother would get mad and say that she couldn't go up to my school every day because she had to work and ultimately told my grandmother to mind her business and worry about her own kids. "What is *your* son doing to help?" she used to always tell her.

But I felt loved at my grandmother's house. I can remember the gospel music playing on Sunday morning when I woke up, my grandmother singing "Amazing Grace." And even though I never saw my father over there, Grandma's felt like the place I was supposed to be. It was also the place to find the best Sunday dinner.

My great-grandmother, Irene, and Aunt Raquela would spend all of Sunday morning making plates and plates of food, and by mid-afternoon the entire Hollaway family would be over talking loud and watching football. Grandma always let everyone bring their friends over for the meal so it was a full house. There'd be all kinds of gossip going down, shit-talking about so-and-so's boyfriend or girlfriend. My uncle Collie would always start banging on the table, impatient to start eating. Then he'd get in trouble and have to wait till last. It felt like family, *real family.*

But Sunday dinners weren't just special for me, they were also the hot ticket in the neighborhood because cats knew that if they went to Mrs. Hollaway's house they would get to eat *good.* So throughout the afternoon and evening, people would come over with their hat in their hand. All they had to do was know one of us and right away my grandmother would invite them into the kitchen. As long as you were hungry, she would feed you. (That's probably why I do the same to this day. If I see anyone on the street who's hungry, I'll give them whatever money they need to buy a sandwich or get a meal.)

My mother rarely let me stay at my grandmother's for more than a weekend, but me, Collie, and Buzzy made sure we made the most of our time together. If we weren't staying up all night watching *Godzilla* movies or *Saturday Night Live,* betting each other over who could be the man and stay awake the longest, we'd be playing "Truth or Dare"—although I don't ever remember any truths being told. I was always the "double dare" man, constantly challenging the two of them to try something crazier or more dangerous. Because I was a year older, I was bigger than both of my uncles at the time, taller and probably stronger, too, so I had an unfair advantage when it came to anything physical—and I was more reckless.

When my grand-mother left Lamar-tine Terrace for a larger house on Warburton Avenue a few blocks away, there was a back balcony that stuck out about ten feet from the top of the garage. It wasn't far to jump

321 WARBURTON AVENUE

but there was a long drop if you slipped. That was a dare that Collie and Buzzy always lost but I would jump across like it was nothing because I knew that the ability to make it across wasn't the issue, it was more the fear of falling and at twelve years old, at least around my peers, that was something I was quickly losing.

My grandmother may not have been as strict or as physical as my mother was but she did know how to teach a child a lesson.

MY FAVORITE JUMP

The whole time she lived on Lamartine, she told all the kids in the house not to go into the neighbors' yards. The houses on the block were built very close together so it was easy to end up running around on someone else's property, but Grandma was adamant.

We had our own place to play and that's where we needed to stay. As a kid, I was fascinated by all different kinds of insects: flies, mosquitoes, roaches. I was just curious about them, how they moved around with their tiny bodies and little legs. I always wanted to catch them and see if I could make them drink or eat something. (Experimenting one day, I learned that if you put two cockroaches in a jar with a wet napkin and a small piece of hot dog, suddenly you will see little white things all over the place: Those are baby roach eggs!) Outside, there was nothing more fascinating to me than a butterfly. They were just so beautiful. So many colors, the way they danced in the air; and one afternoon sitting on my grandmother's back porch, I saw a huge one fly right by me. It must have been the largest one I had ever seen.

I had to catch it.

I chased that butterfly all over our backyard, then up and around to the front of the house and down the sidewalk. It just kept darting around out of my reach. But I couldn't give up. I chased it around to the back of the house again, over the back porch, and then . . . into the neighbor's yard.

"Earl!"

My grandmother saw me and started yelling.

"Earl, come here now!"

But I almost had it.

"EARL, IF YOU DON'T GET YOUR BEHIND . . ."

Just as my grandmother was about to come and get me, I caught it. Holding that butterfly in between my two hands as gently as I could, I ran back to the house and raced past my grandmother into the kitchen. I could feel it twitching in my palms.

"But, Grandma, look what I caught!"

"That's very nice, Earl. But you know what I told you about going into other people's yards."

"What? I wasn't in nobody's yard."

"Earl, you know what I told you about going into other people's yards . . ."

"Yes, Grandma."

That was the first time my grandmother ever put her hands on me, but I didn't care. All I could think about was that butterfly. Once my spanking was over, I quickly found an empty spaghetti sauce jar to put the butterfly in. She was really big so I had to crumple her wings a little bit to fit her into the jar, but I did it. She was so beautiful. I couldn't stop staring at her. Collie and Buzzy were very impressed.

That night I put the jar next to my bed and went to sleep happy.

When I opened my eyes the next morning, the first thing I did was lean over to inspect my prize and then I saw something terrible.

"Oh, no. Please, no . . ."

Her wings, which were thick and bright the night before had lost their color and had fallen flat. And she wasn't moving. I tried to shake the jar to get the insect moving again, but it was no use. When my grandmother heard me screaming, she came running into the room.

"Grandma, look what happened!" I cried.

She looked at me, looked at my jar, then put her hand on my shoulder.

"Baby, did you put holes in the top of that thing?"

I was crushed. I couldn't believe that I had forgotten to do that.

37

Because of how excited I was when I caught it, because all I was thinking about was how cool it was to have, I didn't even give that butterfly a chance to live. Now my butterfly was dead. Grandma tried to console me, but I cried and cried. Being selfish, I had fucked around and killed the most beautiful thing I had ever seen in my life.

```
If you love something, let it go
If it comes back to you, it's yours
If it doesn't, it never was . . . Hold me down, baby⁷
```

5

Earl v. the Board of Education

BY THE MIDDLE OF THE FIFTH GRADE, SCHOOL 18 STILL DID not know what to do with me. It was like the higher I scored on tests, the further I threw the eraser, and after I left Mrs. Smith's class, none of my teachers ever took me aside anymore. There were no one-on-ones or heart-to-heart conversations, they just punished me and sat me in the back or sent me to the office. I guess my teachers felt it was too much trouble to get into my head and figure out what was wrong. Not that it would have been easy.

School 18 was no more than your typical ghetto school and in Yonkers, the only city in America to have not abided by *Brown v. the Board of Education* and desegregated their public schools, it was hard to find good teachers. The best teachers rarely come to teach poor black kids.

But it was the school's main office that started to notice how often I seemed to come into the building with a busted lip, or couldn't sit down because of the welts on my behind. One day when my lip was badly swollen, they pulled me into a meeting with the guidance counselor and asked me what happened.

"I got a beating, what do you mean what happened?" I answered them.

"This is not the first time that you've come to school this way, Earl, so we would like to take a look at you."

When the nurse pulled up my shirt, she saw bruises on my back and on my arms. There were marks going down the back of my legs. That was when the court started talking about taking me away.

My mother said that if I just stopped being bad, she wouldn't have to punish me so much. She just didn't know how to get me from doing wrong. So it was suggested that she take me to see a child psychologist and the next week we went downtown to see a man who worked out of St. Mary's Church next to the hospital. It was cool to miss school, but we left the house really early in the morning and it felt strange. Everything was so quiet.

When we got there the guy talked to my mom first and I sat in the waiting room. He had a lot of toy cars laid out on the table and I started playing with them while I waited. When he came out to take me into his office, he asked me if I wanted one of the cars. I got excited because I had been having fun playing with this big red fire truck. It was bigger and nicer than the other plastic ones on the table and I thought about how I could take it home and add it to my collection of paper airplanes and little green army men.

"Yeah, I would like this one," I said.

"*Which* one do you want?"

"This one . . ."

The man looked at my mother and smiled.

"Ooooh, you can't have that one, Earl. Why don't you take one of the smaller cars?"

I started crying right away. I mean, why did he ask me if he wasn't going to give me the one that I wanted? Right then and there I decided he was full of shit and I don't know if that was the only reason, but although we went there a few more times, I never spoke to that man about anything.

After that, my mother felt she had no other options for me and by the end of the fifth grade, I had thoroughly zapped out. I was fighting all the kids, throwing chairs at teachers. I just didn't care about anything, so I took it as far as I could. The worst thing a teacher could do was to try to restrain me.

"Don't fucking touch me! Are you crazy? I'll fucking kill you, you flat-ass, coffee-drinking bitch! I hate when my mother touches me.

Get your hands off me, you motherfucker . . . FUCK YOU!!!"

"We think next year, instead of coming back here . . ."

School 18 had had it. The judge told my mother that since she was incapable of keeping me out of trouble, the courts had to intervene and so I was sent to Julia Dyckman Andrus Children's Home, a school/dormitory facility about twenty minutes away from our house. The term was eighteen months.

It was the beginning of my incarceration. I was ten years old.

JULIA DYCKMAN ANDRUS CHILDREN'S HOME

6

Three Meals a Day *and* a Snack

IT WAS THE LAST DAY OF SCHOOL THE FIRST TIME I WENT TO Andrus. It was hot, the sun was shining. I remember standing on the corner waiting for the cab to come pick me and my mother up, watching all the kids come home from school. For the final few weeks of the school year, School 18 had sent me home with a tutor who used to come to my apartment on School Street to teach me my lessons, so I hadn't seen any of the other kids in a while. They were all laughing and joking around. Their arms were filled with the books and papers they had from clearing out their desks for the summer and I was sad I couldn't be with them. Then I noticed a girl walking by wearing this long blue-and-white robe. I had seen her around school a few times before and she always had that robe on over her clothes. I guess her family must have been Muslim or something, and then, like every other time I saw her, I just couldn't stop staring at her.

Andrus wasn't like anything I had ever seen in Yonkers. It was a very old, countryside-looking place. There were big, churchlike buildings everywhere where the kids took classes. The living quarters were organized in "cottages" or halls and sat on the side of this big, green field. The counselor that had taken us on a tour explained to my mother that Julia Dyckman Andrus prided itself on rehabilitating children who were unable to make it within the regular school system. I didn't see any black people. I remember really not wanting to go there until the counselor started talking about trips.

"Earl, did you hear what I was telling your mom? In a couple of weeks we're all going upstate to a place called Lake George for a vacation. They have a wonderful amusement park up there. It's called the Great Escape. Have you ever been to an amusement park?"

"No," I answered curiously, suddenly thinking that the place might not be so bad after all.

"Do they have bumper cars?"

"I'm sure they do."

The first thing I remember about living at Andrus was how good the food was. So even though this was the first time I was away from home, I really didn't give a fuck, because I was eating.

"What? We about to eat *again*?!?" I would ask my teachers. They'd give us three big meals a day *with* dessert and then we would get a snack at night. Shit, I was straight! Plus there was a color television in every cottage that didn't have a hanger antenna or a ball of aluminum foil attached to it. We could watch what we wanted during our free time and sometimes they would even show us movies. There was a stereo in the common room of every cottage that the kids could *actually touch*—not like my mother's eight-track joint that I wasn't allowed to use by myself. And every kid would get his own set of

clothes with pajamas for bedtime. All of this was way beyond what I was used to. (The only thing I didn't like about life in the cottages was the everyday shower thing. I mean, I'm ten years old; give me a week, I'll stay dirty.)

There were chores that every kid had to do, too, but I didn't mind doing those because they would give us money for them. Each week you would be given an allowance of $3.50 to do a different chore like cleaning the bathroom, vacuuming the living room, or doing the dishes in the cafeteria.

There was one chore I did hate, though, and that was waxing the dining room floor. We called it doing "the buffer." The janitors would cut up all these gray blankets into squares and you had to put your feet on them and walk them around the whole floor. Back and forth, over and over, pressing down as you slid the wax all around. There would be three kids buffing at a time, but it would still take us almost an hour to finish a room.

But this was the first time I ever made any money for anything and $3.50 a week started to add up. Andrus kept your money in separate accounts they set up for the kids and every Saturday I would take two dollars out of mine and buy some candy and a *Mad* magazine. I would read the *Mad* from cover to cover and try to draw the puzzle picture they always had on the back page that you had to fold together. The school didn't mind what you bought, instead they encouraged you to buy the things you wanted so they could show you the benefits of working for a living.

For Christmas, every kid would be given an extra twenty-five dollars on their account so that you could order gifts out of this catalog they had. You were supposed to buy something for your parents and siblings first and then get one thing for yourself. That first year I ordered this racing car set that came with this track you had to put together. It had a big jump in the middle. "Watch the world's fastest car defy gravity!" the box said. I must have played with that thing for months.

That spring, the school did take us to Lake George and the Great Escape rollercoaster was definitely as much fun as the counselor said it would be. I remember I fell into this heavy crush on this girl when we were up there. I don't remember what her name was, I just remember getting this sick feeling in my stomach. If I was older, I probably would have realized that feeling meant I wanted to fuck, but at ten years old, I had no idea about sex. I mean I had barely hit puberty. After spending that first day at the amusement park, they took us down to the water and I just spent the rest of my time catching frogs.

But surprisingly the best times for me at Andrus weren't when we went away somewhere, they were when we had family visits.

"Hi, man!" my mother would say.

Whenever she was happy to see me, my mother used to call me her li'l man.

"How are you doing? I miss my li'l man."

By this time my mother had had another little girl named Shayla. She was born when I was six, and when my mother would bring her and my sister Bonita up to campus, the four of us would hang out together. We would play catch or Frisbee on the lawn and, in the wintertime, we went sleigh riding. One time the school had to give my mother a whole new pair of boots to wear so she and I could slide down the hills in the snow and she wouldn't mess up her shoes.

It was like my mother liked me when I was at Andrus. I

MY LITTLE SISTER, SHAYLA

thought maybe she even felt bad for sending me there and after her and my sisters would leave, I always felt sad. I missed them and even if this place did have a lot of nice things and three meals a day, it was still strange and I wanted to go home.

Andrus had mostly white kids, but race wasn't an issue for me. Maybe because of how many kids wouldn't fuck with me growing up, I told myself that I would be cool with anyone who was cool with me. It didn't matter whether they were black, white, brown, or purple. The first white kid I ever really knew was a kid from my 'hood called Anthony Butler. He was bad like me and occasionally him and I would hang out together in his house on Oak Street. Well, one afternoon his mother was home, and all hell broke loose. The second she saw me walk in the house, she started screaming, "Anthony, what the fuck? Get that nigger out of here!"

I didn't know enough to understand what she was bugging about, but I knew enough to leave.

"Get that nigger the fuck out this house!" she kept wailing.

The funny thing was that Anthony wasn't one of those rich white kids from the other side of town, he was just as poor as I was. Oak Street was just a few blocks away from the projects.

"Mom, why are you bugging out?" he yelled back at her.

Anthony was cool about it. He didn't care that his mother was a racist or what she thought about him having black friends. A few minutes later, he just came outside, called his mother a name, and the two of us went off and hung out.

So I had no problem with my roommate at Andrus being a chubby white kid from Long Island or the fact that he played the song "Stairway to Heaven" every night on his record player. We had a stereo in the common area that all of the kids shared, but Glenn's parents decided to get him one of his own. That meant that he could play his ten-minute Led Zeppelin song over and over again. After a while I started to like the record, even though every night I had to get the sound of that electric guitar out of my head so I could go to sleep.

Glenn and I got along pretty well: he was the person who showed me how to smoke a cigarette and, later, would show me how to get high, so that's probably why the first few months at Andrus went by pretty fast. After a few weeks I was used to the routine of classes and meals and chores. I had forgotten about School Street and the dramas of School 18 and was having a good time. It was like the campus became my whole world and, before I knew it, I had been away from home for almost a year. It was one night while buffing the dining room floor though that my trouble started.

Adam was this Chinese kid who lived in the cottage next to mine. He was a year older than I was but for some reason we were always assigned to the same chores and from the first day I met him I didn't like him. It wasn't because he was Chinese, there was just something about the way he looked at me that bothered me. We were similar in a lot of ways, so maybe that was it, but I don't think Adam could accept the fact that I was as smart as he was and so he always competed with me, like he always had something to prove. Because of that, Adam and I would always argue, and at least once or twice a week our arguments would turn into fistfights.

But on this day, instead of arguing, Adam and I spent our time getting creative. We dreamed up all kinds of crazy stuff we could do around campus and then for some reason we thought about setting the basement floor on fire. We didn't want to burn anything, we were just wondering if the floor would turn blue if we lit it up. Shouldn't a blue flame turn whatever it burns blue? And wouldn't that make it easier to clean?

We thought up a plan.

We knew we would probably find something flammable in the garbage room in the hallway. Add that to a can of paint and we would be good.

Well, we made a fire with a blue flame, all right, but the floor didn't turn blue, it turned *black*. And the fire wouldn't stop burning.

Twenty-four hours later, after the whole building almost burned down, Andrus charged me with arson. They knew it was an accident, but they said that one of the janitors heard me say, "Where's the match?" and that was the evidence that they used against me.

But Adam wasn't charged. It seemed the janitor didn't hear him say anything so he got away with it altogether. That's when I decided that I hated him. Right away we started fighting again and after our third fight in as many days it became a major problem. I didn't want to shake his hand and say it was over like the teachers wanted me to. That was bullshit. It wasn't over for me. *I don't like you, motherfucker, and I'm gonna kill you.*

We were in an arts and crafts class. Mother's Day was coming up and they had us making flowerpots to give to our moms on the next family visit. Adam came over and looked at mine.

"Yo, that looks kinda nice, Earl."

"Thanks," I said back.

When he walked away, something just hit me. See, all these years I had *thought* about killing without being able to do anything about it but now I was old enough to pull it off, so I just got out of my chair, went to Adam's table, and grabbed him in a chokehold. I squeezed as hard as I could. When they finally pulled me off him, his face was blue—just like that flame—and he was already unconscious. When the teachers revived him a few seconds later, all this blood started gushing out of his nose.

Adam had been adopted by two old, wealthy white people and they weren't trying to let their kid get attacked, let alone attacked by a poor black kid from the projects. So they didn't hesitate pressing charges on me for assault, and now I had a problem.

Andrus decided that Earl Simmons was no longer fit to be a part of the normal school population. I had to immediately move out of my room in the cottage and for the rest of my term, live in the school infirmary. I was no longer permitted to take classes with the other kids, eat meals with the other kids, or see them at any time for recreation or otherwise. Just like School 18 put me out a little more than a year before, now Andrus was through with me.

After they realized that I couldn't stay in the infirmary all day ("The kid's not sick, he can't stay here and take up a bed!"), I was moved into a small, unused office in the administrative building where I had to stay during school hours. I was to do all of my work there and then just report to the infirmary in the evening. The infirmary was in the same building, so all I had to do was go upstairs and walk down the hall. That one-minute walk from the office to the infirmary was the only exercise I had for the next three months.

The office was on the third floor with a window that looked out onto the front courtyard. They had a lot of antique furniture in the room and I remember sitting for hours in this dusty wooden chair looking at all of the weird designs. By the afternoon, I would finish the work that they prepared for me and then just stare out of the window, wishing I could go outside and play with the other kids.

Talk about lonely.

Just like they wanted, I didn't see any kids at all during the day because there were no classes in the administrative building. The only children who were there were the ones that were there for an interview or orientation or something and they never came by the office where I was anyway. I didn't see many adults either. The only people I saw were the same two or three teachers that would come in my room every day to give me my work and this big, fat nurse that would give me my meals. That nurse never showed any feeling toward me, no emotion, never asked why I was there or what my problem was. She, like the rest of the people in that place, was just a middle-aged white lady doing her job.

"Here's your lunch."

THE ADMINISTRATIVE OFFICE

Since I wasn't in the cafeteria, of course I couldn't choose the food that I wanted, it was always just the basic tray—and she always forgot the salt, pepper, and ketchup. *Fucking bitch!* So much for enjoying the food.

After about a week going through that, I just couldn't take it anymore. I couldn't stand not being able to do or eat what I wanted, couldn't stand being locked in, alone, for so many hours with nothing to do. That's when I started to finish all the work they gave me as quickly as I possibly could, just to spite my teachers.

"Here you go. Here's your assignment, lady. I'm done . . ."

Suddenly, I could hear the other kids playing outside my window and I started getting angry, started pacing the room. *Fuck you. Fuck my work. Fuck everything.*

The next time my mother came up for a visit, I told her how they were punishing me and begged her to let me leave.

"I'm not going to uphold you in your wrongdoing, Earl. You made your bed hard, so now you have to lay on it."

If my mother's first visit reminded me of why I loved her, this one reminded me of why I hated her.

I started feeling like a caged animal. I was trapped. There was nothing that I could do or say to get out of that office. I began to listen to my instincts and my anger started to explode. Not only did I stop giving a fuck about everyone and everything around me, I began to believe all the bad that was ever said about me—Earl is manipulative, Earl is a problem, Earl has made his bed hard—and I swore that I would have the last laugh.

You thought you saw a young kid from the ghetto that you could save? Huh? You thought you had a Yonkers kid from School Street that you could just "rehabilitate"?

Yeah, okay. I bet you didn't know what my name is. My name is Crazy Earl. Crazy Earl, that's what they call me. And trust me when I tell you that you don't even know who the fuck you're dealing with!

7

Crazy Earl Tries It On

THE EIGHTEEN MONTHS I SPENT IN ANDRUS GAVE ME A REP with kids in the neighborhood. Back then you had to be an extra-special bad ass to be sent away to group home and while I was away, Buzzy started threatening everyone he fought that he was going to put his crazy nephew on them. When I came home I made sure that I lived up to that reckless reputation. When we would throw snowballs at other kids and random passersby from the top of one of the hills near our house, I put rocks in mine. When we wanted to learn how to put somebody in a sleeper hold—knocking someone unconscious for a second by squeezing a special vein in their neck—I suggested we practice on each other. It was like whenever we thought of doing something, I convinced my uncles to take it a step further. Whenever they wanted something, I had a plan to get us that and a little bit more.

One day I dared two of Buzzy's friends to sneak up on this woman and steal her pocketbook. I didn't know anything about robbing, I just wanted to see if I could get somebody else to do something that bold. I told them that the woman wouldn't see them if they did it quick, and even if she did, she wouldn't be able to catch them. I told them it was the perfect plan.

When they agreed to do it, my uncles and I made sure we weren't stupid enough to be nearby. But when they came back to where we were hiding, I was shocked to find out that not only had those two kids taken the woman's purse without being caught, but now they were holding $150!

Hey, I want some of that!

"You know you can't go home with that much cash in your pocket," I told the dumber-looking one. "Your mother is going to find out and whip your ass."

Buzzy and Collie looked at me and tried not to laugh.

"But, see, *my* momma ain't gonna do that," I went on, "so I think that money that you *stole* is really better off with me . . ."

After berating them for almost an hour, I got those kids so shook about getting busted by their mom, they actually gave in and gave me all of their earnings. I took their whole $150 with pride, and then gave them each back a five-dollar bill for their hard work.

"Here, now get the fuck outta here, stupid!"

When me and my uncles got back to my grandmother's, Rhonda and Raquela saw us counting it and taxed us for more than half of what we got, but it was cool because me and my uncles still had enough dough to roll some singles behind our ear and do our thing at Al & Floyd's Grocery Store down the street. That's where the Crazy Kong machine was. See, most days hanging out in there we'd have to watch other kids play video games because we never had money, but that day we had more quarters then we knew how to spend.

It didn't take long for me, Collie, and Buzzy to get the run of our block, at least among the kids who were around the same age as us. And if anyone wanted to test us, the "Buzzy Surprise" was a good way of keeping them in check:

"Yo, man. Come here for a minute. You want the Buzzy Surprise?"

"The what?"

"The Buzzy Surprise. Everyone's getting one . . ."

When the unsuspecting kid would say yes, Buzz would reach back and punch him dead in his eye. The kid would almost always fall backward and by the time he got up to see who hit him, we would be three blocks away and around the corner, laughing, already recapping how Buzz's fist looked smashed against the kid's face.

• • • • •

My uncles and I definitely thought we were slick, but we weren't *that* slick because sometimes we would end up on Alexander Street. Alexander Street was where the Yonkers City Jail was.

I SPENT MANY NIGHTS HERE

Yonkers is the only city in the state, besides New York, to have its own city jail. When you're arrested you have to stay there until your arraignment in front of a judge and your case is either thrown out, you're released on bail, or you're sent to Valhalla, the prison that serves all of Westchester County, to await trial.

Across the street from the city jail is the Youth Division. That's where anyone under the age of seventeen gets held until a parent comes to pick them up. I was seven years old the first time I was there, busted for shoplifting out of the Finast supermarket in the Square. I thought I was the man at the time, but now I can imagine how obvious I must have looked with a whole box of Entenmann's pies stuffed down my shirt.

I was always scared when I went down to Alexander Street because there was nothing there besides a few run-down factories and the MTA train station. No one lived that close to the waterfront, so you got the feeling that anything could happen to you and nobody would ever know. A few of the cops that dealt with the kids did have good hearts but they would try to scare you first.

ALEXANDER STREET YOUTH DIVISION

"You want me to bring you across the street? Huh? You wanna go see the big boys? . . . Well, keep doing what you're doing then . . . I'm telling you, those men will fuck you in your ass!"

Later they would get more real: "What are you doing, Earl? You seem like a good kid. You wanna do this shit for the rest of your life? You want to be in and out of jail?"

I remember I got one of those talks when Andrus sent me there for the arson charge. I had to sit in this small holding cell listening to this officer preach to me until they contacted my mother. Then, when my mother came, she started whupping my ass before we even left the building.

"Okay, Mrs. Simmons. You can punish him when you get home," the officer said. I guess he didn't want to be witness to anything.

After I came home from Andrus, I tried to stay at my grandmother's house as much as I could because at home things had gotten worse. Not only had my mother had given my toy pickup truck away ("You don't play with it, Earl." "But how could I have played with it if I wasn't home? When I left you told me, 'Don't worry about a thing,' and that was my favorite truck, Momma!") but Richie the mailman was still making house calls.

The difference was that I wasn't eight years old anymore.

"No, man. NO . . . Get away from me. You ain't my father!"

As usual, he had just finished getting briefed by my mother and was standing in my doorway with a belt in his hand. But I was tired of being nervous around this guy. I was tired of being scared around anybody, period.

"Fuck you."

He was shocked.

"What did you say to me?!?"

I just couldn't take it anymore. So I summoned all the courage I had and screamed as loud as I could.

"FUUUUCK YOU!!"

I couldn't believe the results. Richie yelled back at me and told me how bad I was, but I didn't get the beating. That belt never touched me.

A few minutes later, him and my mother were at the kitchen table wanting to talk.

Oh, so this is how it goes down? I zap out and then you want to talk. A few minutes ago, you were coming to whip my ass, now you want to ask me what's wrong. Hmmm. Maybe getting reckless is not such a bad thing after all?

But it seemed my mother had another plan: punishment.

First it was for a weekend: my mother sent me to my room all day Saturday and Sunday. Even though I hated hearing all the other kids playing outside the window downstairs, that wasn't too bad, because by the time I started to get bored with all my cars it was already Sunday evening and Monday I was free.

Then my punishment was extended to a week and that was tougher. I could only leave my room to eat and go to the bathroom. No TV, no playing with Bonita, no nothing.

When a week didn't work, then my mother took all the cars and toys out of my room and extended my grounding time to a month.

"You didn't learn yet, huh?" she would ask me, frustrated that I was still doing everything that she told me was wrong or bad.

Thirty days I had to spend in my room with the door closed, alone. The only thing I could do was come out to eat and get some water. I stayed getting water. Being punished at home was worse than Andrus because this was home and I knew my sisters were right outside the door doing whatever they wanted, probably laughing at me the whole time.

I was so bored, I remember spending whole afternoons just sitting on the floor studying the cracks in my wall. I knew exactly how all of the paint bubbles looked because I made them look like faces. When I got tired of that, I used to peel the paint off my ceiling. Once I saw it chipping in one corner, I'd peel it off to see how far it could go because it was a game and I hated when it stopped. *Fucking paint.*

Other times the zipper on my pants became a fire engine to me. The top was the truck part and the zip was the ladder. I would just pull the ladder up and down and let my imagination do the rest. Or I would find a piece of string and pull it through the air. When the string used to float, I would imagine it was a starship.

If I still had textbooks lying around I would spend a lot of time doing schoolwork. I liked the *Readers Concept* stuff because I could do all of the problems and then check my answers in the back. First

I saw how many I got right, then I tried to figure out why my other answers were wrong. I kept reading as much as I could. While in my room on punishment, I must have read the book *White Fang* like five times.

After a while, the length of my grounding didn't make any difference to me. Andrus had introduced me to this kind of isolation and I was getting better at creating my own world. Occasionally, when Uncle Pinky was over he would pop his head into my room and ask if I needed anything.

"No."

I became good at shutting everyone out, and everybody else in the apartment did the same. Anyone who came over to School Street during those years shouldn't have been surprised to find me in my room on punishment, Bonita and Shayla in their room minding their business, and my mother in her bedroom resting for her night job. All four of us would have our doors closed.

There was one time when we did get to go out, though, that was when we'd go to Aunt Vern's place across town on Cedar Place. Even if I was on punishment, my mother would normally bring me and my sisters with her over there. Through the years, Aunt Vern tried to step in wherever my mother chose out. My mom, being a Jehovah's Witness, rarely celebrated Christmas, New Year's, or any of our birthdays, so most of the time we would go over to Aunt Vern's house to put up a tree or exchange presents.

Aunt Vern was gangsta. Broad-shouldered, almost six feet tall, Vern was one of those whup-a-bitch-ass type of girls. She wasn't crazy with it, but if you brought any bullshit to her, she would put you down. Everybody knew Laverne.

Many weekends I would wake up in her house smelling breakfast cooking. Music would be playing. And Vern always had the parties. The *adult* type of parties where there was always lots of drinking and smoking going down. There would be about fifteen or twenty grown-ups running around and it was funny because one of them was always given the job to play with the kids. They would enjoy it at first, when the party was in the living room, but as soon as everybody disappeared into that private, off-limits-to-kids room that Vern always had, then they got mad.

"Damn. Can't you kids take care of yourselves?"

I always came up with a reason to need one of the adults in that room for something so I could knock on the door and see what was going on.

"Get away from this door, Earl. We in here doing grown folks stuff!"

See, my aunt was a lesbian, and as far back as I can remember she always had girlfriends. And all of her girlfriends had girlfriends. So I grew up thinking lesbian shit was normal. Between all of them, my sisters and my mother, I was like the only nigga at these parties although once I got used to being around a lot of older women, I did kind of enjoy it.

AUNT VERN AND ME

I had my first drink at one of Vern's parties. My aunt gave it to me to be funny.

"Here, Earl. Take a sip of this . . ."

My mom just sat there, like, "Vern, you crazy," and everybody laughed at how I reacted to my first taste of poison.

"Look at him wobbling!"

I wish I could have turned around to everybody and told them how they were probably fucking my whole life up, turning me into a drunk at *seven* years old. But I didn't know any better.

This is what's up? This is where the in-crowd is? Okay, fuck it. I'm gonna do what y'all are doing.

But after a few more sips of vodka, suddenly I had to lie down. I thought I was tired. But I wasn't tired, I was drunk.

That was okay, because once everyone at the party thought I was asleep, then I got to hear the dirt, then I got to hear what was really going on. All I had to do was put my ears on radar, and I had a method for that: First, you have to close your eyes to block out any distractions. Then you focus; punch out all of the music and the extra sounds that you hear in the bathroom or in other bedrooms and just focus on what you hear in the kitchen.

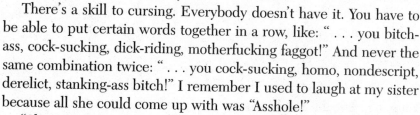

Blip . . . blip . . . blip . . .

Your radar is now on. That's how I found out how well my aunt could curse.

There's a skill to cursing. Everybody doesn't have it. You have to be able to put certain words together in a row, like: " . . . you bitch-ass, cock-sucking, dick-riding, motherfucking faggot!" And never the same combination twice: " . . . you cock-sucking, homo, nondescript, derelict, stanking-ass bitch!" I remember I used to laugh at my sister because all she could come up with was "Asshole!"

"Shut up, Bonita," I used to tease her. "You can't curse!"

But Vern had it. She made it where a nigga would believe it. "Oh, no! Not today, you good-for-nothing, sorry-behind, lazy-ass mother-fucker . . . !"

So I knew with that mouth that she could get down for me, no matter what. I just wish she was around that day I needed her most.

After I left Andrus, it was decided that I go to a "progressive" school on the rich side of town. That was not a good idea. I didn't know anybody, there were only two other black kids in the whole school, and after all that I had just been through in group home and all I was still going through at home, I was ready to zap out.

I lasted in that school about two weeks.

"We're going to send a tutor to your house," the vice principal told me the day she gave up and put me in a cab. It was a little after twelve in the afternoon and my mother wasn't home so they tried to contact my aunt. She wasn't home either, but Paula, my aunt's girlfriend at the time, was in the house and she told the school that they could send me to her.

Well, as soon as I got over there, Paula broke this big, wooden billy club over my head. I guess she felt I needed more discipline. But I didn't know what the hell was going on, she just attacked me when I walked in the door. I tried to run away from her and hide under the kitchen table, but she followed me with the club and kept hitting me on my arm that I was holding up to block my face. She hit me so hard, so many times, the wood started splintering off of the club down to the fucking metal inside. When she saw that, she stopped, but by this time, blood and wood splinters were all in my aunt's carpet and my elbow had swollen so large it looked like it had a big salt ball on it. She beat me like I was hers. She beat me like I was grown.

I didn't deserve that one.

When my uncle Pinky came by a few hours later, I pulled him into the bathroom. I felt like he was the only help I had.

"Please, Uncle Pinky. Help me, please. She beat me."

My uncle looked at me and said he would "talk to her," but by then Paula had left the house and when I got home, my mom didn't say *nothing*. It was only when I went to my grandmother's house the next day that anyone raised hell. I knew my grandmother wouldn't ever let anyone put their hands on me like that and there was a big family controversy. It was like my father's side against my mother's side. My mother just told everyone that it wasn't none of their business. She was raising me the best she could.

In 1981, my mother grounded me for the entire summer: June, July, and August. I didn't even know what I did. That was the most frustrating part. I mean, I could be locked up in the room by myself. I didn't care what things you took out of it or how long it was for, but to be forced to be punished without knowing the reason why? That was fucked up.

Sometimes I was guilty, I knew that, but other times I didn't do whatever it was she was accusing me of and my mother just didn't want to believe me. One time I remember she had given me a beating in the kitchen in front of the stove with one of those thick wooden spoons that folks hang on the wall for decoration. But I didn't do what she said I had done. *I didn't do it.* I kept trying to explain that to her, but it was no use. So when she finished, I just ran down the hallway screaming as loud as I could.

"Momma, you're a liar! You're a liar!"

Then she came in my room and beat me some more for talking to her that way until she finally heard what my explanation was.

"Well, next time say that!" she told me.

"But I did say that, Momma. That's what I was trying to say to you the whole time!"

It never mattered.

My little sister, Shayla, was about five when she started waking up to the sounds of my mother going crazy. When I started getting old enough to outrun her, and the grounding wasn't working, my mother decided to beat me while I was sleeping. In the middle of the night, while I was still in the bed, she'd just pull my covers up from the bottom, sit on my back, and just wear my behind out. Before I even knew I wasn't dreaming anymore, I would feel the hits on my ass and the back of my legs. If I had been sleeping on my back, then she'd hit me in the chest.

"Ma, stop . . . Please . . . I can't breathe. No, Momma, no. I can't breathe!"

"Well, when I get finished whipping your behind, then I'll take you to the emergency room for your asthma!"

And that's exactly what she did. After she was done, she'd call a cab, tell Bonita to look after Shayla, and we'd go to the hospital so they could put me on a breathing machine. I don't remember the doctors ever asking what brought on the attack.

The next time she hits me, I'm gonna . . .

Things got so bad that I began to contemplate my mother's murder. Night after night I would think the act all the way through, play the steps over and over in my mind: first go in the living room, then kick her in the stomach and make sure she falls out of the window. Then all of my pain would be over.

The vision always ended with my mother holding onto the windowsill.

"Earl, help me," she'd call out for me to save her and that was when I would always feel bad and end up pulling her back in. I would see her hanging there, begging for her life, and I wouldn't be able to go through with it.

That's what made me know that I really didn't *want* to kill my mother. I didn't want to kill her, I was just mad at her. I loved her. And no matter what she was doing to me, I couldn't hurt her. I just wanted her to have my back and get down for me. I wanted her to feel like how my grandmother felt about me. Or at least try.

That same year, my father left Yonkers and moved to Philadelphia. He said it was a place where he could make a living for himself selling his paintings. By this time, he had two other sons, Joseph Jr. and Jessie, who he had by his girlfriend, Cathy, the white woman my mother had told me about. They had been living together in this small house on Woodworth Street. I had actually gone over there a few times. Cathy would move two beds together for my brother Joe and me to sleep on. Joe was only a few years younger than me but Jessie was still a baby so he would be in the crib crying. My father was rarely there.

The times my father *was* around in the house, I couldn't find a connection with him. I remember one night we were all watching something on television together, me, my father, Cathy, and Joe, and when he came back from the bathroom he looked at me and asked what had happened on the show. I didn't have anything to say. I knew what had happened, but for some reason I couldn't find the words to say anything to him. He shrugged and we all just sat there in silence.

The times my father tried to do something nice for me always seemed to backfire as well. One time at my grandmother's house he gave me this metal plane that he got from one of his artist friends on the street. It shot sparks out of the back like the cars I liked and had a cool propeller on it that you could twirl. But when we left a few hours later, I forgot it upstairs. The next day when he saw me without it, he got mad and told me that I obviously didn't want the gift. He said he was going to give it to my brother instead.

Well, fuck it then. I don't care anyway . . .

But now my father was moving out of Yonkers altogether. I guess he wouldn't have to worry about going broke and having to sleep in Central Park anymore. That was good I guess, but sometimes I used to wonder if I would've been happier with him, even if that meant that I would have to be homeless. I mean, anything was better than living with my mother. I didn't need much anymore. I really didn't need to be taken care of. I just needed to learn. I just needed to be shown.

8

Earl Finds a Mission

"EARL, WHERE HAVE YOU BEEN?"

"I ran away, Momma."

"But you got a bed right here. You had me worried sick!"

It didn't matter to me anymore. Home was the last place I wanted to be. My father was gone. My mother still refused to let me live with my grandmother, so I took to the streets. I didn't care if I didn't have any money, or I wasn't going to school. At least I would be in control of my own life.

"Why are you doing this to yourself?" my mother would ask me when I showed up at the door after surviving on my own for a few days. "And why do you look like that?"

"It's cold out there . . ."

"Well, it serves you right, Earl. You should have come home."

Many nights outside by myself, I crawled into the clothing bins they kept outside the Salvation Army in Getty Square. It was warm and I knew no one would find me. My mom never looked for me; I guess she felt that if I wanted to stay lost there was nothing she could do about it.

I did a lot of thinking when I was out there by myself. I was lonely, but I was determined not to go home. After a while, though, it's hard not to go crazy when you don't have anyone to talk to.

Then I saw a dog.

He was a gray mutt with dark streaks, and he looked pretty beat up. I saw him walking a few streets away. Something told me to try and approach him, but when I did, he started running.

"Come here, boy. Come here."

Stray dogs are normally scared of people; they're scarred by whatever neglect or abuse put them out on the street. Or if they're lost, they're depressed because they can't find their way home. But that morning I decided that no matter how long it took, I was going to get that dog to come over to me. I was going to convince him to trust me and make him mine.

So for about three hours I followed that mutt all over downtown Yonkers. He just kept jogging away from me, every few steps nervously turning his head around to see if I was still behind him.

"Come on, boy. It's okay . . ."

Finally, by late afternoon I achieved my goal. Not only did the dog stop running so I could pet him, but he let me tie a wire around his neck that I used as a leash. For the next few hours, we walked all around Yonkers and later that evening I found some scraps of food for him to eat. He stayed with me all night. The next morning I was so proud of my new friend, I took him with me to School Street.

As soon as I got up there, some older dudes started messing with me.

"Yo, look what Crazy Earl got!"

The three of them walked over to us.

It's okay, boy. Don't be afraid.

"Hey, li'l nigga, are you sure that mutt is yours? What if I just . . ."

I tried to reassure my dog that everything was all right, but before I realized what was going on, one of the guys kicked him right in the ass. Immediately, my dog wriggled out of the piece of wire, started running, and within a few seconds he was clear out of the projects. I tried to chase him but the faster I ran, the faster he ran. For blocks, he kept the same amount of distance between us until he finally just disappeared down an alley. He wasn't going to let me catch him twice.

I never saw that dog again, but now I had a mission. I started looking all over for strays that I could catch and train for myself and suddenly I had a reason to go back to my mother's house: I needed somewhere to keep my dogs. Once I found one I would just tie them up in the front hallway of our apartment so they wouldn't get away and every night I would leave them a bowl of cold water to drink. Most of the dogs I found would be good and wouldn't make any noise,

but it wasn't long before my mother told me we couldn't have them in the house. It seemed School Street didn't allow pets.

"Earl, that dog better not be here when I come home from work . . ."

"Okay, Momma."

"I mean it, Earl."

Most of the time, when I didn't want to listen, my mother made real good on her threat.

ONE OF MY FIRST DOGS

"Where's my dog, Momma?"

"I said to you that the building would kick us out if they found a pet in this house, Earl, so I had to take care of it . . ."

"So you got rid of my dog? That was *my* dog!"

"That was not your dog, Earl, and you have to learn to follow the rules of this house."

So then I started hiding them from her. I knew my mother's schedule, what time she came home and went to sleep, what time she got up in the morning. I just had to make sure that Uncle Pinky wouldn't snitch.

"Didn't your mother tell you not to bring that dog in the house?" he would say when I walked in the door with a new friend.

After midnight, everyone would be asleep, but Pinky would be lying on the couch.

"Yeah, I know, Uncle Pinky, but I can't let him go. He has nowhere to go."

One dog I hid under my bed for a few days actually gave birth to puppies. I didn't know she was pregnant until one night I peeked under the bed and saw the whole litter. The puppies were still covered in all the blood and placenta. It took me a while to get rid of them all.

When it became too much trouble to hide the dogs, then the roof became my place. School Street only had twelve floors and we were on eleven, so I only had to walk up two flights to get up there. It was never locked. I just brought a blanket and some pillows from the house with me and me and my dog would camp out up there all night.

I liked the roof. It was always dark and peaceful and I used to do a lot of staring at the sky. Some nights lying alone, I thought about the girl I used to see in that blue and white robe. There was just something about her that sparked my imagination. I dreamed that I was a wild lion that only she could tame. I was a savage, and she was my princess, the only woman who could ever control me.

But it was on the roof that I also started to think that I could fuck with a dog before I fucked with a person because it seemed the more love I gave them, the more love they gave me back. And dogs didn't know betrayal. All I had to do was hug them, feed them, and I knew that I didn't have to worry about a thing because as soon as that roof door started to crack, my dog would growl and start to protect me.

It was the same way on the street. Once I got a dog to trust me, he was loyal to me and wouldn't let any harm come my way. And when I noticed how everyone was scared of them anyway, how when I was with my dog the older kids that would normally try to dis me and take advantage of me suddenly started to move away, that gave me the heart as a young nigga to deal with anything that came up the 'hood.

See, there's a little bitch in everybody—you just have to find where it's at. Most of the time a person is more scared of a dog then they are of a gun because if you put a gun in someone's hand who's not ready to use it, or doesn't know what he's doing with it, that gun is useless. But it's never like that with a dog. Bullets go straight, but a dog will always stay on target. A dog will look at you and say, "I'm gonna kill you," and if the master says so, will chase you around for hours. A dog is gonna chase you through buildings, across streets, over cars. Hit the fence? The dog got you on your leg. Turn the corner and bust your ass? It's over.

Growing up in the 'hood by myself, without my dog, I probably would have been taken advantage of, would have been forced to snap or wild out on niggas to get any respect. But with my dog, the respect came a lot easier, and that changed everything.

9

What's My Name?

SHE SAID WE WERE JUST GOING TO LOOK AROUND.

But the day we went to visit Children's Village School for Boys, my mother had me wearing a pair of orange slacks, with a yellow button-down shirt and black shoes. Not only did the outfit make me doubt that we were just there for a tour, but it also gave the other kids a first impression of me that would be very hard to overcome. I was the only one on the campus who wasn't wearing jeans and sneakers, but I was supposed to be the straight thug!

It was lunch hour when me, my mother, and a social worker named Charles White walked into Crolius to meet Miss Santos, the head of the cottage. All of the kids were in the dining room eating and when we came through the door they looked up and I could hear them all laughing. Then when my mother asked to see the rest of the facilities, Mr. White seemed very eager to show her around. The two of them thought it would be best if I stayed behind to "see if I could blend in," so I was left standing in the doorway like an asshole.

Miss Santos introduced me to all of the kids and most of them just shrugged their shoulders and didn't speak to me, so I just went into the living room and minded my business.

I should have known it wasn't going to be a short walk. My mother and Mr. White didn't come back for over an hour.

"So how do you like it, Earl?" my mother asked me when she got back.

"It's all right."

"Well, I think you're going to stay here for a little while."

"WHAT? Momma, you mean I'm not going home?"

"Let's just see how you like it."

I was in shock. I knew we were coming to a group home but I never thought my mother would drop me off at one with no warning! I didn't even have any of my clothes with me.

"You mean I'm staying right now?"

"You're staying right now."

The worst part was that my mother told me this with all the kids staring at me, so I couldn't get upset or start crying in front of them. I couldn't let anyone think I was a bitch.

"You're really going to enjoy yourself here, Earl," Mr. White said.

I could have killed that motherfucker for saying that bullshit, but within the hour, my mother was gone. For the rest of the day, Miss Santos tried to make me feel better about my new home. She said Children's Village wasn't like other group homes; she said it had been dedicated to children for over one hundred years and everyone here treated each other like family. Miss Santos claimed CV was a place where I could expect unconditional love.

I wasn't impressed.

The bedrooms were upstairs and I would be sharing a room with three other boys. There was a locker with hooks and a little shelf where I could keep my things. Since all of the cottages at Children's Village were arranged geographically, the other twelve kids in Crolius were from Westchester County and Long Island. Miss Santos said there were actually three other kids in the cottage from Yonkers, three brothers: Sheldon, Hampton, and Tyvian. But I didn't care who I would be sleeping in a room with. My mind was busy figuring out how I was going to survive in this new, hostile environment. In Yonkers, I had begun to create my own rules, I stayed out on the street, did whatever I wanted. No matter how much trouble that put me in, I was committed to living my own life. Now I had to be in bed by 9 P.M. How was I going to make it in another institution?

First, I knew I had to get out of these damn clothes. Of course, I

69

MY HOME FOR EIGHTEEN MONTHS

couldn't get fitted for anything until the following morning and then when I got to the quartermaster's office, he didn't have any shirts, all he had was underwear, socks, and a pair of old pants that didn't fit me. So I ended up wearing that orange shirt and yellow pair of slacks for the next two days. When I finally did get the standard Children's Village outfit a few days later (plaid shirt, farmer john jeans, and skippys), it wasn't much better because the clothes were so new and stiff, I looked crazy. I noticed that some of the older kids got to rock Levi's jeans and suede Pumas. But not me, not the new kid who didn't have any things of his own.

I decided the only way to cope was to stay to myself. The small library in the living room of the cottage wasn't as nice as the one I had at Andrus, but reading was a salvation for me. For the first few weeks, while the other kids played cards or challenged each other at the Ping-Pong table, I spent my time sitting in this big lounge chair reading. I didn't speak or hang out with anybody, rarely got interested in the cottage's activities, and never, *ever* shared the anger that I was feeling inside.

I really missed my dogs.

Everyone at Children's Village went to school from 9 A.M. to 3 P.M. We would walk over as a cottage together to the school building and then split up into our respective classes. You rarely went to class with the same kids you lived with; instead, you were grouped according to ability. I was placed in the advanced RCT class, which meant that in addition to doing the usual eighth-grade coursework, I had to prepare for the ninth-grade statewide exam at the end of the year.

My teacher's name was Mr. Mossblack. He was very strict and he tried his best to teach us every subject. I remember enjoying math and history the most but I was more concerned about the other kids in my cottage not finding out what class I was in—so they wouldn't have anything to tease me about at dinnertime—than I was about the work itself. That's one of the reasons why I didn't carry any books with me. Just like in School 18, Mr. Mossblack always wanted to punish me for being unprepared, but I still knew most of the answers in his class.

After a few weeks of trying to stay to myself in the cottage, two kids I had never spoken to tried to mind my business.

"Hey, man. What's wrong with you? All you ever do is read. What? You wanna be a white boy, or something?"

"Leave me alone."

"You don't say nothing to nobody. What's the deal, Earl?"

"I said leave me alone . . ."

"Come on, man. That shit is corny."

"I said LEAVE ME THE FUCK ALONE!"

I jumped out of my chair and was ready to fight both of them right there in the living room. These kids didn't know me. They were messing with the wrong motherfucker. Miss Santos heard me yell and rushed over, but there wasn't anything to break up. Stunned at how ready I was to throw down, the two kids just stood in front of me with their hands at their sides looking at me like I was crazy.

Yeah, that's right, bitch. Let me introduce you to Crazy Earl.

That incident woke me up. There was no reason for me to go in a shell and shut myself off from everyone when I could be running the place. Why not be the leader, the smartest *and* the craziest one, just like I was with my uncles back home? So I changed my attitude and told Miss Santos like I told Mrs. Smith in third grade: if I'm getting my work done, I should be able to go to class without books. If I'm getting up on time in the morning; I should be able to stay up as long as I want at night, and as long as I'm finished eating, I should be able to start my after-dinner chores whenever I'm ready. Why do I have to wait for everybody else?

Miss Santos had some trouble with my new behavior.

"Earl, you better come sit down," she used to yell at me when I would jump up from the dinner table to rush and start the dishes so I could be the first to get chore money. Then in the morning, I would try to be the first to make up my bed so I could be the first to get to school. I would just run across the campus and felt good when everybody else who had to walk with her arrived in class at least five minutes behind me.

Children's Village was where I discovered the joy of running. Up until then, all I had ever done was run up and down the stairs in School Street. Since I was the only boy in the house, laundry cart duty was mine and when the elevator was broken I always had to lug that whole cart of clothes up eleven flights. As I got older, it got to be where I could run up those stairs without breaking a sweat, and after a few weeks running around Children's Village, I saw how strong all those stairs must have made me and I started sprinting everywhere I could.

Then I joined the track team and every afternoon I had to run around the whole campus on purpose. After a few weeks of practice, I was running five miles a day with no problem.

I loved to run. There was just something about feeling the wind hit my face. It made me feel free, powerful. And when we would have races, in that last lap I would just push myself as hard as I could and sprint to the finish line. I almost always crossed first.

At Children's Village, you were not allowed to leave your cottage unsupervised for any reason. You were considered "out of program." But because of the special class I was in, I could bend the rules a little more than most of the kids—I could arrive a little later to places without being questioned or disappear for a little while without teachers being suspicious of where I was. They would just give me the benefit of the doubt because I was one of the "gifted and talented." But the times I would really test the rules—like when I visited friends on the other side of campus, raided other cottages' kitchens for their cereal, or just took it upon myself to go into town on an I-know-I'm-not-supposed-to-be-here pleasure trip, Special Services would always pick me up and take me back to Miss Santos for punishment.

Sometimes I could smooth-talk my way out of trouble with a "How could I do that if I was over here?" type of alibi, but most of the time Miss Santos wasn't buying it.

"If I let you do little things like this now, Earl, when you get older, you're going to do bigger things."

That's why I wasn't allowed to go home for my first home visit.

When you're first enrolled, Children's Village kept you for a month without letting you see your parents so that you would get used to being away from home. You could speak to your relatives on the phone but you couldn't leave or have any visitors. Since I had already been in trouble and out of program a few times, Miss Santos and Mr. White decided that after my first month, I hadn't earned the privilege to go home. (Mr. White fought on my behalf, though, probably because he figured my mother would come and get me and the two of them could take another stroll.) But at that time, I really didn't care about seeing my mother. I had even told Miss Santos that I didn't need to speak to her on the phone. I felt that if she wanted to send me away, then I would force her to deal with being apart from me. This was the way *she* wanted it, right? That feeling lasted until the holidays.

It was Thanksgiving 1984. I had been at Children's Village for almost six months and my stubbornness had faded away. Now I was just homesick.

For weeks, Miss Santos had been using the upcoming holiday as an incentive to stay on our best behavior. "You better behave, boys; remember, you have a home visit coming up . . ." And we listened.

I was looking forward to being back in Yonkers, going over to my grandmother's house, running around with my uncles, finding some more stray dogs. But on the morning that everyone was getting ready to get on the bus, Miss Santos got a phone call. She had spoken to my mother a few weeks before to get permission for me to come home; now my mother was calling to say that she had changed her mind.

"There's a family emergency, Miss Santos. Earl is not going to be able to come home today."

"But he's all packed and the bus is already here to take him, Mrs. Simmons. Your son has been anticipating this trip for a long time."

"I'm sorry, but when I say my son can't come home, Miss Santos, he can't come home."

My mother never gave a good explanation. It was early in the evening before I cooled down and stopped throwing things around the cottage. I felt angry—more than fucking angry, I felt rage.

Only the orphan kids didn't get to go home for the holidays. And now me . . . I wouldn't get to see my dog, I wouldn't get to chill on the roof. I would miss Sunday dinner . . . But I tried to remember that it wasn't Miss Santos's fault. She always treated me with respect. That night, she took me and all the stay-back kids to the movies.

Children's Village encouraged the kids to call their guidance counselors "Mom" and "Pop." They felt it would add to the family atmosphere of the place. But Miss Santos never allowed me or any of her other kids to call her mom, even though for those two years I spent with her, at times, I felt she was doing a much better job raising me than my mother ever did. I don't know whether that was what she meant by "unconditional love," but it was definitely something.

Unlike Andrus, only about half of the kids at Children's Village were white, and even though many of them came from families with money, we all shared the same kinds of problems at home: abuse, neglect, young or single mothers. Living with twelve other people, though, still forced you to learn and get along with many different kinds of personalities. I never got real tight with anyone in my cottage, but after those first few weeks, we all became friendly enough.

There was Michael Wiznewski, Patrick Chaney, and this big, doofy white kid we used to tease about having a big nose, named Charles. It didn't help that his last name was Sniffen. "Sniffffen!!" we used to yell at him with our noses stuck up in the air. There were the three Corey brothers from Yonkers who used to keep getting dismissed from CV and somehow end up right back a few days later. Aron was this smart tattletale kid in Mr. Mossblack's class who never wanted to leave me alone.

A lot of kids in Children's Village came from all over the country, so not only did a lot of folks have different accents but they also liked different music. It wasn't uncommon to hear some weird punk or country stuff playing out of another cottage. That's why I was glad the cottages were arranged geographically because there was one thing the kids from New York and Westchester had in common, and that was a love for a new kind of music: hip-hop music.

This was the "I want my MTV" era. Tina Turner was making a comeback with her "What's Love Got to Do with It" record and Prince and Michael Jackson were tearing it up. Rock and big-time R&B were all over the place. But if you were a black or Puerto Rican teenager growing up in the early 1980s, you were quickly moving away from rhythm and blues because when you first heard a beat and a rhyme you knew that hip-hop was your shit.

Most afternoons in the cottage after school, someone would bring their boom box down to the common room and turn the radio to 98.7 KISS-FM or WBLS, New York's two R&B stations. At the time, those stations weren't playing hip-hop, because the music was considered "too ghetto" for their twenty-five-year-old audiences and was thought of as nothing more than a passing trend. But occasionally a jam with a hard enough bass line would come over the airwaves and kids could spit a rhyme over the top of something by the Gap Band or Donna Summer. I didn't know anything to say, never thought of a rhyme in my life, so I would just stand to the side and jam to the music. Miss Santos tried to discourage us from rapping. She said it was silly to talk over someone else's singing, but rhyming to the radio became more and more fun as kids started challenging one another to see who could say the flyest or freshest rhyme.

It didn't take long for me to start feeling left out, so the first weekend I was allowed back to Yonkers I made sure I stayed up to tape-record Mr. Magic's Rap Attack show off the radio.

Each week, during his three-and-a-half hour set, Mr. Magic debuted a few exclusive tracks he knew his audience would have never heard before. The night I was taping I heard Whodini's "Five Minutes of Funk" for the very first time and I got an idea.

"Ain't nobody gonna know about this," I said to myself before I spent the next few hours memorizing the song's second verse. It was brand new, in the middle of the mastermix, so I just knew I could take it back to Children's Village and say it like it was mine.

```
Now sit back, relax, put on your headgear
Get ready for a trip through the atmosphere . . .
```

The plan worked like a charm. The kids in the cottage gave me props for coming up with a hot rhyme and my love for all things hip-hop had begun.

During my next home visit I began to notice that more and more kids in Y-O were getting into hip-hop. Everyone was rhyming or DJ-ing or break-dancing, tagging on a wall or doing the electric boogie somewhere in the park. And if someone didn't have any of those talents, then they were just becoming b-boys.

A b-boy was somebody who just stood on the corner looking cool. He didn't do anything, just stood there and represented hip-hop. But he knew the right outfit. He knew how to rock the Gazelle glasses with the Kangol hat and the shell-toe Adidas. He always kept his heels together and his feet pointed outward. Maybe he carried a boom box or occasionally tagged up somewhere, but his main job was just to stay in that b-boy stance.

Seeing all of this go down, I knew that I had to find my niche, so one day I started beatboxing.

At first I didn't know what I was doing, but once I taught myself how to make three or four different sounds with my mouth, I got more confident. It's all how about you press your lips together. After a while, I could mimic some of the beats that I heard on the radio and I started going up to cats on the street challenging them to a mini beatbox battle.

"Yo, you beatbox?"

"Yeah. A little bit . . ."

"All right, well let's go head to head. Let me hear something."

It was around this time that I met Ready Ron.

Ready Ron was from Brooklyn and he was the best rapper that I ever heard. I thought he was nice to the point that no one on or off the radio could fuck with him. Ron liked the aggressive attitude he saw me have around the way and one night asked me to do a beat for him while he rapped. Ron could rhyme for like five or six minutes straight, so I remember having to keep my mouth moving for a real long time. But I did it, and right after that he asked me to be his partner.

Ron was twenty-seven, more than ten years older than I was, but it was cool because I didn't hang out with many people my age anyway and when he said he wanted me to roll with him, to be with him wherever he would perform or do small shows, I agreed without a second thought.

But I needed a name.

DMX was the name of one of the best early drum machines a lot of the kids were using and since I felt I was nice with the beats, I took that. It was strong, powerful. I liked the three letters and thought that it would be cool to make them stand for different things. So when I went back to Children's Village after my home visit, I was no longer Earl Simmons or even Crazy Earl. I was DMX. *DMX The Beat Box Enforcer.*

10

In the Game

WHEN I WAS YOUNGER, MY MOTHER'S FRIEND THELMA USED to come over to our apartment all the time. I remembered Thelma because she always used to cheer my mother on when she was giving me a beating.

"You better go ahead and teach him a lesson, 'Nett."

She had two daughters of her own, so when they came over, my sisters and I would have a sleepover with them in the living room. But my big thrill didn't come from sleeping so close to girls that weren't my sisters, it came when I walked into the bathroom one morning while Thelma was getting dressed. She was pulling up her stockings and I noticed that she didn't have any panties on. It took her a couple of seconds to realize that I was staring between her legs, but by that time, I had seen all I needed to.

That was my first look at pussy, but it wasn't until my last visit home from Children's Village that I actually got my first piece.

The woman was twenty-six and lived in the same building as me in School Street. I would see her sometimes, she used to talk to me in the elevator about how her husband was fucking up and wasn't home a lot, then one day she just invited me up to her apartment.

I was fourteen, right in the middle of puberty, and was sprouting out kind of big from all of the running and working out I was doing in group home. But I was surprised that she kept smiling at me because I know I must have looked like a straight lumberjack with my CV outfit on. When we got inside her place, she started acting kinda funny, said the kind of pain medication or something she was taking was making her horny and when she pulled me into the kitchen and started kissing me, I didn't know what the fuck was going on. I never had sex before, I hadn't even been around girls that much. In CV they had weekend dances with some girls from a local group home but I rarely went. So when this grown woman started touching me, I got thirsty right away.

Then she took me into her bedroom. She was wearing a long red dress and when she turned to me and pulled it up, I saw that she had stockings on with no drawers.

"You see this?" she asked me.

"Oh, shit," I thought. "I guess I'm a man now."

I was nervous as hell. She got me on top of her and I did it—real quick—and almost died in the process. But I was in the game.

Nothing was ever said between us after that day, she wouldn't even speak to me in the elevator anymore. A few years later, when I brought my man over to her house to try to show her off to him, she fronted on me, claiming that nothing ever happened. Looking back, I think that she kind of took advantage of me that day, but fuck it, I enjoyed it.

After that, I became a wolf for the pussy. Who? What? Where? I was a fucking hound. At that age, you had to talk to a girl for like six hours to get any action. Once you played around and wrestled with her all day, then maybe in the hallway on her way back home she would give you a chance. But there always had to be a lot of touching and kissing, and there were still no guarantees that you would get in her drawers.

"But I'm sayin', Ma," you had to say over and over.

When you got older, you could just say, "Take it off, girl, and get in the bed," but as a kid you had to start rubbing the neck, massaging the shoulders and then slowly move down. Slowly, very slowly . . . I remember having so much trouble unhooking a girl's bra.

"Uh, you need some help?" the chicks would ask me, and my game would get knocked down a few notches. Then one day I sat and just looked at the clasp. *Oh, that's how it goes!* You pull it together first, twist, then push it out with your thumb. Ping! (Then the challenge became to open a bra with one hand *through* the shirt.)

Niggas like me weren't getting much love anyway, though. In 1985, girls were on that Menudo shit. Those were the *Purple Rain* days when you needed a long Jheri curl with the ruffled collar to get any attention. Spanish dudes, Puerto Ricans, were the only ones getting pussy. If you were light-skinned, maybe you had a shot with the honeys, but regular guys like me were assed out. You needed the wavy hair and the green eyes. I had none of that.

So I had to run up in the 'hood rats who hung out in the street, find the dirty bitches who didn't mind fucking a nigga outside. They would fuck in the park, on the roof, in the staircase. If it's on, it's on.

"Ain't nobody coming, girl. Let's just do it right here real quick."

The rats always kept it real.

11

1985

Silver shadow
Glowing shadow
Shining brightly
For all the world to see[8]

IN THE FALL OF 1985, I WAS RELEASED FROM CHILDREN'S Village. A few months before I had decided to obey as many rules as possible so that Miss Santos and the other social workers would see consistent behavior and recommend my release. The eighteen-month maximum was coming up anyway, but it was time. I had outgrown the place. My mother was hesitant about having me home again, but I think she knew that if she didn't take me back now, she would lose her last opportunity to ever have a relationship with me. I was fourteen years old and between Andrus and here, I hadn't been home much since I was ten. The first thing I did was find me a new dog.

I stole Blacky out of a junkyard. He was the first dog that I ever really called my own. When I saw him he was young, couldn't have been more than nine months old, but he was huge, and I wanted him. He was behind this old metal fence and I didn't see any sign of the owner. When me and my friend Jose came near him, he started barking like crazy, but after dealing with so many strays I had learned one thing: be patient.

"It's okay, boy. It's okay."

I kept inching up closer and closer and when he finally stopped barking, I put my hand through the fence and started to pet him.

"That's a good boy."

I petted him for over an hour and when I saw that he was comfortable with me, I slowly climbed over. Jose thought that I had lost my mind but I knew exactly what I was doing. I just had to figure a way of getting him out of there. The fence was old but there was no way of getting around it.

I played with him some more and the dog slowly started to trust me, but I figured the owner would be back soon so I needed to make my move. I knew that if I wanted to pull this off and not have the dog bite me, I had to be fast.

1—2—3 . . .

I grabbed the dog real tight and pushed him right through one of the holes in the fence onto the sidewalk. The dog didn't know what was happening, but he landed on his feet. I quickly scrambled back over, too, and then me and Jose started running. When the dog started following us, I knew he was mine.

"Come on, Blacky."

I didn't know what his name was but I just said, "Fuck it, your name is Blacky now, boy!"

I loved that dog. I fed him. I cared for him. My mother was still bugging about having animals in the apartment so when she kicked Blacky out, I left with him and went straight to the roof. I brought some more blankets up there and just like I did with so many strays before, made me and Blacky a home. Blacky wouldn't ever disappoint me. He was the love and affection and companionship I needed and now that he was mine, I knew that I would never be alone again.

Yonkers High School was the baddest school in the city. It was probably the baddest school in all of Westchester County because all of the projects—School Street, Slow Bomb, Mulford, Cottage, Ravine—all fed into two schools, Yonkers High and Gordon, and Yonkers High always got the worst of it. Every thug and 'hood rat in almost a five-mile radius had their name called out for attendance in that place. I had gotten used to the group home schools so this was a whole new world to me and being a freshman, the lowest on the totem pole, was not what you wanted to be so I went in with attitude.

I'm straight out of my second group home, man. What? Y'all niggas ain't got nothing on me!

That only lasted me a few days after I saw how serious about gun carrying some of the upperclassmen were, but the first week of freshman year I did get up enough game to join the track team. I ran relay, long distance, and the hundred-yard dash. I even jumped hurdles. I was smoking everybody except this one big, cock-diesel dude named Drew. He was a senior and was the only kid faster than me. The coach of the team never cared about how I was doing in school though, so when my lateness to classes slowly started turning into full-blown absences, coach still let me compete in the meets. (You better believe I showed up for school on those days, running sneakers in hand!)

See, after a few weeks at Yonkers High, my biggest concern wasn't track or classes but the fact that I was still broke and there was no way in the world I was going to be in high school either hungry or looking raggedy. This was the real fucking world. There was no quartermaster around that you could hustle for new clothes. There were no more spelling bees to win that could get you something different to eat for lunch. If there was anything like that, maybe I would have stayed in school a little longer, but within a month I realized that there weren't many ways for me to get what I wanted. My mother couldn't help me with money, neither could my grandmother, so I just made the decision that whatever I had to do to get some fucking money, I was going to do it. I was going to take control. I was nervous as hell the day I committed my first robbery, but I just said fuck it. If you got money and I don't, it's on. I'm taking yours.

My first victim was a lady walking out of that same Finast supermarket in the Square where I got busted for stealing those Entenmann's pies. I jumped out of some bushes on the side of the building, snatched her pocketbook off her shoulder, and ran. She never knew it, but I had been sitting in those bushes all day waiting for who I thought would be the perfect person.

From the second I started robbing, I took the activity very seriously. I watched a lot of TV and knew that the more careful you were about who you robbed, and the smarter you were about when you went out, the bigger the payoff. So if I had to lay low in the bushes somewhere for a few hours to win big, then that's what I would do. But the day I robbed that lady I also got real lucky. It must have been the fifteenth of the month or something, the day most of the women in Yonkers cashed their government checks, because she had over one thousand dollars in twenty-dollar bills in her purse. One thousand dollars? For my first robbery? At fourteen years old? *I was the man.*

The first thing I did was go to the pet store and buy Blacky a new leather collar and a harness. Then I bought myself my first pair of Timberland boots, some butter-colored ones from the store in Getty Square. They looked official. This was also when Levi's jeans were big, so I bought a few pairs of those and then topped my shopping off with a checkerboard bomber jacket and a matching rabbit hat. *Man, listen. Life was good!*

The next day I went to school rocking my new gear and at lunchtime I went around the corner and bought a huge turkey sandwich from the store and brought it to the lunchroom with me.

Yeah, what's up? Now I got what y'all got.

It was just such a good feeling to walk around the school with money in my pocket and later that afternoon I went right back out to rob someone else.

Once I got better at robbing, it didn't take me all day anymore because then I knew the best spots and could identify the best victims a lot faster. That's what I liked about robbing and was one of the reasons that I never thought about hustling—*hustling on the corner took too fucking long.* You just had to sit there all day. There was nothing you could do as a dealer to make the baseheads come to you any faster. So I always thought, why don't I let *you* hustle all day and get that money. Then *I'll* come around at the end of your shift and just rob you. Then I'd have the same money it took you all day to make and would have earned it in less than two minutes!

By November of my freshman year, I had totally stopped going to class, but that didn't mean I stopped coming around the school. Now that I was steady robbing, Yonkers High became a great place to get it on.

"You know that kid right there? Is he cool?" I'd ask someone I knew before going up to a potential victim.

I was ready to bang anybody I saw. It didn't matter. One time I took this kid named Al B's furry Kangol.

"Yo, Al, let me see that . . ."

"What's up, D?"

"Let me see your Kangol . . . Oh, shit, this hat is hot man, word . . . All right Al, now you can walk."

"Huh? What are you talking about?"

"You ain't getting this shit back, Al. Now get up outta here!"

I had Blacky with me. I used to bring him to school with me every day. He was my running partner and he was always ready to bite somebody, so when Al didn't want to listen, I just turned to my dog.

"Get him!"

On command, Blacky jumped up and bit Al on the back of his leg. He was holding on tight, so it took Al a second to pull his leg out of my boy's jaws. Then when Al started running away, Blacky just kept chasing him down the street. It's not like I kept my dog on a leash or anything.

I used to put Blacky on bags all the time. I just taught him to grab anything that was in someone's hand. One morning an old lady came up to the two of us while we were walking down Linden Street.

"Oooh! What a nice dog," she said, bending down to pet him. All of a sudden, Blacky grabbed the lady's bag in his mouth.

"Get it, boy!"

The lady was so startled.

"Oh! Oh my . . ."

Blacky and I just ran down the street, his tail wagging back and forth, me laughing.

"You did good today, boy! No more hot dogs out of the freezer, okay? Today you get dog food, *in a bowl.*"

Whenever Blacky did good I made sure to bless him when we got back up to the roof and he loved Alpo. I hated to admit it but that stuff did smell kinda good. When I opened the can I was always like *Hmmm. Maybe if shit ever gets too hard . . .*

After a while, my robbing and stealing started giving me a new reputation around the school. Because of my beatboxing, I was called DMX now, and kids knew to just give it up when they saw me. "Oh, here comes this nigga again . . ."

"Yeah, y'all know what time it is! Who got what?"

Just me and my dog. No mask. No gun.

It was crazy because robbing really gave me a rush. Just before the robbery my palms would start sweating and my throat would get dry.

My heart would beat faster and my mind would start to race. Sometimes halfway through a robbery I would have to stop and take a breath, like, *Oh, shit. I'm going through it again . . . Okay, yeah, motherfucker!* Then I would just zone out. The nervousness, the danger, it was the strongest feeling that I had ever experienced. I just felt it everywhere.

So I made it my job. I did my robberies on a schedule. Just like niggas hustle, but I was straight stickup. I'd rob three times a day: before school, after school, and on the late night. That way there would be three different groups of people to choose from. The morning shift was always really crowded, so that's when I had to do the pressure type of robbery, just walk the same way as someone on their way to school and push up on their back. That worked good. Or I'd just go down to the corner store where the kids with money always were. *Shorty looks like he got five dollars, that's probably enough to get me through the morning.*

After school was cool because then you didn't have all the people going to work around everywhere. You just had to be careful that none of the kids hanging out late saw you catch somebody behind that tree.

Then there was the evening, like 7 P.M. I robbed mostly older people at night. They usually had more money on them anyway and it was more of a rush catching somebody twice your age. Whenever I caught the last groups of people coming home from Getty Square, I hit it big.

Three times a day was how I got down for a long time and I was always a face-to-face robbery nigga, straight up. There were many other ways I could have robbed something but I never wanted to do it any other way. I was just more comfortable robbing somebody in the flesh. Maybe because of the time these cats asked me to help them rob a house and I was so scared I wanted to just snatch the VCR and run. I wasn't comfortable because I didn't know *who* was in that house and I didn't know *what* was in that house. I could have been in the back room and the owner could have been in the front bedroom with a burner under his pillow. Or maybe the owner could have come back from walking his dog or something and popped me in my head.

"Yo, let's get the fuck out of here!" I just kept yelling at the other guys.

You never really know the details about a place you're trying to steal from. "Oh, I can get out of this window," you say to yourself, not knowing that window has been nailed shut for years. And you can't say anything to someone if you're in their house with all types of TVs in your arms. You're just busted and they can do whatever they want to do to you and be 100 percent right.

So I learned pretty quickly that I wasn't a thief. I wasn't going to *steal* anything and I already knew that I didn't like to hustle or sell drugs. Me? I was going to *take* something.

You want to come to school with the new Adidas with the fat laces? Let me get that. The little silver chain with your name on it or the raccoon hat or sheepskin coat? I'm taking all that from you, homes, because I ain't got none of that. I ain't got a sheepskin!

At Yonkers High, if you were one of the ruffnecks that didn't go to class all day, you hung out in a spot called the Castle. It was like a small stone structure with a few benches inside it that sat on the far end of the baseball field, out of sight of the main building. Most days, you could find five to ten upperclassmen chilling up there, smoking and shooting dice. Some of them knew me for doing the beatbox with Ready Ron, but most of them just knew me for all my robbing and stealing. Whichever way, because I had become so reckless, as a freshman it was like I had the respect of a senior.

Sometimes I would go over to gamble with them, but I didn't like to see anyone having fun without me, so me and Blacky would often just disrupt the game. Other times I would go up there to sell some of the stuff I stole and since everyone at Yonkers High was more concerned about putting on a fashion show than they were about anything else, selling shit was a good hustle.

Back then, you needed a Kangol with the matching bomber jacket to be fly. Or a big puffy hat with the flaps that came down. Anyone with a lumberjack shirt or a Triple F.A.T. goose coat was always good.

Sheepskins were the hottest commodities. I wore them for a day or two just to let folks know that I came across one, then I would sell it for fifty dollars or even one hundred dollars if I could. Sometimes the price would depend on what I had to do to get it. Once, I caught a blue sheepskin by rolling up on this dude and his Puerto Rican girl-friend. The problem was that I had to smack the shit out of the girl to get the coat because she wouldn't stop talking shit.

"Yo, get your girl," I told him, but he couldn't control her. He was acting like a bitch and when she started getting too aggressive in my face, I had to hit her. She looked a little younger than me, too, so I wasn't proud of that one . . . but I made sure I got a good price for the coat.

That's probably why I never liked messing with girls my age or younger, because they always acted too silly. I remember one day after school, this young girl was like, "I'll hit you in your nuts!" Now girls always say that when you're playing, but she did it right away. She didn't even wait for me to answer her, she just banged me with her forearm. It hurt so much I stayed on the ground for like ten min-utes, just laying there in a fetal position. My eyes were closed; my nose was running. I couldn't catch my breath. At that age, you really don't know whether or not you're holding—*where you stand within the male community*—and I was messed up.

Leave me alone, it hurts. I just wanna go to sleep.

When I finally stood up, it felt like I had to shit, but I couldn't get anything out. I just threw up all over the place and promised myself that I would never ever mess with a young girl.

Leshawn Johnson was in the twelfth grade when I was a freshman. She used to come over to my house every day, watch TV, and play Monopoly with my sisters. It was cool because Leshawn was grown enough to know when her parents weren't going to be home and wasn't shy about taking her clothes off. I got points on the block just because she was older, but she was fine, too. And normally if they weren't on the Menudo shit, bad bitches like her liked the dudes who sold drugs, hustlers who had a lot of clothes and drove around on scooters in the summer. (In the mid-eighties, hustlers always had the 98 Oldsmobiles with the banging systems, the same cars that the cab services in Harlem used to use with the tinted windows, fat rims, and whitewalls, and they always took their girls to City Island to eat shrimp for dinner. But that wasn't me. I was the type that would catch a nigga for his cash *before* he went to City Island. See the Touch of Class cab pull up and be like, "Hey buddy, let me talk to you for a

minute . . .") But for whatever reason, Leshawn was
down with me. She even
knew that I had formed a
little robbery crew with
my two partners, Nick and
Reg, but she didn't care.

THE CASTLE AT YONKERS HIGH

In the 'hood, it was easy to
find someone who would
roll with you to do your
dirt. But while everyone
talked about getting some
money, when you got out
on the street, a lot of guys would front. They would be scared and
stand around looking stupid. That's why I loved Nick and Reg,
because with them, there was never any hesitation. It was just, "You
ready? . . . Okay, let's get him." And they knew how much I loved it.
If they ever went out robbing without me, they knew they'd have to
make it up to me quick because I was just on it like that and never
wanted to miss a chance to feel that rush.

That night we needed a hundred dollars so Reg could get his
little brother a bike for Christmas. He had just got a job so now his
folks were putting pressure on him to start buying things for everybody. Whenever project parents found out you started working, it
was always, "Son, can you get. . . ?" or "Baby, we need this." Reg
was feeling the heat and I liked his little brother, so I changed into
this blue jogging track suit that I always liked to wear to go robbing and the three us decided to go on a spree to get the money he
needed.

It didn't start off too good. In our first hour, we robbed three different people but came back with only six dollars to show for it. One
lady we caught—her wig came off and everything—had only thirty-
two cents in her pocket! So we stopped at Leshawn's house and took
a break.

This was the night I tried mescaline for the first time. Reg said you
should drink a beer right afterward, so I guzzled down a forty-ounce
and a little after 8 P.M. we went back out.

After a few minutes we saw this woman walking down South Broadway. She was wearing white stockings and matching white shoes, so we figured she worked in the hospital downtown and we started following her. Ten blocks later, she stopped for a moment near the bus stop right down the hill from School Street. Now was the time.

Me, Nick, and Reg had this robbing technique called the Death Run. After you walked behind a person at the same pace for a while, you would put about a half a block between you and then start to jog toward them. You had to jog softly enough so that not too many people noticed you running, and time it so that your victim wouldn't hear you coming up on them until you were right behind them, but once you started that jog, the Death Run was on. There was no turning back.

BOOM!

One of us would hit the person low exactly at the same time the other person grabbed their bag. It was like a football play and it worked every time with either a man or a woman because once a person falls like that, their arms automatically raise up to protect themselves from hitting the ground and their bag will normally fly right off. You're not thinking about your bag, all you're thinking about is breaking your fall.

But nothing would go smooth that night.

The woman wasn't tall, about five-four, but she was husky and she had on this big, thick wool coat, one of those grandma joints that closed real tight. I was doing the grabbing and when she got hit, she fell to the ground hard. The problem was that she held on to her purse.

"Let it go!" I yelled at her.

That lady must have had the super grips on her pocketbook because even though I kept shaking her wildly, she just kept holding on—*with one hand.* Now it was a scene. The people at the bus stop started screaming.

"Come on, lady!" I yelled at her again.

I ended up dragging her into the middle of the street. I kept pulling and pulling. Then, while I was still yanking on her purse, I saw my mother coming down the hill. She must have decided to go to work early that night.

Oh shit. I better hurry up . . .

"COME ON!"

Finally, the strap to her bag broke and I got the purse and started running toward Main Street after my two partners. I could hear my mother's voice behind me screaming for help with the rest of the people.

I never turned around.

One evening, after a more successful robbery, I rolled back into School Street and heard this song playing out of one of the ground-floor apartments. I didn't see who was playing it, but this was the second or third time that I had heard the song and I thought how much I really liked it. I didn't listen to the words then, but there was something about the record that drew me to it. It was called "Silver Shadow."

```
I remember gazing on those quiet nights
The stars were as bright as they could be
Wondering if things would ever go right
And if there was a spot up there for me
```

Yeah, that's that shit right there!

12

Turn Out the Lights

NINETEEN-EIGHTY-FIVE WAS THE BEST YEAR OF MY LIFE. I
had survived my time in group home. I was back in Yonkers. I had a
dog I called my own. Nineteen-eighty-five was the year I started robbing, running, fucking, the year I first heard "Silver Shadow," and the
year that I bought my first pair of Timberlands.

But 1986, well, that was something else . . .

It was Peanut's fault. He lived in building 10. He had been talking
shit to me all morning so me and Blacky chased him right upstairs
into his hallway. His mother heard us arguing and came out with a
frying pan in her hand, so I went back downstairs to catch him later.
Ten minutes later, the police rolled up. When they saw me and Blacky
posted in the front, they immediately drew their guns and opened
their car doors halfway to shield themselves.

"Put the dog up against the fence!"

My first instinct was to run, but I didn't know if Blacky could keep
up with me and I didn't want them to start shooting at my dog.

"Tie your dog against the fence and step this way."

I did what they said.

They put me in the back of the police car and when I asked them what was going on they said that the pound was on the way. Someone had called in a complaint about my dog.

When the handlers arrived, they put a loop around Blacky's neck to try to catch him but he was big and strong and when my dog saw that I wasn't getting out of the police car, he started going wild. They couldn't pull him in the paddy wagon. Blacky just kept barking.

"Yeah, boy. Get him, boy!" I yelled at him from behind the window. I wasn't going to let them take my dog.

The handlers wrestled with Blacky for ten more minutes, then I saw one of them nod to a police officer.

"Everybody please stand back . . ."

They hooked Blacky to the fence again and when I saw one of the police officers move directly in front of him I started screaming.

"NO! DON'T KILL MY DOG! NOOOO!"

Two shots later, Blacky was dead. They shot him right in front of the building. That's why I hate Peanut to this day because he got my dog killed. *Fucking bitch.*

In 1986, though, being broke wasn't my only problem.

A few years before, Ready Ron introduced me to something that was far more damaging to my life and my spirit then not having money. Until then, I drank forties with cats on corners, smoked whatever weed I came across, and experimented with bullshit drugs like mescaline when the mood arose, like the day me, Nick, and Reg went on that robbing spree. But that didn't make me much more than your average project nigga. There were no lingering effects of getting drunk one night off a bottle of malt liquor or passing a blunt with my niggas from School Street.

But when Ready Ron spoke of the great high I could get from a "woolie," the "new thing on the block," he didn't tell me how differently it would affect my life. He didn't tell me of the war that I would have to fight to kill my desire for one of the most addictive drugs on the street. He didn't tell me how quickly it would ruin what little was left of my relationship with my mother, my sisters, and even my uncles.

When I smoked a blunt laced with crack cocaine, he didn't tell me how much I would suffer. How wrong that was.

"I fucked up."

Collie found out about my problem the day I went into the shoe-box he kept in his closet and took some of his stash. My uncle occasionally hustled to put some money in his pocket, mostly nickel or dime bags of weed, but every now and then he would flip the harder stuff.

"What do you mean you 'fucked up'?" he answered me back.

Then he saw what I had taken. Collie and me had never had a fight. We would disagree and argue like brothers, but we would never come to blows. That day I could feel his anger and disappointment fire at me like a shotgun blast.

He said he knew it wasn't me. I told him it wasn't a big deal.

But it got worse.

Now I had another reason to rob. Not only was I trying to eat, trying to keep some money in my pocket, but now I also had a habit to feed.

It didn't help that my aunts were also struggling, or that I bumped heads with my uncle Pinky in the same apartments on Ravine where I was getting high. At one point, Pinky lived next door to one of the buildings that served as my main stomping ground. Sometimes he would come and try to take me out of the hallways I was in, tried to pull me out of hell.

It was never easy.

I never talked to anyone about my problem. But I couldn't hide it. One day I saw my little sister Shayla walking home from school. She must have been no more than nine or ten years old. I didn't think she saw me.

"Earl."

I couldn't let her see me like this.

"Earl. I know that's you."

I had to hide my eyes. I wasn't the older brother she thought I was.

"Go home, Shayla."

"Earl, please come upstairs. Please come upstairs and I'll give you something to eat. Talk to me for a minute."

"No, not right now, girl. I'm not coming upstairs right now."

But at my darkest moments, I did go upstairs. These were the times I ran out of money, the times someone's wallet wasn't enough to pay my bill. The problem was that I knew whomever I needed to pay would accept anything that I could give them: VHS tapes, shoes, sneakers, even giant-size bottles of bleach or laundry detergent. I took them. I would lift coats out of my mother's closet, sweaters from my sisters, or swipe old clothes of my own that were still in my room—anything that would get me closer to that next high.

It didn't matter to me. There was a voice in my head louder and more powerful than anything I had ever heard before, and it wouldn't stop yelling.

A week after Blacky's murder, I walked into the lunchroom of Yonkers High School with a sawed-off shotgun taped to my leg. The gun came from the floor up to my knee, so it made me walk with a limp, like I was crippled. I didn't give a fuck about nothing or nobody. I was ready to rob anybody I could.

Niggas thought I was bluffing.

"What, man, what? It can happen . . . Run your fucking pockets!"

I came home with about four dollars. A few days later, I was behind bars.

It was dark and hell is hot.

13

Betrayal

I WASN'T AFRAID TO TELL MY MOTHER ABOUT MY ROBBING and stealing. I wasn't ashamed of it. If she was home the times I walked in the house with someone's pocketbook, I told her the truth. I needed some money. I was hungry. Maybe I was being spiteful. Or maybe it was a lesson I learned from her, since she always told me that the worst thing anyone could ever be was a liar.

"As long as you tell the truth, Earl, I will always support you."

But we both knew that wasn't true because she always followed it up with "But if you're not with me, I cannot say that I know what you've been doing. If you're not with me, I can never tell anyone, 'that was not my child,' so if the cops come saying you did something, Earl, I'm going to show them to your room."

I couldn't have imagined how much she meant that one.

Industry Institution is a minimum-security facility for juvenile offenders. Located just outside of Rochester, New York, Industry was the furthest I had ever been sent away from home. I had already been to Woodfield, Valhalla's juvenile unit, for a few months, but this sentence was two years. I wasn't trying to stay for two days.

Bobby was one of my cellmates. He was from one of those small, upstate all-white towns, and he was almost as reckless as I was. The first day we looked out of the rec room window and didn't see any gates or fences or barbed wire holding us in, we knew we weren't going to stay long.

The wardens felt Industry was way too isolated for any child to think about leaving. They were confident that since there wasn't a town, let alone a city, for many miles, escape was not an option.

Yeah, okay. You don't know me. I don't care how far I have to walk. I'm not doing two years!

Bobby and I made an agreement: If we leave together, then we go all out together. If we got to hitch a ride and the truck driver wants to try something with one of us, then we both fuck him up. Whatever we need to do, we'll do it.

It was early December, less than thirty degrees outside. At night, we knew the temperature would even fall below that, so it took us a few days to get the clothes together that we needed. But once I had hoarded three pairs of long johns and got my boots, I was ready.

All we had to do was knock over one guard.

When Bobby pushed him over, we were home free. I remember looking at him shivering on the ground. It was so cold, he didn't even try to get up, but he must have hit an alarm or something because they sent the dogs after us in a hurry.

It was pitch black out there in the woods, Bobby and I couldn't see the dogs coming, but we heard them barking behind us. I remember thinking if I had Blacky with me, he could have handled his business, but after a few minutes I saw one of the hounds right behind me and before I could think of what to do, he bit me on the back of my leg. The dog wasn't that big, but his bite was crazy. I fell face-first onto the ground and just started kicking as wildly as I could.

"You fucking motherfucker, get away from me!"

Kick . . . Kick . . . KICK.

I went nuts. A few times I felt my boot hitting the dog on the head and by the fourth time, he stopped barking and I heard him whimper. I was still on the ground, my leg was bleeding badly, but that dog wasn't going to bite me anymore. I don't know what happened to the others.

Bobby and I walked for three more days. He lived somewhere upstate so we tried to find roads that were heading south toward where he lived. We didn't go on the highways because we were scared a cop would stop us, so we stayed on local streets. But upstate

New York is nothing but a bunch of small, rural towns in the middle of nowhere and once the towns ran out there'd be nothing but miles and miles of farmland. At the end of what felt like a week being without anywhere to sleep or anything proper to eat, we finally got to Bobby's hometown.

He said we couldn't go to his house, but we could chill in one of his friend's basements. I didn't care, I was just happy to be somewhere warm. It was a large basement, the kind that ran underneath a whole house, and when we got there I just went to the back corner and huddled under some old blankets I saw lying on the floor.

Bobby stayed with me for a few minutes and then said he was going to go home and get us some money.

"I think I know where some of my friends might be, too."

I never saw Bobby again.

The next morning, I didn't know what to do. I had no money. I had no food. I didn't know where I was. All I knew was that motherfucker had left me. That motherfucker left me all by myself.

Then I heard a voice.

"Oh my God! Somebody's back there!"

It was two girls, teenagers, my age. The taller one, whose house it was, told me that Bobby was her friend and had called her and told her I was in her basement, but she needed to know exactly who I was. Her mother was upstairs and she had to tell her something.

Her friend, the fatter one, didn't say anything. She just kept staring at me, looking at me up and down, like she wanted to fucking eat me or something.

I just begged for something to eat.

Miraculously, the mother didn't flip out.

"He's down in the basement starving! Mommy, please! We have to give him food."

The mom could have easily called the police and squad cars would have been at their house in two minutes to take me back to Industry. But she didn't. Instead she let me come upstairs into their house and after she saw that her daughter was calling Bobby on the phone without being able to reach him, she told me I could stay with them until I figured out what to do. I ended up staying with them for days. We just smoked a lot of cigarettes together and played cards. At night, we watched television. It was Christmastime and even though they didn't have a tree or any decorations around, they kept on listening to this radio station that was playing nothing but old Christmas carols.

It's the most wonderful time of the year . . .

One night, when I told them my sixteenth birthday had passed a few days earlier, the mother and daughter even made me a cake.

After a while, though, things got weird because I noticed that the mother never got off the couch. She ate there, slept there, spent her whole day there, and their house was kind of nasty. When I went to take a shower I saw all these little tiny bugs crawling on the towel. They were smaller than the roaches I was used to, and they were all over the place.

But who was I to complain? These people saved my life. I just couldn't forget that motherfucker Bobby had left me. He probably found his peoples and just said, fuck you. Fuck Earl. I couldn't believe it. Here I was willing to die with that nigga.

The last two days in their house, I just slept. The fat friend kept bothering me but I never paid her any mind. Then just before New Year's, the mother surprised me and gave me some money so I could get on a bus back to New York.

"Here, Earl," she said. "It's time for you to go home."

I was so grateful.

It was 3 A.M. when I got back to School Street. My clothes were torn apart and the big gash on my leg where the dog bit me was now an infected, dark color red. I knocked on my mother's door.

"Well, look who it is . . ."

My mother was shocked to see me, but it wasn't because she was surprised that I escaped—she had already told Industry that her son was "a runner"—she just never thought that I could ever make it all the way back home.

"How did you get out, Earl?"

After everything that I had been through, "How did you get out?" was not the kind of cold reaction that I wanted. How about "I'm so happy to see you"? Or "Are you okay?"

So after I said what's up to my sisters, I left immediately for my grandmother's house.

"I just couldn't take it no more, Grandma. It was freezing up there in that place. They didn't feed you right, they wanted to work you to death. I had to go. I had to leave, Grandma."

My grandmother was happy to see me. It had been almost two weeks since I had escaped, so the rumors about what must have happened to me had been pretty bad.

"Okay, baby, well you just stay right here."

Collie and Buzzy were thrilled to have their running partner back. Now that I was an escapee, my reputation in their eyes had grown to where they thought I was capable of doing absolutely anything. I probably was—but only the things that were in my control.

Three days after New Year's, there was a knock on my grandmother's door. It was my mother. She had the police with her.

I could hear my grandmother arguing with her.

"I know he's here . . . you just let him do anything he wants to do! Well, I'm his mother."

I walked to the door.

"It's better to do it like this, Earl," my mother told me. "Honey, this is all because of you and you have to pay the consequences. The holidays are over. Now it's time for you to go back where you belong."

My mother would never understand. I didn't come home for fucking New Year's! I was facing two years . . . I was trying to be out for good!

Then I looked at my grandmother.

"Go back, baby. It's okay. We'll get you out."

She looked at me and tried to smile. The cops got out their handcuffs.

I guess my mother thought that she had to teach me another lesson, but it was a lesson that I would never, ever forgive her for.

14

DMX the Great Is Born

UNLIKE INDUSTRY, MCCORMICK JUVENILE INSTITUTION wasn't afraid of bars. There were gates and barbed-wire fences everywhere—and guards with guns. McCormick made sure you weren't going nowhere, so I had a lot of time to think.

I thought about Bonita and Shayla and my crazy aunts and uncles. I thought about my grandmother on Warburton and my father in Philadelphia. I thought about Blacky and and why I hated Peanut so much. And I thought about my beatboxing career. But when I thought about that there was one issue with that I couldn't get out of my head: why was I letting Ready Ron get all of the attention?

It was like every time we did a show, girls were all over him. I used to watch it go down. He would always get the flyest chick in the

POSING AT McCORMICK

crowd and at best I got to talk to Shorty's ugly sister—and still had to beg all night for a kiss.

That wasn't right. I was the one providing the crazy intro for the rhyme. I was the one throwing the hot break in there. What's up? Where was my love?

But no girl wants to talk to the dude that ends up with a handful of spit every night. So it dawned on me that that was all you got from being the beatbox: no pussy and a handful of fucking spit!

Oh, no. We got to switch this up. Maybe *I* could write a little something, then on the break, Ron could do the beat for a minute and I would say the rhyme. Why not? It made sense. Ron had already shown me what you needed to do to move the crowd. Why should I be playing the background? All I had to do is write.

"I think I'm gonna be an MC," I told Collie in a letter I wrote to him from lockup. "Fuck the beatbox shit, I'm going to be a rapper."

After that I spent my days and nights in McCormick writing rhymes. I had brought a boom box with me from home that had this one big bass woofer in the middle of it, so I used that for background music and just wrote about everything I knew, everything I saw in the world around me: Yonkers, School Street, lockup, group home. Robbing, stealing, running, hustling. It was fun and it felt good. It gave me a way to talk freely, gave me the tool to express all of the thoughts that had sat unheard in my brain since I was seven years old.

Okay, this is what's up. No more Beat Box Enforcer.

When I came home from McCormick in 1988 I was an MC, an MC by the name of DMX the Great.

I'm DMX. For short, just call me DM
I keep the party jumpin' from A.M. to P.M.
Then back to A.M. competition I play 'em
The commandments of the religion of rap, I obey 'em . . .[9]

15

"I Want to Do That!"

MY UNCLES AND I WERE AT THE NEPPERHAN COMMUNITY
Center the day it opened its doors. Down the street from my grandmother's house on Warburton Avenue, the Center was the kind
of teenage refuge the likes of
which you rarely see anymore. It
was recreational as well as edu-
cational, board games sat on the
shelves next to reading work-
books, a pool table shared space
with a chalkboard, and it was
always warm inside.

My favorite activity was hanging out in the career room in the
back where I could shut the door
and excite Collie and Buzzy with
stories of my life upstate, robberies I had done, and adven-
tures I wanted to plan. We had
tried to come up with new ways
of entertaining ourselves on the
street, whether it was climbing

MY EARLY TAG

on top of the roof of a building or throwing our middle finger up to cops driving by, but Nepperhan gave us the opportunity to have fun simply playing dominoes or Connect 4 all afternoon.

Nepperhan was also the place that had all the paper and pens, which meant it was the place I could write more rhymes. I still occasionally drew pictures of people on sheets of notebook paper or on that rough yellow stuff the counselors gave you to draw on, but words quickly became my true passion. I tried to write a whole new rhyme every day and I used Collie and Buzzy as my audience and number-one critics.

Mrs. Gains, the head counselor of Nepperhan, was forever kicking me out of the Center, especially when she figured out that all the yelling she heard outside her office was actually me finishing one of my raps with a string of "fuck," "bitch" and "motherfucker." She

always said she knew whenever I came in because I was like a tornado blowing through the doors that knocked down everything in its path. She was right because whatever was happening, I had to be a part of it. Whatever conversations were going on, I had to interrupt to make sure my point of view was heard, and then I would probably convince whoever was talking that they weren't talking about the right shit anyway.

But whenever she kicked me out, I just came right back the next day, checking her office in the back to make sure she was at her desk.

"Hi, Mrs. Gains."

"Good afternoon, Earl. I already knew you were here . . ."

I liked the Center.

Every year Yonkers sponsored an African-American Heritage Day in Trevor Park and the Center would set up a stage where their kids could perform and show off their various talents. They also had a poetry contest. That year, Mrs. Gains asked me to write a rap.

"Just make sure it rhymes," she said.

I was stunned later that afternoon when she told me that I had won. My rhyme had beaten out twelve other poems from all over the city. It felt like I had just won the spelling bee again and made me think that maybe my writing was actually pretty good. Maybe this MC thing could be all right?

Then I saw the movie *Krush Groove*.

I went to see it at the Park Hill Theater downtown. I had never been to a real rap show; the closest I had got was me and Ready Ron doing our thing on the block for a crowd of people, but this movie was like a concert.

Starring Run-DMC and Sheila E., *Krush Groove* was the story of Russell Simmons and how he started his own rap record label with his partner, Rick Rubin. Kurtis Blow was in it. LL Cool J and the Fat Boys were in it, and every time one of them performed, the audience in the movie theater jumped out of their seats and started cheering at the screen. It was so hot.

"Now DJ Run's my name . . . Jam Master Jay is his . . . He's DMC, it's like that and that's the way it is!"

I want to do that!

The next day at the Center I asked Mrs. Gains if she could set up a microphone for me. At first she said no, because she didn't want to hear all that cursing and screaming, but when all the other kids started asking her, and Collie and I promised that I would say a rhyme that didn't have any bad words in it, she gave in.

That afternoon, she set up the PA system in the parking lot and all of the kids brought their plastic chairs outside. They were mostly

ONE OF MY FIRST BATTLES

younger than me, but once I became a full-fledged teenager, I always liked the little eight- and nine-year-olds. (During family days at Children's Village I always played with other people's younger brothers. We would run around together and I would protect them from the other kids who used to like to bully them and punch them around. "Don't worry, little man, ain't nobody gonna mess with us," I used to tell them.) So even though this wasn't exactly the kind of grown-up audience Ready Ron used to get, I was excited to be putting on my first show.

The song I did was a rap I wrote while in McCormick that used Burt and Ernie and the rest of the *Sesame Street* gang as characters. I just flipped it—without telling Mrs. Gains—and made them all drug dealers.

> Yo, I had this dream that I've been having a lot
> That Sesame Street turned into a crack spot

Collie and Buzzy knew what I was saying, but I don't think any of the kids figured it out. At the end of the rhyme, the Count steals all the cash and everyone gets shot. Money and friendship don't mix.

> All of them dead not a sound to be heard,
> From the Monster, the Count, the Grouch or Big Bird.[10]

Everyone enjoyed watching me perform and despite the content, Mrs. Gains was pretty impressed.

After that I started asking her to let me throw a real party at Nepperhan. I told her that I could print up flyers and hire a DJ. We could charge people five dollars at the door and everybody in the neigh-borhood could come and rhyme and she and I could split the money fifty-fifty. It would be a big hip-hop jam, I would get paid, and she could buy some new things for the Center.

She wasn't with it.

By this time, Mrs. Gains was used to hearing my plans for making money and getting out of the ghetto. One night I had rolled into the Center just before closing time and found her and two other coun-selors talking about how awful it was that parents were spending all of their money on sneakers for their kids. These families didn't make more than two or three hundred dollars a week (sometimes less than that on public assistance), but they would spend all that money on a new pair of Nikes when they had no food in the refrigerator. (Nineteen-eighty-eight was the height of the Air Jordan era and any new pair of kicks kids were lusting after was a hundred dollars or more.)

But I didn't want to talk about why parents were spending their money. I wanted to talk about how to get a piece of that pie.

"I'm gonna open me up a store," I told them. "I'm gonna open a place and just go down to Manhattan and buy sneakers where they're cheaper. Then I will bring them back to Yonkers and kids will buy them from me for whatever price I want."

Mrs. Gains smiled.

"That's a good idea, Earl."

"Then when I get everybody in the store, I could sell drugs in the back and make real money . . ."

Hearing that, Mrs. Gains almost dropped her bag in disgust.

"Why would you do that? Selling drugs is illegal, young man."

"What? It's not like I would have to hustle to find customers. They'd be coming to me."

"Earl, all that's going to happen with that plan is I'll have to end up visiting you in jail."

"So what? I'm probably going to end up there anyway. But I'm try-ing to be a millionaire by the time I'm twenty-five, Mrs. Gains."

"Oh, really? Why do you want all that money, Earl?"

"Mrs. Gains, how much money do you make?"

"That's not your business."

"You probably don't make no money, Mrs. Gains."

"Earl . . ."

"I bet if I did my sneaker and drug thing I could make more money in one night than you make in a week—"

"But what good is that if you're in jail?"

"Twenty years from now, I bet you're probably going to be doing this same job, making the same money. You bust your butt from morning to night and all you get is minimum wage!"

Mrs. Gains couldn't help laughing.

16

"Stolen Novas"

PARTLY BECAUSE IT WAS DOWN THE STREET FROM THE CENTER, by the time I was a teenager, my mother finally let me live at my grandmother's house for a little while and Collie and Buzzy knew I would be there every day when they came back from school. I'd either still be asleep in the bed or up eating breakfast at the kitchen table writing rhymes while I ate my cereal and French toast.

See, after my time in McCormick, school was over for me. They shut down Yonkers High School after I went to juvenile, turning it into a middle school for younger kids, and while if my mother really pressed the issue I probably could have gone to Gordon, the high school where my uncles went, it wasn't going to happen. Juvenile offenders like me weren't exactly welcome additions to a school population—especially when their new hobby was stealing cars.

My friend Jose taught me. Up until then, the dirt I did in the streets was about things I felt I needed to do. Robbing people was a way of getting money, taking someone's jacket was a way of staying warm. It was a thrill, but it was also a job. Stealing cars was different, it was just fun. I didn't try to sell them or strip them or really need them to get around anywhere. There wasn't anywhere to go. I just wanted to ride.

All you needed was a dent puller and a screwdriver, the two tools of a car thief. The dent puller was for the front door; the screwdriver was for the ignition. Once you learned how to use them, almost any car on the street was yours for the taking.

Toyota Corollas, Camrys, and Nissan Maximas were my favorites. If the puller was heavy enough I could break into slightly nicer cars like Volkswagen Jettas or Volvos. When Slick Rick's "Mona Lisa" record was big, I always wanted to find a Chevrolet Nova to steal. That way I could profile in a "stolen Nova" just like in the rhyme.

Collie and Buzzy learned how to steal cars, too, and after a while it wasn't uncommon to see us come down the block, pushing stolen cars back to back. We would find one around the way in Yonkers to steal, or troop over to White Plains or the Bronx. We would keep each car for a couple of days, until it got hot or ran out of gas. Then we just went and found another one.

One time I went to pick Buzzy up from school in this nice blue Honda I had stolen. You should have seen the expression on his face. The next day, I gave it to Collie and he parked the car in the school's lot like it was his. Another time the three of us and another friend, Ant, picked up this little red Datsun sports car from in front of Ravine and we almost got hit by an eighteen-wheeler truck when we tried to speed on the highway.

My grandmother almost busted me one afternoon. Collie and I had just gotten off the bus from the Square and I saw a car double-parked with its engine still running. Now, my grandmother's house was only two blocks away, but I didn't care. As soon as I got into the driver's seat, though, the owner came out. My grandmother was looking out of her kitchen window when she saw some man chasing a car up the block. Luckily, she didn't see who was in it.

"Some crazy boy just stole a man's car," she said to Collie when he got back to the house.

After a while, my love for stealing cars got so intense I couldn't just keep it to myself anymore so I started teaching everybody else on the block how to jack. Then none of the vehicles in the surrounding area were safe—even our own. One time I had to punch this kid Mel in his face when he stole a car from me that I had just stolen! It was crazy.

I was in a Trans Am GT early one night when the police pulled up behind me. They must have assumed (correctly) that this was not my car, so they started flashing their lights to pull me over.

But I wasn't stopping.

I gunned that Trans Am up Ashburton Avenue and drove right through the middle of Slow Bombs projects down a one-way street. I slammed on the brakes in front of building 7, jumped out of the car, and instead of running, just kinda hung out with the cats who were standing in front of the building. The kids who were with me in the car made a dash for it. The brothers outside looked at me like I was crazy.

"Yo, you got the po—"

When the cops pulled up, they saw a bunch of brothers standing around and two kids running up the block.

Hey, don't look at me, officer. I'm chilling.

You know that, being stupid, they're just gonna chase whoever's running.

"I see them. They're over there!" one cop said to his partner, and the two of them ran right past me.

I got some points for that move.

The next time I had a police confrontation in front of the projects I wasn't so smooth, though. "Yonkers teen incites riot . . . " that's what the local newspaper, the *Herald Statesman*, said after I got knocked in a Toyota Corolla in front of my building. I started yelling, "Police brutality!" when they almost broke my arms pulling them behind my back to arrest me. Folks from School Street actually started chanting, "Leave him alone . . . leave him alone," before the cops threw me in the back of their squad car and took me away.

I actually learned how to drive a stick while stealing someone's car. The Hyundai Excel had just come out and one night in White Plains I saw a brand new two-door joint. I knew that would be a hot car to bring back around the way, so I pulled out my tools and got busy. I got into the car without a problem but when I was in the driver's seat I noticed it wasn't an automatic. Now I had to figure something out fast because I was sitting right in front of the owner's house.

Screech. Stop. *Scrreeeech.* Stop.

I didn't know what I was doing. I just knew the police were going to see me lurching up and down the street. I must have driven in first gear for blocks before I figured out how to use that damn clutch.

I should have taken that as a sign that the car was going to bring me bad luck because three days later that new Hyundai Excel got totaled.

I had taken this young kid from School Street out for a lesson. I often let people drive in the cars I stole. I wasn't selfish with them. We could all share in the fun for a minute and it's not like anyone on the block would forget who did the stealing. The kid was keeping it mellow, calmly driving around the projects getting his shine, but it just so happened that this was a day the police chose to come through and harass everyone.

The chase was on.

High speed chasing, racing through the streets
Death's in the air, I can taste it through the heat
My partner's going fast, I don't think he's gonna last
And if he don't, I'ma hit his wife with half[11]

Now, Yonkers is full of hills. Everything sits above the Hudson River at varying degrees, and if you don't have proper brakes on your car—or don't really know how to shift a manual transmission effectively—you're going to have a problem driving eighty miles per hour through the neighborhood. With the cops right on our tail, my man turned onto North Broadway and started flying down this steep hill. Two blocks ahead we had to make a left turn.

We never made it.

Instead, we went headfirst into one of those huge brown telephone poles. I had never seen anything come at me that fast before in my entire life. I just saw the pole coming right toward my face, it flashed in front of my eyes like a dream. Then . . . IMPACT.

Everything got slow. I saw my man hunched over the steering wheel. My brain was trying to tell me what to do but everything just felt like I was on angel dust, like life was moving in slow motion.

"Get . . . . out . . . . of . . . . the . . . . caaaaaaaarrrrrrrrr!"

I tried both of the doors but they were jammed shut. Luckily my side window was broken, so I punched out the last pieces of glass and dove onto the sidewalk. The car was a crumpled mess.

It took the cops a few seconds after they screeched to a stop to make sure they were okay themselves before they approached the car. But as soon as I hit the street and felt that cold air, I got my senses back. I saw the police walking over and immediately started running. Once the cops saw that my man wasn't going anywhere, all smashed up and bloody in the front seat, then the two of them came after me and I hit the Aqueduct.

The Aqueduct was one long dirt road that stretched all the way from Yonkers to White Plains. It had been the original waterway early residents had used to run water from house to house. It was like an artery that ran through the city, past people's homes, through the middle of backyards. As kids, we used to play on "the Ak." We would play hide-and-go-seek in the brush or see how long we could follow its path before getting scared. Sometimes we had fun throwing rocks at the barking dogs that were tied to people's back fences. You just had to calculate how long it would take the dog to get to you once he broke free and pushed through that hole in the fence.

After a while you got to know the Ak like the back of your hand, so when I saw those two cops chasing me from the bottom of North Broadway, I knew I could hit it for a minute and then pop back on the street and know exactly where I was.

Okay, run down here for a second, cut through this person's backyard, go back up the hill . . .

Once it gets dark, the police ain't running the Ak. They wouldn't know their way and would probably be scared of what could be waiting for them. (You could always find a lot of dead things on the Ak—animals, even bodies, and because of how dark it was at night, it's also where a

THE AK

lot of girls in Yonkers got raped.) So it didn't surprise me that once I got as far as Lamartine, I didn't see those cops anymore. I just cut through my aunt Renee's backyard, came down the steps, and was home.

That was a close one.

My man who was driving, though, broke three ribs. When he came back from Woodfield a few weeks later, his chest was still swollen. Telephone poles don't move.

As Earl walks back to his car, something in the brush catches his eye. There, laying motionless a few yards away from the highway, a thick brown snake is curled up on top of itself, partially hidden by the desert plants. Intrigued, the artist walks over to inspect the animal, but before he can get close, it starts to move, revealing a jagged, bone-colored tail.

"Oh shit! That's a rattlesnake!"

I quickly move away along with Earl's security guards, thankful that I didn't step on the creature by accident, but Earl does the exact opposite. He keeps inching closer, curious to see its head, curious to find out if everything that he had heard about poisonous killer snakes on the Discovery Channel was true.

"Dog, what are you doing?"

Crouched down, with the look of wonder in his eyes, Earl moves a few feet away and discovers that the snake has been hurt. Part of its body is crushed and deformed, probably run over by one of our cars when we pulled off to the side of the road.

"Yo, you dare me to pick it up?" he asks.

But the snake is still alive.

"All I gotta do is grab it by its neck . . . "

Instead of responding to the challenge, security just rushes to get out the camcorder. They know their boss doesn't really need anybody to cosign his idea, and this they have to catch on tape.

A few minutes later, with cameras ready and everyone in the entourage crowded around, DMX reaches out his hand and with one quick movement grabs the snake at the base of its head. The animal thrashes around to try to get out of his grasp, but X holds on tight. Its tail starts to rattle in protest and its mouth opens wide, but X holds up his trophy and just smiles. Later, back at the house, we watch the tape in slow motion and see venom shooting out from the snake's fangs.

"Earl, you're crazy," I say to him.

"Yeah, I know."

17

A Weekend in the Hamptons

THE NUMBER OF STOLEN CARS I DROVE AROUND YONKERS, it's ironic the first time I was actually caught for the crime was in Long Island.

It was Friday night and I was with a friend I met at Children's Village named Dre. We had just picked up a nice Toyota Corolla Limited Edition and were bored with driving around Yonkers, hollering at the same girls, seeing the same niggas on the corner. So Dre came up with the idea to drive to Long Island. He said he had family we could chill with and could definitely find a hot party to go to. I didn't have a better suggestion so we got on the highway.

We probably should have thought how long a trip it was, though, because since we didn't leave New York until after 3 A.M., we didn't get to Long Island until the sun was coming up. So much for going to a party. So we just crashed out at his people's house. They lived in this small country-looking 'hood on the outskirts of East Hampton.

In the morning, we chilled with his peoples for a little while and then decided to go get some beers. I didn't think anything of it then, but none of his family came with us.

In the late eighties, the Hamptons was even more the home of the rich and the white than it is today. Even though East Hampton was probably the most metropolitan of the four towns in the area, it was still extremely unlikely to find two teenage black kids driving around in a brand-new car (the rappers-driving-Bentleys invasion hadn't happened to the Hamptons yet). Black folks, like Dre's peoples, lived on the other side of the train tracks and that's where the ruling townsfolk expected them to stay.

But we didn't know that.

I had already learned what you don't do when you're not familiar with where you are, but Dre was fifteen, two years younger than me, and the whole trip he had been driving real extra and I could tell he was thirsty to act out. When he pulled in front of the grocery store, I told him to chill.

"Yo, when I come back with the beer, we can go to a park or something and relax."

Of course, when I came out of the store, Dre was gone.

So here I was, early Saturday morning, standing in the middle of Main Street, East Hampton, holding a bag of beer. *Not the move.*

Then just as I started to walk up the block to look for him, I saw a police car drive past and guess who was in the backseat? This motherfucker went and got knocked! My first instinct, being the loyal kid that I was, was to try to find my way back to his people's house to get help. The problem was that I really couldn't remember where their place was, all I knew was that it was in a row of raggedy houses that didn't look like nothing nearby and after about an hour of walking around the neighborhood getting lost, the same police car finally rolled up on me. This time, no Dre. I was still carrying that bag of beer.

"Hey, kid, where are you going?"

"I got some family that lives out here," I replied.

"Yeah. Well, what do you have in the bag?"

"Beer."

"Aren't you too young to be buying beer, son?"

"Well, then, you better get the guy in the store. I don't have nothing to do with that!" I said with an attitude.

That answer pissed them off, but I was right. There was nothing illegal about me holding an unopened bottle of beer, the clerk was the one that was supposed to get in trouble for not checking my ID.

"Well, you're gonna have to come and show us who sold it to you then."

"I don't remember where the store was."

Now the bullshit started.

"Well, why don't you let us help you then. If you don't, we're gonna start taking this bottle of beer of yours a little more seriously . . ."

"Uh . . . well, okay. I guess I can show you where."

And that was my first mistake.

I got into the back of the squad car with no handcuffs on or nothing. Then, of course, instead of pulling up in front of the store where I bought the beer like they said, the cops pulled up in front of the police station.

"Officer, this is not where the store is."

"Yeah, we know. But we want you to come inside for a minute."

"But the store is over there!"

"We're not going to the store anymore. Now come inside and shut your mouth."

When I got inside the precinct, they led me to a small interrogation room where they started grilling me about the car. I knew they didn't see me in it or anywhere near it so I just kept denying everything. The only way they could know about me was if Dre told them something.

"I don't know anything about any car, man. I don't know nothing and I didn't do nothing!"

"Are you going to make us go find your fingerprints on the door handle, boy? Then you'll be a liar, and I hate little liars . . ."

"I don't give a fuck! Do whatever, man."

I wasn't going to let these cops massage me more then they already had. "Do what you gotta do. I wasn't there."

Then I saw Dre's shadow in the mirror and I realized that the bastard was snitching me out.

After a few minutes they brought him into the room.

"Is that him?" they asked him.

"Yeah," he answered looking squarely at me. He stood right in front of my face. "That's him. His name is Earl."

"I don't know what he's talking about, man!"

I got desperate in a hurry.

"That wasn't me . . ."

I was already on probation and was not trying to go to jail.

"THAT WASN'T FUCKING ME!"

Dre was a minor, he was getting off once a parent came to get him anyway, so why did he have to turn me in? But the most fucked-up part was when his grandfather came to the station and I noticed that he was wearing a badge. Dre's grandfather worked for the sheriff's department in another county so Dre knew he was straight all along!

But it was over for me. I was getting locked up. Earl Simmons was now a convicted felon.

When I was younger, my mother and her friend Thelma had me scared to death about getting locked up. "Tell him about what they do to boys in jails," Thelma always said when my mother was beating my ass. Just like the officers on Alexander Street, the two of them thought a good deterrent was making me think that on the first day I walked into a jail, somebody was going to fuck me in the ass. Well, it didn't happen like that, but I did arrive at the Farm with a real hard-ass attitude.

Don't say nothing to me . . . don't even fucking look at me . . . I'm not saying nothing to nobody and I ain't going to ask you for shit, so don't ask me for shit!

"The Farm," the minimum-security division of Suffolk County Correctional Facility in Yaphank, Long Island, was similar to the barges New York State used to house inmates who were convicted of nonviolent crimes like theft or drunk driving. It wasn't meant to be as secure or restrictive as the main unit of SCCF. Instead of cells, inmates lived grouped together in dorms or "mods." You could freely associate with the other guys in your mod, use a Walkman, read or play cards, and while in no way did you have your freedom, life in the Farm, at least on the minor block where I was, wasn't the most difficult experience for me—especially after what I had been through over the past two years in Industry and McCormick.

(Now that I was grown, though, the hardest thing to endure was being without pussy for all those weeks and months. That was tough. There were some pretty female corrections officers in jail, too, and a lot of them were freaks. The freak COs would be the ones that lived right in the same 'hood as you and knew all of your peoples from around the way. Behind bars was the only place that I ever considered paying for some ass, because I definitely would have tossed a couple of dollars to one of them to knock it down. I never got that chance, though.)

After a few days in the Farm I hooked up with two guys named Pos and Rondu and we started running game on the other kids in the dorm. I was familiar with the commissary routine from my time spent in McCormick.

"Yo, you better order me two packs of cigarettes and I want six Milky Way bars," I would tell the kids that I knew had money in my mod.

Surprisingly, there are a lot of weak people in jail. Not everyone is the kind of crazed lunatic you need to be afraid of. If you had a good amount of game on the streets, you would normally be able to find someone to take advantage of on the inside. It's like there are a lot of phony gangsters around whose card you can pull, like the dudes who always have something extra to say, but only ever say it into the air.

"Yo, word to my mother! Y'all motherfuckers need to recognize . . ."

The bitch will see three dudes by the phone and feel like he has the occasion to start complaining:

"Y'all can't be hogging up that phone time, man, y'all know what's up with that . . ."

"Actually, no, we don't know what's up with that phone time, homes. Why don't you let us know? And, as a matter of fact, which one of us are you referring to?"

So I didn't have much difficulty finding the inmates I could pressure into putting things on my commissary. The bigger challenge, though, was to get one of them to smuggle you in some weed during visiting hours. A good bag of smoke was worth far more than a chocolate bar or an extra pack of Newports.

For two weeks me, Pos and Rondu had this white kid in our pocket.

"Have your sister bring us in some smoke or I'll break your fucking neck." Scared of us three thugs, our friendly assistant never spoke unless spoken to and always politely stayed on his side of the mod. So I should have known something was wrong the day he walked over to us out of the blue.

"So, you said you wanted me to get my sister to bring in the weed, right?" he asked us one morning.

"Yeah, motherfucker, we already told you that. What, are you stupid?"

"Okay, because she says she's gonna bring in the weed today."

"Yeah, you better have it today, too, you bitch-ass nigga."

Ten minutes later, after the riot squad rushed in, locked the whole mod down and tossed and strip-searched everyone, Pos, Rondu, and me were on our way to the big house. The charge? Extortion.

Since I was transferred with a write-up, my first week in the main unit of Suffolk County Correctional Facility was spent in the hole. Four floors up on the lockdown block, in a six-by-nine-foot box by myself that I was never allowed to leave. This was not a mod, the hole is where you have to grind for real. There's little room to move. It's dark. Don't expect even the semblance of humane treatment from the guards, and hope your sink is clean, because if it ain't, you're not going to have anything to drink.

But there was something kind of peaceful to me about being locked up in there. It was like loud silence. Maybe, all the days I had spent in that office at Andrus, all the months in my room in School Street, all the years in group homes and juvenile had got me ready for what would be a nightmare for most human beings.

But I thought a lot and I wrote more than I ever had before. Song after song, rhyme after rhyme, I produced pages of lyrics alone in that box. I shifted flows, changed styles, tried to experiment with new ways to win a battle or excite a crowd. For me, rapping wasn't going to be no pastime paradise. This was for real.

```
D to the M, from the M to the X, from the X to whatever
    MC is next to step up so I can rip up, snatch up, whip
    up my style, versatile
Get wild, I'll sew your lip up[12]
```

After two weeks in the hole, I was transferred out of the lockdown block into the minors. In Suffolk County, since kids were constantly fighting and getting out of control, the warden of the minor block set up a twenty-three-hour lock-in schedule. That meant each inmate had only one hour of recreation a day—sixty minutes when you were allowed outside—and the rest of the day you had to spend in your cell. It was just you and your cellmate and often—since Suffolk County prison was so ridiculously overcrowded—the three other inmates that were forced to share your two-man space with you.

This wasn't juvenile, this was maximum security, the big boys' jail, which also meant during those twenty-three hours the correction officers let you have it.

"Come on, you fucking asshole. Get inside the damn gate!"

It was always the little ones.

"Hey Simmons, I said you. Your shower is fucking over, now what did I say? Get inside the fucking gate!"

I couldn't take much of that, not from somebody half my size.

"What? Fuck me? No, how about fuck you?"

One time one of the guards rushed me for cursing at him and I spit right in his eye . . . and then I got beat down. I mean, BEAT DOWN by five members of the riot squad in full battle gear who loved every minute of fucking my ass up.

The minors went to yard with the "PC" niggas. PC was Protective Custody and was where all the sick motherfuckers were, the older guys, guys on medication or morphine, or just the scared dudes who had to be kept out of the regular population. We weren't on the same side with them, because Suffolk County's yard was split into two sides by a thick, barbed-wire fence (we would have fucked around and probably killed them), but we shared the same sixty-minute time period.

At the Farm, I had heard about this guy who was making a name for himself on the rap tip called K-Solo. Supposedly, he was the cousin of an MC named Erick Sermon who was a big star at the time with the duo EPMD. K-Solo was Erick's heir apparent and the word was that he would have blown up already if he wasn't locked up. Everybody in the minors knew that I could rhyme because I had taken everybody out on the cell block that thought they had lyrics. So brothers got real excited the day we saw K-Solo on the other side of the fence. I didn't know what he was doing with the PC niggas but he was there, and the day he said he wanted to battle, it was on. We went back and forth through the fence for the whole hour. I remember he had this little fat black dude with him.

"You can't fuck with my man, Solo!" the kid kept yelling.

And, of course, I had my mans with me: "What? Is you crazy? This is DMX's house, punk."

It was a good thing that I had been writing the whole time I was locked up because K-Solo had a lot of rhymes. Every time I hit him with a hot one, he had a response. He was no joke and after forty-five minutes, there was no clear-cut winner. But there was time for one more round before we had to go back in and I had just written a song called "Breakin' It Down" where I used a different style in every verse. I was kind of skeptical about how well it would go over, but it was the only rhyme I had left. Luckily, the last verse killed it:

```
There's one more way of breaking it down
This is how a rapper will leave you spellbound
So yo, bust it, what I'm about to do
Is to S-P-E-L-L it out to you . . .¹³
```

The style was to spell out almost every word in the rhyme in letters. I liked it because I knew no one had ever heard anything like that before, and well, it's not like I wasn't into spelling shit.

"Yo, that verse was hot!" K-Solo said to me afterwards, admitting defeat. "How you do that?"

"Most of the letters rhyme anyway," I explained to him proudly, "so just write out a cool sentence and then spell it. Just make sure you stay on the beat . . ."

K-Solo and I never battled again. In the days after, the two of us would just chill and talk through the fence. It was like rapping had given us a mutual respect for each other. I felt good and I spent the last weeks of my bid in Suffolk County writing more rhymes and just trying to stay out of trouble. Now that I had my first official win under my belt, I just wanted to get back to Yonkers and show everybody that DMX the Great was a *bad motherfucker*!

ONE OF MY EARLY MIX TAPES

18

"Wanna Battle?"

WHEN I WAS RELEASED FROM SUFFOLK COUNTY THERE WERE two things on my agenda: the first was to find someone that could help me make tapes of my rhymes, the second was to find Dre. Unfortunately, the latter came first.

My first day home I was with Collie and I saw him talking to a girl in a car on Glenwood Avenue. As soon as he turned around to walk down the hill, I caught him. Punched him right in his face. Dre never saw it coming.

"What's up, money?"

The bottle of juice he was holding fell out of his hands and smashed to pieces on the sidewalk.

"Who got who now, huh?"

Instead of stepping up, like a bitch he started circling around this parked car to avoid me. I chased him around about ten times before I ran out of patience.

"Don't worry, nigga. I'm gonna see you . . . and I bet you don't walk on this block no more!"

Collie and I started walking toward Ravine. Then just as we got to the end of the block, I heard Dre yell out, "Hey, X. What's up now?"

I turned around and saw five of his boys with bottles in their hands crouched down gorilla style next to some trees. Dre had been hustling for some older dudes in the neighborhood and I guess now I was messing with one of their workers.

"What's going on with you and my peeps," this kid named Kenny asked me. Kenny and I knew each other, but he was about hustling and I was about robbing. That meant we didn't get along too well.

"Your man snitched on me,"

"I'm saying, what's up, though?"

"He turned me in, right to my face."

"So what's up?"

"Well, wassup nothing, nigga!"

The brawl was on. I had a little size on me from my time locked up, so I took on a few guys. Collie called Buzzy and my other uncle, Buckeye, from out of my grandmother's house and once sticks and bats and kitchen knives came into play, things got ugly.

I was supposed to be the one getting jumped, but I never left my feet once. That was a weak consolation prize, though, because I got arrested again. The cops always believe the loser. I hadn't been home twenty-four hours.

Things always seemed to happen to me that way. I would come home from jail and get arrested again, come home and get arrested again, often within a few days of each other. It was like if I stayed out of trouble that first week, then I'd be good. But all of my jail time only increased my resolve to do music—and gave me more time to write my rhymes.

When I came home in the summer of '88, I was determined not to get knocked again because I had fifteen or twenty whole songs written and I had a plan for them: I was going to make my own mix-tapes and sell them on the street to make money.

The first step to making a tape was to find a DJ with a microphone and a pair of turntables who knew how to loop a bunch of instrumentals together. Then, since I didn't have any music, hope that he had copies of the hot songs on the radio that I could use to kick my rhymes over.

When I finally found a DJ and first heard my voice recorded over a banging beat, I knew I had something special because it sounded dope, *real dope*. Now all I had to do was make copies of them because even if they hadn't heard of me, I knew that people would want to buy my shit so they could get all of the hot music from off the radio. And that was the hardest thing to do because you had to find someone that had a double cassette deck. So right away I got real friendly with who-ever had one and went over to their crib and spent hours dubbing as many tapes as possible. If I didn't have a blank, I would just find a prerecorded joint and stuff a piece of tissue into the holes on the top so that I could tape over it. Old Billy Ocean albums became DMX the Great mix tapes. I was manic about it because I loved hearing my voice on tape and knew that I could get at least five dollars each for them. It was cool if it took a few hours to crank out eight tapes because then I could just go up the block and come back down with forty or fifty dollars in my pocket.

Selling mix tapes was the best idea I had in a long time, and after a couple of weeks hustling them, almost the whole city was buzzing with my music. It was like the more tapes I sold on Warburton, the more I took down to Ravine. The more I sold on Ravine, the more I brought up to Mulford. Once School Street was feeling me, then I took a bunch of tapes to Slow Bomb. Soon, I was walking all over Yonkers making money from my raps, flipping hot songs on the radio into my own DMX the Great joints. But even though I believed right away that my versions were better than the originals, a lot of times to get somebody to buy a tape I had to show and prove—and that didn't bother me at all.

"Do you rap?"

If I saw a group of guys hanging out on the corner, I would run right up on them.

"Wanna battle?"

If somebody even *acted* like they rapped, I wanted to get it on. I didn't care if I knew the brother or not, if he was from School Street or any other part of town. I just wanted to challenge anybody I could—especially when I knew that if I slaughtered him, the next time I came around him or one of his friends would probably buy a tape.

See, I wasn't scared about battling someone on their own turf because I quickly realized that MCs thought they had an advantage on their block when they really didn't. They didn't understand that because they were the "block MC" and were always kicking their rhymes to everybody, their rhymes and punch lines weren't so hot anymore. Everybody had already heard what you had to say. If your boy could finish off your rhyme for you or whisper in your ear when you start to run out of things to say to tell you to "say the one about his mother," that never looked good. So I knew the crowd was going to go for me when I came around with flows and styles and lyrics that no one had heard before.

Battles had become war to me. I didn't play fight. I would never *half* dis somebody. I wanted to embarrass you as much as I possibly could, and make sure that you wouldn't want to shake my hand afterwards.

Fuck you and your bitch girlfriend . . . and why doesn't your mother suck my dick!

I always made it personal. Nothing was too rude or vicious for me because I didn't care. This was a battle. There were no rules, and I wasn't going to let someone bite me on the rap tip because I played with him.

In the late eighties, the more I battled, the more I won. And the more I won, the more energy I had for it. Battling made me feel powerful, like my rap skills were grenades in my pocket that I could throw at any time. I just wanted to finish everybody, shut down every MC I came across and make them want to give up rhyming for good. That's why I loved when fake MCs had their girlfriends with them. Once I started killing them, either their chick would get embarrassed and start looking around like, "Aww, man"—that was bad enough—or she would just break down and start laughing at her man. That was terrible because then the brother had to walk away with a loss *and* hear the jokes from a shorty who was now ready to be his ex (I don't remember getting any pussy like that, though, but it still made me know that I was the man.)

Always, after I was through with a battle, then I would sell whatever tapes I had and just roll out.

"DMX the Great, baby, and I'm not to be fucked with 'cause I'm deadly with a motherfucking mic!"

While hip-hop was becoming more and more popular, there weren't too many people around that were interested in *making* the music. Guys like Imperial JC or the Moet Posse had stuff to throw parties with and they did a few shows, but they were much older than me, and the brothers that just freestyled on the block didn't have any equipment to take it further. But there was one guy I heard about who had his own microphone and tape deck in his apartment. He called himself Lord Kasun.

The first thing I noticed when I walked into Kasun's apartment was the number of records he had. Hundreds of albums and twelve-inch singles were all thrown about the floor, others were tucked together in rows of milk crates he had stacked against the wall. To test him, I asked if he had this funk joint called "Mardi Gras" and this Billy Squier dance record called "Big Beat" that I had heard on the radio the week before. When he pulled out two copies of each of them, I knew he was legit.

By this time, I had rhymes that I knew would go over well with certain instrumentals, but messing around with random DJs, I just didn't have access to all of the music that I wanted. But not only did Kasun have the right music, but he could perfectly cut up and loop whatever I wanted. I was so amped because now all of my rhymes could really come alive and I could spit full songs with proper verses and hooks. The first day I met him, Kasun and I must have stayed up half the night putting jams on tape.

"Yo, X, man. That flow is dope!" Kasun said after I finished spitting the third verse to a joint I called "Spellbound." I just extended the spelling style that I used on K-Solo in Suffolk County into three verses and added a hook. Kasun came up with the right beat and, just like that, the two of us had put together a banging song.

```
Yo, can you see me?
No, I'm the d-i-v-i-n-e d-o-p-e MC,
R-u-g-g-e-d on the m-i-c, r-o-p-h-o-n-e
And I'm g-o-i-n-g p-l-a-c-e-s
Why? B-e-c-a-u-s-e I am the best.
```

"Just keep coming with the beats, K, 'cause, dog, I'm telling you, I got fucking rhymes!"

I used to really study how rappers made songs. I would hear a jam on the radio and try to figure out how many bars there were in each verse or predict when the break would come. After a while, I realized that most good songs followed a certain pattern, that there was a method to creating a great piece of music: three verses, sixteen bars to each verse, with eight-bar hooks and either a four- or an eight-bar intro. I applied those rules to my own lyrics and it helped me grow as a writer. With other people's songs, I began to hear where an MC fell off beat or cheated and said fifteen bars instead of sixteen and just grunted their way into the hook. "Unh, unh . . ."

"See, he messed up right there . . . he can't fuck with me," I used to tell Kasun when we'd be listening to the radio together. (A lot of rappers who are out now *still* don't understand what the purpose of bars is because they write in odd numbers. Or they try to get away with an eight-bar verse and an eight-bar hook. Now their song is only two minutes and they'll have to repeat themselves or sing their way to the end. That was never good enough for me. Say something to the people, please, because without a proper science to your music, you're not really giving us enough.)

A few weeks after I met Kasun, he told me that a friend of his named Daryl D Mac wanted to battle me. I knew the dude was wack, but I thought, instead of us battling on the corner, why didn't Kasun invite him over to the apartment and we could go at it on tape? He had a little rep and that way we'd have something to sell afterwards.

It was a good idea.

With the battle, Kasun and I put some of the new songs that we had done together on the tape like "Spellbound," the *Sesame Street* rap I did at the Center, "Breakin' It Down," and another joint called "Unstoppable Force," and it became a big hit. The tape sold all over Yonkers. It was the biggest and best mix tape that I had ever made. People kept coming up to me asking if I had copies, wanting to know when I was putting out another one. I was proud of myself. I was learning, making money, my reputation as an MC was growing.

Was this it?

I was expressing myself with a freedom that I had never felt before. I was being heard. My words, my thoughts were being listened to.

Motherfuckers never listened before!

Could this rhyming shit really get me what I wanted?

. . . didn't know I was special 'til this rap shit came to be[14]

The Palace was an R&B club in New Rochelle. Every other week they held a talent show that was "open call," which meant that anyone could show up and perform. My cousin Mike told me that he heard some pretty good MCs in there a few weeks before and I wondered if I could get the same kind of response in a club that I was getting with my mix tapes on the street.

It wasn't too crowded when Mike and I walked in a little before 8 P.M. They had a small stage set up toward the back of the dance floor and a DJ booth on the left-hand side. I had on my normal outfit: black jeans, sweatpants, Tims, and a black hooded sweatshirt. I always wore a pair of sweatpants underneath my jeans to make my legs look a little thicker. The show had already started and I was scheduled to go on after a rapper named Top Quality. Mike went to find a spot at the bar but I just chilled near the stage to check out the competition.

Most of the performers were sorry, but Top Quality was good. He kicked a rhyme over the beat to Teddy Riley's "New Jack Swing" and the audience got up and started dancing to it. I couldn't figure out what he was saying, but I had never heard his kind of flow before and it matched the rhythm of the song real good and the way the crowd reacted I could tell he was the man to beat. I knew that I could take him just on rhymes, but this wasn't a head-to-head battle, or the kind of Yonkers ghetto crowd that I was used to. This was in a club, in New Rochelle, so I was nervous and I wanted to come up with something different. The only thing that kept coming into my head was "Spellbound."

Well, when I got on stage and started spelling almost my whole five-minute rhyme, the crowd started cheering and hollering. I think I spit two extra verses that I had never said before, just building on the energy of all those people. When the judge came out and announced that I was the winner, I nodded my head like I always knew what was up, but it felt good. "Spellbound" had done it again.

```
I'm the D-M-X, will f-l-e-x on whoever is
n-e-x-t to the m-c-e-e a-g-a-i-n-s-t me,
I'll f-l-i-p like an a-c-r-o-b-a-t with a critical r-h-y-m-e
Leave competition d-e-a-d
Or had them wishing they w-e-r-e[15]
```

When I was coming off the stage, this guy approached me and said he was looking for some rap acts. He had a studio he worked with nearby and wanted to get artists in there to try to get them a record deal. He wasn't trying to sell me a big dream, but he thought that I was talented and should call him. His name was Jack MacNasty.

I took his business card but didn't pay much attention to what he was saying because I was busy talking to a shorty trying to get some pussy off my win, but a few days later my cousin brought his name up. He said at the Palace that night he had bet some guy named Jack fifty dollars that I would win the talent show. It seemed Jack lost his money on TQ. (I was wondering why Mike was looking so happy that night. He didn't share any of that money with me!) But that reminded me of our conversation, so I found Jack's card in my jeans pocket, grabbed a quarter from my cousin, and went to the phone booth.

"Yo, this is DMX. You still talking about that studio?"

"Who is this?"

"DMX, the nigga from Yonkers that was at the Palace that night."

"Oh, yeah! What's up? I was hoping you would call."

Jack was an older guy born and raised in New Rochelle. He had an accounting background but he and his brother promoted parties in the Bronx and were making connections with some record company folks. He had only been managing artists for a year but I was impressed with the list of people he said came through his spot: Biz Markie, Just-Ice, Big Daddy Kane, some of the biggest names in hip-hop. I would definitely want to do a show in that kind of place and knew that I was better than the kid Top Quality who had already gotten down with him, so I figured I didn't have anything to lose by fucking with him. He wasn't asking me to sign nothing.

A few days later, Jack scooped me up from Yonkers and brought me over to his house in New Rochelle. I remember it had these big wooden poles in the front of it like an old ranch. Inside, music was blasting, TQ was spitting rhymes, and this DJ kid named Shabazz was spinning records on the turntables. I stayed in the battle mind-set, so I did my thing and went head-to-head with TQ for a couple of hours. TQ's lyrics were much more abstract than mine, filled with multisyllable words and strange metaphors. I realized I liked the more direct approach. I wanted to be able to tell a story and talk about subjects that a crowd could understand.

When I left, I gave Jack a new tape I had made. It had about eight five-minute songs on it that I had done with Kasun and a bunch of freestyles. Later he told me that he really underestimated the extent of my writing ability.

Cooler than a bottle of Coors, I'm refreshing . . . just like the great outdoors . . .

Over the next couple of weeks, Jack would pick me up from Yonkers and take me and TQ to the recording studio that he was renting in White Plains. Since TQ had committed to him before I did, Jack let TQ do his thing first, but it wasn't long before Shabazz and I started making it happen in there. We did another version of "Spellbound" and songs called "3 Little Pigs" and "Creativity." I didn't like the way Shabazz cut the beats as much as the way Kasun rocked it, but now that I was in a proper studio, I was building a strong collection of material that sounded good. After a few weeks, Jack wanted something to send around to different record labels to try to get me a deal so he took three of my best songs and put them on a tape. This was my demo.

One of the first places Jack sent my demo to, though, wasn't a label, it was the hip-hop magazine, *The Source*. At the time, *The Source* was just a black-and-white newsletter, but they had a new-artist column they ran every month called "Unsigned Hype" and Jack thought if I won that, we would have no problem getting attention from the record companies. The magazine needed a picture of me, so the next day Jack brought a photographer to the studio, I borrowed TQ's long black trench coat to go over the white turtleneck that I was wearing, put on a hat with a skull and crossbones patch on the front, and we took some shots. Now I had a full-blown demo tape *and* a black-and-white glossy photograph. *DMX the Great was official,* more official than I had ever been—but that still didn't give me any more props with the chicks.

T G & F
Entertainment Consultants
Management & Direction
Bruce Tabbs
Terrence Gibel
Donald Fortune

DMX
THE GREAT

PRODUCTION:
House
PARTY
PRODUCTIONS

MY FIRST PUBLICITY SHOT

133

19

A Bowlegged Cutie

I think about when a nigga didn't have
When a nigga told a joke, and the bitches didn't laugh[16]

DAPHNE WAS A BOWLEGGED CUTIE I MET ONE AFTERNOON in front of my grandmother's house. Short and brown-skinned, with a small waist and a fat ass, she had just moved to the block from Connecticut and was walking home from the store. At seventeen, you were a real nigga if you could bag a chick that wasn't from the neighborhood on the walk-by.

"How you doing?"

Looking at her long, wavy hair, I knew Shorty must have had a little Indian going on in her family.

"I'm fine. How are you?"

I was gassed when she let me walk her the rest of the way home, and when we got to her building we ended up sitting on her stoop talking for more than an hour. That's where it all started.

"So, um, you think I can call you tomorrow, then?"

I was open. Daphne was a dime. Over the next few weeks we got together almost every day. We would call each other and go hang out somewhere, get some Chinese food or go to the movies. She always had her mother's car and that was big. For a girl to be driving a dude around at that age? Forget about it. I was doing it. I would be in the passenger seat, leaning back, grinning at all the losers on the block whenever we came through. "Turn in that way," I would tell her so that we would pass by as many people I knew as possible.

She was scared of School Street.

"I don't wanna go through there, D."

"Nah, you're all right, girlfriend. That's my spot. This is where *I* live at."

Sometimes Daphne would get lost coming to pick me up and end up driving through the whole project looking for building 80. That was cool, though, because, by the time I came downstairs, everyone had seen the honey with the Connecticut plates.

"Yo, who's that?"

"Yeah, that's me, nigga!"

A lot of times we would go to her house and I enjoyed that because her moms was real cool with me.

"Earl, are you staying for dinner?" she would always ask me.

Moms even smoked weed. Whenever I went over, I made sure that I had a nickel bag so the two of us could smoke together. It was real. I felt a part of something. Then Daphne and I would just lay on each other for hours and watch television in the living room. It wasn't like we had to go out and do a lot of things, we could just spend good, quiet moments together.

Whenever I knew that we were going out, though, I made sure I robbed at least two people that day so I would have money in my pocket. I couldn't be up in her face broke. If I was, I had to hide it. One time we were riding around and she said she was hungry, and since I didn't have any money to stop anywhere, I just kept looking out the window like I didn't hear her.

"D, don't you want to get something to eat?" she asked me again.

"Huh? What?" I replied without turning around.

"I'm starving. Don't you want to stop at a restaurant or something?"

"Oh, nah. I'm good," I said finally looking at her. "What, your moms ain't cook?" I was starving, too.

Twenty dollars was all I would need, though. With that I could pad my wad of money with a lot of singles in the middle so the stack looked bigger when I pulled it out, or I could just turn around when I paid for something. I made sure that Daphne and I always stayed local where it was cheaper and I wanted to show her off anyway. Nobody knew me in the Bronx or Manhattan, so we wouldn't go down there. I couldn't get any points that way.

Since she had just moved here, I was one of the few people

Daphne knew in Yonkers and so it was good for her that I was thorough in the street. One night in the back of School Street, some bum came over and started beefing with me about something. When it got violent, I kept kicking him in his back to the point where Daphne had to come over and pull me off him. You know how a man gets when his girl has to break up a fight.

"Damn. I'm sure fucking glad that you were here, Shorty, because I would have *killed* that motherfucker . . ."

"I know baby, you really let him have it. Are you okay?"

"Yeah, I'm good. I'm good," I said, trying to hide my smile.

The only bad thing with Daphne was that she made me wait for the pussy. She had me on that gentleman thing so I didn't get to have sex with Shorty for almost two months! But I was good with it. Everybody in the 'hood knew she was my girl and I got official kisses in public so nobody knew the difference. It was the best relationship with a woman that I had ever had.

Then I went to back to jail.

It was only a ninety-day bid, which by this time wasn't nothing for me, but after the first month I was feeling extra good because Daphne had already written me three letters and had come to see me. She was keeping me well taken care of and I didn't hesitate bragging about her on the cell block.

"What? Y'all niggas is crazy! I'll be out of here in a minute, man, and none of y'all can touch the shorty I got at home!" I put her picture right where everyone could see it.

I didn't hear from her as much over the next two months, she sent me a few more letters, but didn't visit again or send any more pictures. But I knew that she had started working and probably must have gotten busy.

The first day I got home, I went to go find her, but when I got to her block I was surprised to find that she had moved back to Connecticut. *Okay, that's probably why she hasn't kept in touch*, I thought to myself. "I'll just find her number in Stamford." I had never dialed a 203 area code before.

"Good afternoon, Mrs. Coaty?"

I was always very polite when I called a girl's house.

"Oh, hi, Earl. How are you? . . . No, Daphne is not here right now. She's at work at the mall. Would you like her number?"

Moms was just as sweet as ever.

"Yo, wassup," I said to my girl when she came to the phone.

"Who's this . . . Earl?"

"Yeah, wassup. I'm back. I want to see you."

"You're back already?"

"Yeah, and my man Rick has a ride, too. I'm going to get him to bring me up there tomorrow so we can see each other . . ."

"Tomorrow? Oh, um, okay . . . I guess that's cool."

Her voice didn't sound right, but Daphne was my girl, and now that I was used to getting pussy on the regular, three months without it was a long time so I was thirsty.

When a new kid moves into the projects who doesn't know anyone, the only way he'll survive is if he hooks up with the right person. Rick was fresh from out of state, but he had a car so I let him roll with me, and in exchange for having his back in the street, I always had a ride. That day, I didn't want to go through the hassle of stealing something, especially when I just came out of jail, so I told Rick what was up, hooked up with my man Forrest, and the three of us drove to Connecticut.

We got to the mall around 2 P.M. Rick had to rush back to Yonkers, so me and Forrest went in on our own and as soon as we got inside, I saw Daphne walking with a girlfriend. She was still fly.

"Daphne."

"Oh . . . hey, what's up, D? You made it, huh?"

This was only my third day home. My clothes were hard and I didn't have a haircut. I still had on my jail sneakers, but I was still *me*. I was still the nigga that chilled in your house and drove you around the projects. I was still the nigga that made tapes and had a rep. Why was she sounding like that?

"Well, why don't you meet me when I get off. Around 9 P.M.?" she said, stepping away.

"Where should I meet you?"

"Um . . . I'll just come right back here."

She sounded real shady and then as soon as she was gone I realized that it was only 2 P.M. Neither me or Forrest had a dime in our pocket, we were already starving, and now we were stuck in the middle of some bullshit mall.

"What the fuck are we going to do now, D?" Forrest asked me.

I just tried to think positive thoughts: Daphne's got a car; she'll drive us back to her house; her moms probably made dinner. We'll be straight.

3 P.M. . . . 4 . . . 5 . . . 6 . . . 7 . . . 8 . . . 9—seven hours later, we weren't so good.

At 9:15, there was still no sign of Daphne and with the gates coming down on most of the stores, security came and told us we had to leave.

"But I'm waiting for my girl!"

"Not in here you're not . . ."

The mall was closed. I was furious. Stamford was not Yonkers: Everything was all spread out, there were no other stores or people on the street. There were buses out in the parking lot, but we wouldn't know where to go and we didn't have money anyway, so Forrest and I just followed the signs to the Metro North station. Maybe we could hide in the bathroom of the train or hope for a nice conductor. Either way, I was getting the fuck out of there.

A block or two away from the station, we saw a big crowd of folks standing outside of this nightclub. It was a Thursday night and I could see that a few of the chicks on line had some bad-ass outfits on and we could hear music playing inside. Me and Forrest went over to make it happen.

Fuck Daphne. I'm DMX the Great. One of these bitches is going to give me some pussy . . .

We hadn't been over there ten minutes when Daphne and her girlfriend walked up. I couldn't believe it. The second I saw her, I got heated.

"Wassup, girl!" I yelled out to her.

"Oh, wassup, D . . ."

"What do you mean, 'Wassup, D'? I thought we were supposed to be hanging out tonight, Daphne? I've been waiting for you all day!"

"Oh, I'm sorry. Something came up."

The other people on the line started to watch us argue.

"You're sorry? That's fucked up, Daphne. Me and my man don't have a way of getting home or nothing now. I thought—"

Before I could finish, she cut me off.

"What you thought, D? That *I* was going to drive you home?"

Oh, shit. I never felt so small in my entire life. She said it loud, too. Then she made it worse.

"And what kind of nigga comes all the way to Connecticut with no *money* in his pocket?"

That hurt. That hurt bad. The other girls on the line looked at me waiting for my response, but all I could manage was a real fragile "fuck you" under my breath.

"Come on, yo," I said to my man, slowly walking away. "Let's go rob something."

So much for being a big-time rapper.

Despite how well my plans with my music were going, and despite all of these people around me who seemed to have my back like Kasun, Jack, and Shabazz, somehow I was still more comfortable alone. Most nights, after I finished selling whatever tapes I had, I would walk through the whole city of Yonkers by myself and not want to interact with anybody. I'd go from Riverdale to Whitney Young to Warburton. I'd walk through School Street up to Slow Bomb projects then down Palisades Avenue and be happy just being in my own head. It was safe, familiar, and it gave me a chance to think.

I thought so fucking much!

Sometimes while I walked, I would compose a rhyme in my head—from one end of the city to the other I easily thought up twenty-four bars, always starting with the first line of the song and ending with the last—but most of the time I let that solitude give me the chance to wonder about my life. That time alone gave me the space to ask myself all of the questions that I needed answered and I always started with the biggest one: Why?

Why, Momma, do you do the things you do?

Now that I was grown, I was beginning to understand that my frustration with my mother was less to do with all the beatings and the punishment that she gave me, but more because she never could answer that simple question. Her answer for everything was always "Because I said so," but I knew enough to want to hear more than that. I needed her to give me a reason.

Momma, maybe I'm too young to deserve that respect, but please, can't you understand that I need that respect?

Sometimes I wished my mother was around to hear those thoughts, but of course she wasn't. It was just me.

FLYER FOR MY BATTLE WITH BILL BLASS

20

Talk of the Town

THE BIGGEST RAPPER IN YONKERS WAS A LIGHT-SKINNED
pretty boy named Bill Blass. Bill was flashy. He always liked to stay
dipped in the nice outfits, and since his father was a hustler, he had
the game and the confident attitude that gave him a lot of luck with
the girls. Bill made a name for himself by MC-ing at parties throughout the city and almost every weekend he performed at a downtown
club called Browneyes with his partner Cloud. He didn't have a
recording contract and his songs were never played on the radio, but
in Yonkers—a small town that masqueraded as a big city—being a
local star was almost like being a national hero: everyone knew your
name and made sure to give you that respect when you passed them
on the street.

Bill Blass was D Mac's cousin. After he heard about my battle with
Mac on the mix tape, it didn't take long for him to call me out and him
and his boys found me one afternoon in front of my grandmother's
house. Bill wasn't a stranger to battles. He loved to drive through
Yonkers, see someone chilling somewhere, then pull over and kick a
song he wrote called "Jumping MCs" at him. It was like how I used
to get down in the street, but Bill drove instead of walked (his car was
never stolen), used a camcorder to tape the whole scene, and brought
his friends for backup instead of a dog.

"Yo, we're jumping MCs, X. You say you're a dog, but you must be a bitch. You, too, Collie J, you're next because your nephew ain't shit!"

Me, Collie, and these two girls had been chilling on the block when we saw their car screech up. Bill caught me off guard and maybe it was the camcorder he had running in my face or something because I didn't respond. I just stood there sucking my teeth, like, *you fucking clown.* But a few days later, Kasun told me that Bill was talking shit and was showing the tape of them rolling up on me all over the 'hood. So now I knew I had to say something. I had heard Bill's rhymes before and knew I could easily beat him in a battle, but I couldn't deny how popular he was. Those who had heard my tapes felt I was the best, but I was still the dirty, underground rapper from School Street. Bill Blass had the parties and the hype and the fancy name, so I knew it would be close.

"Fuck that," I said to Kasun. "Tell your man Bill he can't fuck with me."

So it was arranged that in two weeks, in the gymnasium of School 12, DMX the Great would take on Bill Blass. Those next fourteen days felt like an entire summer. If it wasn't the flyers Kasun was putting up advertising the party on every corner, it was the mix tapes. Before the battle, Bill must have made at least four or five songs that called me out by name and I heard them everywhere I went: in stores, from boom boxes on the corner, out of cars. The battle became the most hyped party of the year.

It was a Friday night. Collie and Buzzy made sure everybody from Warburton Avenue and Ravine were coming to the show. I had already told all the heads from School Street and Slow Bomb and when I got to the front of the spot I must have had about twenty people with me, but I told them all to go in ahead of me. I wanted to walk in on my own.

I was wearing a black hoody, black jeans, and a pair of butter-colored Tims with some black shades—straight business. I could tell

THE GYMNASIUM OF SCHOOL 12

from the amount of people outside that the gym was probably crowded, but I didn't imagine how completely packed it was until I walked in. People were everywhere: pushed together along the walls, standing on the bleachers, some kids were actually hanging from the supports of the basketball hoops to try and see better. There was no stage in School 12, just a table they put in the middle of the floor where a DJ was set up. Kasun was at the door collecting the money and Collie and some of my other uncles were in the center of the gym trying to clear a space.

I just walked directly through everybody and went straight up to Bill. He had on a red corduroy suit with a red patch corduroy shirt and a big hat. He had a water gun in his left hand and was already talking shit on the mic. He must have thought this was a fucking circus.

"Who do you wanna go first?" he asked me when he saw me.

"I don't give a fuck, let's just get it on, baby."

Blass went first. As he rhymed I couldn't take my eyes off of this big, hairy mole that he had on his face. It must

THE ENTRANCE WAS ALWAYS PACKED WITH PEOPLE

have been the size of a quarter, but when he finished, I knew I had him. Bill Blass was saying the same everyday shit.

I started with what had become my signature intro:

I'm the dopest of the dope, the unstoppable preacher of
rap,the original, author of "Spellbound," the motherfucking
pimp, DMX the Great and I'm not to be fucked with because
I'm deadly with a motherfucking mic . . .

Then I went straight to the disrespectful material. I personalized it by talking about his sister:

Pink and black lip brick-oven butt bitch
When I watch her butt switch, it makes my nuts itch
So I fuck the hooker, every time I look her
in her motherfuckin' face it makes me mad I ever
 took her[17]

People started yelling like crazy. It was a prize fight. Madison Square Garden. *Heavyweight Championship of the World.*

"Back up! Back up! Give them room!" everybody started yelling.

I just kept going and going.

Earlier that day, I had written a song about Yonkers that I knew I could use to get the whole crowd with.

School Street's schoolin', Riverdale's rollin'
Cottage is coolin', Slow Bomb's swollen
Nobody hurtin' Warburton, ain't no joke
Mess around with Mulford Gardens, you're bound to get
smoked![18]

It was over. I successfully shut down the biggest MC in Yonkers. *Me, DMX the Great, a bum nigga with no haircut. The robbing and stealing problem child who couldn't stay out of juvenile and jail and group home. I bet that bitch Daphne wouldn't front on me now.*

After the battle, Bill got on the mic and started talking about unity. Now he wanted the two of us to peace it up.

Yeah, right. Not when I just shitted on you. There's no unity here tonight, motherfucker. You lost. You lost and I'm out!

All of my peoples from School Street left the party with me. As we walked back to the block they spread the news to everybody.

"Yo, how did it go?"

"What? You weren't there? Man, DMX killed him!"

We walked down Ashburton Avenue, through Cottage and Mulford Gardens before ending up outside of my grandmother's house on Warburton. Everybody was open. I was the talk of the town.

Kasun spent the whole next day dubbing a tape he had made of the battle, so by Saturday evening everyone in the city was listening to how I murdered Bill Blass. Then, by Sunday afternoon, everyone wanted a rematch.

This time, instead of letting Kasun get all of the money, I promoted the battle myself, finally convincing Mrs.

THE REMATCH

Gains to let me throw a party at Nepperhan. I got manager Jack to watch the door for me and made sure we got everybody's money before I even went onstage.

"Get upstairs, Earl!" Mrs. Gains yelled at me when she found me in the basement counting money at about midnight. I also had these two girls on my lap and was smoking a Philly blunt. The whole basement was fogged up.

"Okay, okay, Mrs. Gains. I'm coming now . . ." I was chilling.

Everyone from Yonkers came to the rematch, but there were also heads there from Mount Vernon and New Rochelle. I guess the word had gotten out about DMX the Great. (One reason I knew the party was the place to be was because Kasun told me this girl that I knew from Slow Bomb was upstairs leaning against the speaker wearing a big pair of bangle earrings. Her name was Mary and she was the shit around the way because she had just put out her first song called "You Remind Me.")

Bill didn't wear his red outfit this time, and he had written some new material, but it was clear that his era was over.

```
I'm the type of guy you catch cooling with your girl
Those that know me well, choose to call me Earl
Simmons, the womens . . .
```

I ripped that over "Dance to the Drummer's Beat" and the pretty and fly Bill Blass became nothing more than "Barbecue Bill from Locust Hill."

I was on top of the world.

It's almost 11 P.M. now on this hot Arizona evening and DMX decides that he wants to hit the club. It doesn't take long for local folks to get hip to the fact that there's a superstar in town. Besides a few ball players, and the golfers in their khakis and plaids who come around for the various PGA events, Phoenix, Arizona, doesn't get too many celebrities. So because X had already made a few nights' worth of appearances at this local bar, it doesn't surprise anyone in the crew that the spot is flooded with the best and the brightest of what this western community has to offer:

All the local college frat boys are in the place, as are the thugs from the poorer sides of town, the wanna-be MCs and the thirty-something party people whose outfits lag behind everyone else's fashion by at least a season and a half. Then there are the girls, mostly white, some brown, some light-skinned, dressed in the different combinations of stiletto boots and almost-see-the-crack-of-your-ass jeans that they must have seen on TV that day.

Posted at a pool table in the center of the club's VIP room, X challenges anyone willing to bet twenty dollars on a game. But just as he finds a partner who looks willing to double his losses as long as he wants to play, the dozens of fans that have surrounded his table begging for hugs and pictures and autographs start to become unmanageable. One girl, almost choking with excitement, pushes past security and tells him that all she wants to do is touch his head.

On that note, it's time to leave.

"I love the love, I really do," X says, after he has retreated to his car and is safely behind a set of dark-tinted windows. "But often it's way too much for me. It's like you grow up being a certain person and whoever that person is, you know that person. Then you're given something that you've always wanted but so many things change and that makes you almost uncomfortable with yourself. I never got any of this attention before and it gets hard because there are less cracks in the wall now, less hiding places where I can just be me. I felt safer then. It's like there is a certain security in no one giving a fuck about you . . ."

X stares out onto the street.

"I need a drink," he says wearily, reminded that amidst the commotion he left his bucket of ice-cold Heinekens inside the club. "You think I can cash some of my love in for a fucking drink?"

147

PART II

21

Dog Love

AFTER A FEW MONTHS WORKING TOGETHER, JACK MACNASTY invited me to move into his house in New Rochelle. He thought it would be a good idea for me to be closer to the recording studio we were working in. He also hoped that my living with him would help keep me out of trouble and until some music money kicked in, he wasn't going to charge me any rent.

I didn't hesitate.

For a Yonkers nigga, always fresh out of jail, to have a spot in New Rochelle? That meant I was making moves, because to anyone from Yonkers, New Ro was viewed as a pretty upscale city. There were still projects there, but the community was dominated by middle-income black and Latino families that worked to keep their neighborhoods nice. The streets were generally cleaner, the evenings were quieter, and families who moved there could expect an easier day-to-day life compared to their Yonkers neighbors who had to survive through a far grimier set of realities.

The space I had in Jack's house was almost like a one-bedroom apartment, because my bedroom was off to the side of the house next to the kitchen. I had my own bathroom and an enclosed porch area that I turned into a living room. I set up a stereo and a television (I even had cable, the old-school kind with the box with the big brown buttons) and was happy because I was able to chill in private or go through the two porch doors to the other side of the house when I wanted to hang out with Jack.

During the day I relaxed and wrote a lot of rhymes and just like I used to do with my uncles in Yonkers, I ran the streets of New Rochelle.

I don't remember exactly why the man in a tank top and boxer shorts was chasing TQ and me that day, but I knew that we weren't paying him much attention even though he was yelling and screaming holding an aluminum baseball bat in his hands.

He had a fat-ass wife and I think he must have heard us say something disrespectful to her as she went in the house, because he came flying out of there on a rampage. He was at least fifty-something years old with a big, swollen stomach and he was dead serious about chasing us up the street in the flip-flops he had on.

"Ahh hah!" I teased him as I ran all over. "Who you think you're gonna catch with your old ass?"

Me and TQ could have jumped him, but I didn't know how well TQ could fight and besides, I was having too much fun playing. Trying to be slick, I ran into this small parking lot across the street not realizing that instead of concrete, the ground was covered with this loose black gravel.

"Fuck you, you fat bitch! Why don't you just suck my dick!" I danced in front of him, laughing. The old man came up to me and lifted the bat up to swing it at my head. I let him get close but as soon as I saw his arms start to move forward, I went to run to dodge his swing and then . . . *I slipped.* The gravel didn't give me any traction and that first step I took almost put me on my knees.

Whooosh!

I felt the wind of the bat fly right above my head and my heart shot up into my throat. He swung that damn thing so hard, it spun him all the way around. If I didn't slip, he would have cracked my head open like a melon. After a moment, I stopped playing with him and ran out of that parking lot as fast as I could.

I was supposed to be dead at that moment. I felt the wind.

$\bullet \quad \bullet \quad \bullet \quad \bullet \quad \bullet$

Now that I lived in New Rochelle my pussy average rose sharply. I could get play with the local honeys that were bored with the guys that they saw in the 'hood every day, and after the Bill Blass battles proved that I was the baddest rapper around, chicks were much more open. The year before, I probably would have still been bringing rats to the roof in Yonkers, but having a reputation and somewhere to go makes a lot of difference when you're trying to get some ass. That's probably why Kasun started to think that he could play the hook up game with me.

"Yo, X. I got this girl who wants to meet you," he said to me one night at a bar called Arthur's.

Her name was Tashera. Kasun was dating her roommate, Nicole, and one night they had been listening to one of my tapes and Tashera had asked him if he would introduce us.

Kasun played it slick though.

"Yo, Tashera, I got this guy who wants to meet you . . ." He told her the same thing at the club that night that he told me.

"Who? Does he know me?" Tashera asked him.

"Yeah, he said he wants you to come and talk to him."

"Well, if he wants to talk to me, you can tell him to come here."

A few minutes later I walked over.

"DMX, this is Tashera."

She was wearing an orange and black North Face bubble jacket with black pants.

"Tashera, this is DMX."

I had on my jeans and a black hoody.

"Wait. This is the rapper you and Nicole are always listening to?" she asked K when she saw me.

"Yeah. This is my man X."

"You're DMX? But isn't your name Earl? Don't you live in School Street?"

"Yeah, that's me. How you doing? You're the girl that lives on Linden Street, right?"

I asked the question, but I knew the answer already. I knew exactly who she was. She was the girl in the blue-and-white robe that I had always dreamed about as a kid.

"So what have you been up to?" I asked her calmly, understanding that this was not the time or place to reveal the crazy thoughts I used to have about her.

"I'm doing good. I just can't believe you're the one that everyone's talking about."

Tashera remembered me mostly from Yonkers High, a freshman playing dice with the older kids at the Castle and never going to class. She was shocked I had the audacity to bring a dog to campus and she didn't believe all the rumors she heard about my robbing and stealing until she saw me rob an old lady for her purse in front of Betsy's Grocery. I remembered the incident: Blacky did his thing that morning, I just didn't think that anyone saw me.

As we talked, we found out that we had something in common: because of her family's Muslim faith, the rules in her house growing up were almost as strict as mine were. She and her six brothers and sisters were never allowed to have friends over and after her younger brother bust some kid in the head with a rock in the playground, her parents didn't let any of the kids go outside to play anymore. *I could relate to that!*

It was a good night and I knew it was some different shit because after a few minutes the two of us actually got up and danced together.

`Can't keep my hands to myself when I'm with you . . .` [19]

I wasn't a dancing nigga and she certainly wasn't a dancing girl, so we just did the real cool thing and just moved our shoulders from side to side. That worked for one song.

I was glad that Kasun introduced us that night, and when I went home I was definitely feeling Shorty, but then after that we didn't speak for *weeks*. It wasn't like I didn't try, I just couldn't get her on the phone.

"Hello. Can I speak to Tashera, please?"

"Who's this? Earl? Oh, you just missed her, she went to the store."

It didn't seem to matter what time I called. Nicole or one of Tashera's sisters, Faatimah or Shabazza, would always answer the phone and tell me that she wasn't there. She was either asleep, at work, or busy doing something in the kitchen. That wasn't right. I knew she was trying to play it cool. But I couldn't forget our conversation. Or that blue-and-white robe.

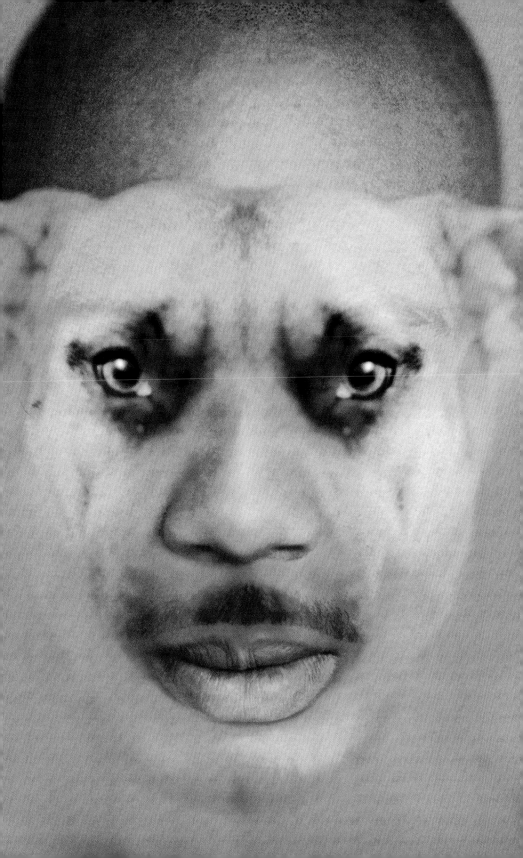

By chance, a few weeks later, I saw her on the bus on my way to the mall. After we talked for a minute, she agreed to come with me. I just didn't tell her that I was going to rob something.

"Are you crazy?"

When Tashera realized what I was doing, she got mad and refused to come into any stores with me, but I ended up swiping a Gap hoody for her anyway when she wasn't looking. That must not have helped my case any, though, because after that day her sisters stayed giving me the phony excuses.

A few weeks later, I was hanging out in front of Steve's Market on Ashburton Avenue. I was feeling good because earlier that day I had robbed a young nigga in Cerrado Park for his black leather coat. He didn't put up a fight once he saw me, just ran his pockets and walked away grumbling. So first I went to McDonald's on South Broadway for a big-ass lunch, then I took myself to the barbershop for a cut. Life was good.

While I was standing outside the spot I looked up and saw Tashera and Nicole walking down the street. I knew she saw me because the closer she got the more she kept trying to play it off. I hadn't spoken to her in almost a month.

"Yo, what's up?" I called out. "Yo, Tashera . . ."

When she turned, she had this shy, guilty look on her face.

"Don't you know that I've been calling your fucking house? Why you keep fronting?"

When she finally lifted her head, she quickly looked me up and down and I could tell that she wanted to smile.

"Oh, shit. For real? What time did you call?" she said, trying to hold back a laugh.

"Yo, you're a fronting-ass nigga, man. I ain't got no time for that."

Nicole tapped her on the shoulder as if to push her on.

"All right, I'm going to beep you tomorrow then," Tashera said.

"No you won't."

"Watch. I promise. I'm going to beep you and we can go out or something."

Tashera kept her word, but the night she invited me over to her house, she told me she had her period so we couldn't mess around.

That was probably a good thing, though, because I had stolen the Tims I was wearing that night and they were a few sizes too big for my feet. To make them fit, I balled up some sweat socks and stuffed them in the front of each boot. She didn't have to see that.

During our conversation that night, Tashera told me that she wasn't going with anybody seriously, that she just had "friends." I didn't care. Even if she did have a man it wouldn't have made any difference to me. I knew that I could get Tashera to feel me more than any other clown that she may have been seeing.

The next day, I stole a nice Honda Accord in New Rochelle and wanted to surprise her with it. When I called and asked her if she wanted to go for a ride, she told me to come over. That was 7:30 P.M.

At 8 P.M. I got to her house.

At 8:20, I was still standing in her doorway ringing the bell.

Oh, hell no. I'm not going to get played out again. This ain't Connecticut!

I knew she was home because I could see a light in the living room window and saw a shadow going back and forth behind the peephole.

Fuck that. You are not going to do me greasy.

I started banging and banging on the door.

"TASHERA!"

No answer.

Okay, this is how you want it? Now you get payback . . .

Around this same time I had met two other girls whose names sounded similar to Tashera's. One was this cutie named Indira that I met on the bus one day; the other was this freak named Lavera. When I told Kasun how heated I was about being stood up and said that I had written a rhyme that told a story about each of them, he said he had the perfect beat: Boogie Down Productions' "I'm Still #1." We recorded it that night.

Once upon a time I knew a girl named Tashera, always fronting so she didn't know the person in the mirror . . . [20]

A few nights later, I was invited to perform at Browneyes. It was a reunion party for these old-school Y-O rappers called the Tribal

Brothers. It was also a birthday party for Nicole's baby son, so I knew Tashera would be there.

With lyrics about people that the local crowd could relate to and Kasun cutting up such a hot beat on the turntables, "Once upon a Time" blew up.

> At first I thought she was just another fan, but then I
>   started to like her
> She didn't have a man and this is the reason why I say that
>   she was frontin'
> She had me confused about what she was really wantin'
> Like one night if her period was off she would have fucked me
> But then she spent the whole next week tryin' to duck me[21]

The crowd loved the record and as soon as I hit the bar my man told me that two of the girls were in the club. Indira wasn't bothered by the attention, but Tashera . . .

"Can I talk to you for a minute?"

Tashera followed me outside as I was leaving. To avoid her, I started circling around a car parked in front of the club.

"Nah, for real, D. I want to talk to you."

She was heated.

Oh! So now the tables are turned, huh? Now I'm the one that's got something to laugh about.

"Yo, was that song about me?"

"What do you mean? Which song?"

Everyone, including Nicole and all of Tashera's other girlfriends, was outside watching us.

"That song with all the girls . . . was that about me?"

"Come on, ma. Why you acting like that?"

Seeing her all embarrassed, I couldn't be mad—now that I knew that I got her back good.

"I didn't say *Ta-shera*," I answered playfully. "I said *Ta-mira!*"

Everyone laughed. Tashera started chasing me around the car faster and faster. "I swear when I catch you, DMX, I'm gonna fuck you up!"

Revenge is sweet.

"I only did that because you're always fronting," I told her once she calmed down.

"No, I'm not."

"Yes you are . . . but to prove it, why don't you come over to my house tonight?"

"Where? I'm not going to School Street."

"Nah. Not Yonkers. I have my own crib in New Rochelle."

"New Rochelle? At this time of the night? What are we going to do? I'm hungry."

"How about I cook some French toast?"

"Yeah, right. You don't know how to make breakfast, Earl."

"No, I do. Watch. I'll make the best French toast you've ever had . . ."

That was April 29, 1989—one of the best nights of my life. Not only did Tashera come over and enjoy my breakfast, but the two of us stayed up all night just talking and bugging out. We watched TV. I showed her all of my rhyme books and pictures of my dogs. She asked me if I wanted any kids and was surprised when I told her that I wanted a daughter.

"'I'd rather my little girl knocked up pregnant than my son be dead or in jail somewhere."

Tashera told me that when she was fourteen, her mother had left the family without a trace. One morning she said she was going to the store and would be back in a few minutes but never returned. There was no warning, no note. Her mom just vanished. Tashera and her sisters spent days looking for her—in parks, in the local mosques, even in morgues—but they couldn't find her. After that, her father was never the same. He stopped selling the oils and incense on the street that he had been making a living from and stopped bringing food into the house for the kids. As the oldest child, Tashera quit school, took on her mother's role in the family, and started cooking, cleaning, and working a full-time job. But after a few months of taking care of everything, her father started to take his pain out on his daughter and began to disrespect her so Tashera left the house and had been living on her own ever since. I could relate to her pain and when she opened her heart to me that night, I felt closer to her than any other woman in my entire life. That's when I told her I loved her.

"You're just trying to get some ass," she replied, sucking her teeth.
I wasn't, but I couldn't prove that to her. Not yet, anyway.

Tashera and I spent the next three days together. We couldn't get enough of each other because it was like we felt the same way about things, laughed at the same jokes. If we both saw something funny, we knew what it was without telling the other person. In many ways we were total opposites. She always dated light-skinned guys. I was dark-skinned with a bald head. She liked the pretty-boy type. I never ironed or even cared about my clothes. But there was a special connection between us. With Tashera, I found myself being able to have fun with a woman in ways that I never thought possible. If we ever ran into a girl I used to mess with, we would hang out with the chick for a few minutes, maybe smoke a blunt, then on the way home I would reveal to her that I used to fuck the girl and we'd laugh. One time I remember this tall, light-skinned chick I had been messing with actually showed up at the spot in New Rochelle. I knew she still liked me so I told Tashera to watch from behind the door. A couple of days before, the girl had told me that she wore a wig.

"Hey. What's up, girl? Listen, before you come in, can you do me a favor? Can you take your wig off for me?"

"Why, D?"

"'Cause your hair just looks so real, ma. I want to see if you were telling me the truth the other day."

The girl hesitated for a few seconds, looked around, then grabbed the piece from the back of her head and pulled it forward. She was baldheaded and had on a white stocking cap underneath. I thought Tashera was going to get us both busted by laughing so loud.

"There. You happy? Can I come in now?"

"Uh, damn. You know I think my manager is going to be home in a little while . . . Can you call me tomorrow?"

Jack started calling Tashera Häagen-Dazs, because he said she had to be my favorite.

"Nigga, what are you doing? You got Häagen-Dazs in there again?"

I'd be in the kitchen making more French toast. It was becoming our regular breakfast.

"Yeah, man. She's hungry."

After a couple months of dating, it became official that Tashera was my girl. Everyone in New Rochelle and Yonkers would always see us rolling together and right away brothers in the street knew they couldn't come at her sideways with no nonsense. I didn't even let anyone *ask* if she was fucking with me, because I'd be liable to crack someone's head open if I thought they were trying to push up and I'd creep anyone for being disrespectful.

(I never could tolerate a nigga that got down like that, even if it wasn't with my girl. My uncle Pinky was about to throw down one night outside of Bo Digs bar with some guy that grabbed his girlfriend's ass. Now she was a drunk, one of those bad, reckless drunks that talk real greasy when they drink—*Motherfucker . . . why don't you suck my motherfucking dick*—so she wasn't helping matters, but before my uncle and the guy could finish arguing, I just sneaked up behind him and punched the guy right in his face over my uncle's shoulder. Pinky didn't even see me coming, but the ass-grabbing bastard was laid out on the pavement.)

I was more protective of Tashera and our relationship than I even was of myself because this was the first time in my life that I cared about someone this deeply. I was hungry and fresh out of group home when I was with Leshawn; Daphne burned me, but she was more of a trophy for a young nigga than anything else; and fucking rats on the rooftop was just that—fucking rats on a rooftop. But with Tashera, I felt the trust and respect and understanding that I longed for. I could only describe it one way. Tashera gave me "dog love."

ME AND TASHERA IN NEW ROCHELLE

22

"You're Not Going to Boo Me!"

By early 1990, Jack had started managing a few other artists in Yonkers and New Rochelle and when we did a show at one of his parties he would bill us as the "House Party All-Stars" after the name of his company, House Party Productions. The best party he and his partners threw was on Thursday nights at a club called the Castle, on 138th Street and Walton Avenue in the Bronx. "Sneaker Thursdays" was popular because there weren't many places in New York at the time where heads could go to party and listen to hip-hop without having to abide by a dress code or suffer through hours of R&B, and every Thursday Jack would have us open for whoever the headliner was. Biz Markie, Big Daddy Kane, Nice & Smooth, and Special Ed were all artists that I opened for at the Castle.

I never thought anybody who rolled with Jack was nice, though, that's why I always made sure that I went on last. I wanted to perform as close to the established artists as possible. But I didn't respect those "stars" that much either. It wasn't anything personal, I just felt like after my wins over K-Solo and Bill Blass, nobody could fuck with me on the rap tip. I didn't care whether someone had a song on the radio or not, I knew that I could tear them up.

One Thursday I proved my point.

It was a night the Castle sponsored a big DJ battle. Folks had packed in the club from 10 P.M. while contestants took turns cutting and scratching their favorite dance breaks. I wondered why Kasun wasn't there because I knew he would have gotten some applause for scratching the record with his teeth, but this was also a regular party night, and you can't dance to a bunch of DJ tricks, so around midnight, the crowd was getting restless. After Jack announced the winner, though, instead of starting up the music, he wanted me and TQ to perform. I knew that wasn't a smart idea and the minute TQ got onstage with a mic in his hand, the crowd started booing him. My man barely made it through his first song. Then it was my turn.

Okay, I understand that you've been listening to a DJ battle for two and a half hours and now you're ready to get your groove on, but y'all are not going to do me like you did TQ. I got something to say.

Lord Finesse was a Bronx MC who had a rep throughout New York for always dropping hot verses on popular underground mix tapes and when I got onstage I noticed that he was chilling at the front with his partner, Andre the Giant (later known as part of the duo Showbiz & AG). The two of them were just standing there staring at me. So I decided to go into attack mode. Forget my normal routine, I was going to direct my rhymes straight at these guys like they had challenged me to a street battle. It worked like a charm because once the crowd peeped what I was doing, they started hollering like crazy. It seemed that Andre the Giant lived around the corner and here he was getting dissed with all of his peoples in the club.

Suddenly Kid Capri, who was the house DJ, cut the beat off. He knew the two of them and could see that they were getting heated without having a way to respond.

"Yo, hold up. Hold up. I want Lord Finesse and Andre the Giant to come up on the stage and we're going to do this shit for real."

On cue, everyone in the club rushed to the front of the stage, curious to see who had the balls to challenge their man in his home spot. They didn't know me. I was from Yonkers. This was the Bronx. They hadn't ever bought any of my mix tapes or heard of Bill Blass and I could see Jack shaking his head. In the early days of hip-hop, your street rep was the most important thing you had as an MC and Jack always tried to discourage me from battling. He knew that if I lost a battle in a place like the Castle with so many artists and label folks around, my whole career would be put on ice and I definitely wouldn't be able to perform anywhere in the Bronx anymore. But I wasn't thinking about all that. I was just trying to get out of the bad situation he had put me in, and well, if it's on, it's on.

Running through niggas is how I do niggas
And two niggas got nothing for me
When they saw me, they looked the other way and tried to
    ignore me[22]

Since there was always a dick-riding dude in the street battles that I had in Yonkers, I already had rhymes where I would talk to one person and put his man in it, so battling two people didn't faze me. And I kept it ugly.

I put holes like foot holes in niggas' buttholes
Stomp a mud hole and when I cut holes, the fucking blood flows

The three of us went face-to-face and I shitted on both of them at the same time. It was no contest.
Yeah, you're not going to boo me, not tonight, not ever . . .
After that, I could do no wrong in the Castle. "Sneaker Thursdays" became more and more popular and artists that Jack wanted to headline at the club started telling him that they wouldn't perform if I was going to rhyme that same night. It felt good to have that kind of reputation in the Bronx, the birthplace of hip-hop, and it wasn't long before I took my skills down to Manhattan.

It was the 1990 New Music Seminar on 99th Street and Amsterdam Avenue in a large school playground called "Rocksteady Park" after the break-dancing crew. The seminar was an annual talent conference that was very influential in the hip-hop world at the time because it was supported by the major record labels and attended by different kinds of people from all over the country who were just hungry to get into hip-hop.

I easily made it through the early rounds of the contest, but in the semifinals, the DJ kept messing up my music.

A battle when you have a DJ is different from being on the street with a radio or a beatbox, because then you're at the mercy of whoever's spinning the records. But the DJ is a crucial part of an MC's performance in a battle. If he plays a beat for you that the crowd already likes, you will have a distinct advantage over the next man, because as long as your flow sounds good, the crowd will be into what you're doing. It doesn't matter what your lyrics are, if the music is hot enough, the crowd will think you're freaking it. But three of the four times I took the stage that day, as soon as I started getting into my verse, the beat started skipping.

"Yo, what's going on, money?"

I looked back at the DJ heated, just glad that I saved face a little bit by saying some halfway decent rhymes before the beat messed up and I had to start all over. Then, after two more bars, the beat skipped again.

"Yo, DJ, turn the beat off, man. I don't want no fucking music . . ."

That crushed it. The crowd saw me taking matters into my own hands as a real move because if I could be dope with no beat, then I had to be a pretty good MC.

Two rhymes later, the contest was over and I won the award for Best Rapper (somebody stole the trophy, though. I was mad because I was going to bring that joint back to Y-O as my first badge of NYC officialness) and when I came offstage, Jack had some more good news. He said *The Source* magazine had called and they wanted to interview me for "Unsigned Hype." We had sent my demo and picture to them months before and when I didn't hear anything back from them, I figured that I didn't get it. But now it was real. DMX the Great was about to be known as "The Best Unsigned Rapper in the Country."

"Yo, Jack, I want you to hold these for me," I said to my manager when we got back to the house that night. I had ten black-and-white composition notebooks that I had been writing in since my days in juvenile. Almost every rhyme that I had ever written was in them.

Jack looked at me puzzled for a second.

"You want *me* to hold them?"

"Yeah, I do," I said, realizing that I trusted the brother. "I do."

Tashera had never seen me perform a big show, but at the time I was supposed to take the stage at Commerce High School,

Kasun and I were three towns away in a weed spot getting lifted.

The event was headlined by Nikki D, Isis from X-Clan, and a group called Leaders of the New School whose first single, "Case of the PTA," was quickly becoming one of the hottest songs in the country, thanks in part to the energy of a young MC called Busta Rhymes. This was different from the type of shows I had been doing at the Castle or School 12 (and definitely Browneyes, the only place Tashera had ever seen me perform before). This was a *concert* where fans actually had to line up and buy tickets.

In the spot, Kasun kept asking me what time we had to go on, but I didn't know so I told him not to worry about it. The green was real sticky and I was enjoying my blunt. When we finally got to Commerce, Jack was furious because I was supposed to go on before everybody else, but Isis had already finished her show and Leaders of the New School, who were scheduled to go on last, had gotten tired of waiting for me and had already begun setting up their equipment.

I didn't care. Y-O was still my hometown and I knew Tashera was there with her girlfriends ("Yeah, you sit right in the front, ma," I had told her with a smile) and I was feeling good because earlier that day I had decided to shave my head.

Up until then I always kept a short Afro with the waves. Even when I went to jail, I never wanted them to cut my scalp too low, but something possessed me that afternoon to change my look, so I borrowed one of Jack's razors after he went to work and got busy. My new bald head looked perfect with my black jeans and hoody.

When I took the stage fifteen minutes after LONS had ended their show with their hottest song, I just took it to another level. Kasun and I ripped through our entire repertoire: "Spellbound," "Yonkers aka Y-O," and a

new joint called "Ten Hype Beats" where K would cut together the hottest hip-hop breaks for me to rhyme over. I even did "Once upon a Time" again just for Tashera. The crowd of one thousand-plus went crazy. I actually had dancers at the time: three girls and two guys. I named the guys Poison & Pain and they were hyping the crowd up behind me doing their "wop" and "running man" routines. I never felt so at one with an audience. I could feel their energy inside of me. The more feeling they gave me, the more emotion I put into every verse and by the time I was through, my body was soaked in sweat.

Tashera was impressed. Commerce was the best and the biggest show that I had ever done. After it was over, I started signing autographs and people were asking Kasun and I to pose for pictures. When it was time to leave, police officers escorted me out of the building like I was some kind of star or something. It was all happening.

"Who is DMX The Great?"

Incarcerated in Suffolk County Jail for being in a stolen car w/o it's rightful owner, DMX spent of summer of 1988 behind bars, writing rhymes and battlin M.C.'s. A juvenile prisoner, DMX embarked on the Ultimate in Rap Style delivery "Spellbound". A unique style of M.C.ing in which spelling words, make up the Rhyme. So "stupid" was this new style, DMX wrote entire rhymes of spelling (Spellbound, Dopest of the Dope, and my status D-O-P-E). Then it happened, word in the joint was there was another M.C. on the premises by the name of K-solo, claiming to have some skills. (Church mouthed choir boy turned rapper). The population decided that the County was not big enough for 2 M.C.'s so the battle lines were drawin in the yard. In battle DMX staked his claim to superiority as K-solo, now dumbfounded and in critical condition was relocated to protective custody. (He could only be heard mumbling "Tell the world his name." "Who is DMX the Great?" "The Original Author of Spellbound!"

Later, K-Solo released from Suffolk County prior to DMX, and now a student in the school of EPMD, shopped a deal. In the process laying claim as his own to the style that slayed him, "Spellbound." Claiming to never have heard of or met DMX The Great, "K-Stol-it:"

He didn't bite it, he ate it
But sooner or later, the truth will be found
that DMX is the original author of Spellbound
D = dopest of the dope

"Who is DMX The Great?"

Meanwhile, DMX the Great was discovered by Jack & Spank MacNasty of MacNasty Management in the summer of 1989. His performing career was launched in the Hip Hop War zone of the South Bronx, at "The Castle." The battle lines now extended from Suffolk County to the Bronx, DMX gained the respect of his lyrical peers in battling and performing with the likes of Kid Capri, Lord Finesse, Andre the Giant and Justice, to name a few. DMX was crowned king of the Castle."

M = Murdering M.C.'s

"Who is DMX The Great?"

DMX the Great born Earl Simmons in Yonkers N.Y. (the largest city in Westchester County) 10 miles north of money earning Mt. Vernon. Ruler of the Ruff Ryders posse, the style of DMX combines Old School Delivery and underground Lyrics with new school beats & concepts. In a Live Radio Interview (Dec. 1990) w/Lady B. of the Hip Hop Connection WBLS, DMX kicked Spellbound accopello with Chuck D, Shockey Shay, grandmaster Flash & B chearing him on across airwaves. His print hype includes January 1991 unsigned hype winner in The Source magazine. A raw, rough edged rapper able to send a message in "The Born Loser" a story rhyme of life in the ghetto, or flash back to freestyle in "Catching the Same Hell" with hype beats and hitting lyric's there is no lack of motivation in "Critical Condition" DMX rounds out his project with a show of versatility in fantasy rhymes "Girls", "Once Upon a Time" and "Sesame Street"

X = The X-Factor

"Who is DMX The Great?"
$$D + M \div X \text{ Factor} = DMX \text{ Great}$$

Like Tic Tac Toe, 3 x's in a row
x-man, x-rated, x-marks the Spot!

MY FIRST BIO

23

One Love Boomer

HE WAS GIVEN TO ME AS A PUPPY. A SMALL PIT, BROWN WITH a white streak that came down across his face, Boomer was like a real person, a nigga with his own unique personality and attitude. He was my companion, my ride. Anything I did, Boomer and me did together. Anything I got, Boomer and me shared. We were inseparable. I raised him to be the most dangerous and feared dog on the block, but he was also the smartest and the best trained. That was a rare combination.

My favorite place for him was right on top of the mailbox outside of my grandmother's house. It was one of those blue boxes with a rounded top and Boomer would just climb up there and wait until I came downstairs. Folks walking down Warburton would be scared to death when they saw Boomer sitting on top of that mailbox with no leash on and no owner in sight. More than half a block away people used to cross the street because they never could be sure that my pit bull wouldn't decide to jump down and attack them. That's how I liked it.

"Yo, X! Get your dog off the goddam mailbox, man. People can't even walk by!" a friend of mine named Big Jack used to holler at me all the time from downstairs.

"He's aiight!" I used to yell back from my grandmother's window.

But Boomer would never move until I told him to. If I wanted to go to the store, I could tell him to wait on the mailbox while I walked down the street and every time he was still sitting there when I got back, I would reward him by going to find some mischief for us to get into.

"All right, Boomer. Come on, boy. We outta here!"

A few blocks up from my grandmother's on Locust Hill, there were some buildings back from the sidewalk that you entered via a small driveway in the front. In the basement of one of those buildings there was a small Laundromat. That's where these seven huge alley cats lived.

They were big, hairy cats, about the same size as Boomer, and when you went down you knew right away that those cats were living well because it was always warm and there were lots of mouse-traps on the floor whose traps were sprung without sign of any kill.

When Boomer was four months old, every night I brought him down to that basement to fight those cats. He couldn't quite kill them yet at that age, but he tried his best to fuck them up. The cats would have their claws out and be scratching him like crazy, but Boomer would never give up and he never lost his heart. I knew when to stop it because whenever Boomer was hurt he would let out this high-pitched wail. He didn't stop fighting; he would just yell wildly out of the side of his mouth, frustrated that because he was so young he couldn't do more against the cats' giant claws.

When Boomer got older it was a different story. Then he was strong enough to grab the cats by their throat and just bang their heads into the ground—that would end all the fighting. And Boomer loved to kill. One time I was outside riding a bike through Ravine and a cat he was chasing tried to get away by jumping through this open vent on the side of a building, but Boomer caught the cat by his hind leg and started yanking him. The cat was hissing and crying.

"Get him! Get him!" I encouraged my boy.

When Boomer finally pulled the cat out, the only thing that was holding the animals back leg together was fur. The bone was bit right through. I ran right up on it. When an animal dies, he'll just piss and shit all over the place, and I caught some piss in the face that day.

Then Boomer started to eat the rest.

Boomer always wanted to drag his kill around with him for a few hours after the event. Or he would just quietly stand over the dead animal in a victory pose—until of course, you tried to pull it away and he would start screaming.

Boomer killed a lot of raccoons, too. To him they were just big cats.

See, most dogs have problems killing raccoons. Raccoons are much bigger and heavier than the average cat and their claws are sharp enough to rip through flesh, but any well-trained pit bull should be able to snatch a raccoon off his feet. All that scratching shit doesn't work when your legs are up in the air.

Boom, boom, and *BOOM!*

After the third slam, you're neck is broken. Now all you can do is twitch. Just twitch and shit on yourself. Raccoons have heart, they will still try to fight back, but you'll see that sad look on their face and their eyes will start popping out of their head. There's no more thinking when your head is crushed. All that threatening, arch-your-back routine is dead. All you're thinking about is sleep, buddy.

Boomer's conflicts weren't always nasty, though. Sometimes they were actually pretty to watch. One time he ran up a fence in pursuit of a cat and when the cat jumped off to escape, Boomer jumped with her and somehow caught the cat in midair. That was some fly shit.

I taught Boomer how to climb fences. It's tricky for a young dog to understand how to get up and then down again because they get scared. I started him off with a little gate and then quickly worked his way up. After a few months, all Boomer needed to hear me say was, "Get up, boy!" and he would start climbing. That was an important skill because I needed a dog that could run the streets like I did. I learned that when I lost Blacky. If I had to go over a fence, then my dog needed to be able to follow—especially when the police were chasing, because in Yonkers you could catch a charge for a dog even if the police caught your dog without you. And, like they did with Blacky, the cops would probably shoot him dead. So I made sure that Boomer could roll like I did.

I started to get real close to Boomer the second year that I had him. That's when I realized that the dog was more like me than I ever imagined, and I was like my dog.

It was a night me and Boomer were walking down Warburton on my way to my grandmother's house. Out of the corner of my eye I saw a raccoon run out from a yard and squeeze under this parked car, so I quickly crouched down behind a tree to hide and Boomer came right with me.

Fifteen minutes passed.

I didn't mind waiting.

Fifteen minutes more.

I wanted Boomer to have that raccoon.

After thirty more minutes, now my back hurt, my knees hurt, and I was about to get up and forget it, but I looked at Boomer and he was crouched right there next to me, still eyeing the spot. He wanted that animal just as much as I wanted him to have it. I could see in his eyes that he was ready to wait all night and I had to be as game as my dog.

Twenty minutes later when that motherfucking raccoon finally popped his head out, Boomer was on him. Game over. Our mission was accomplished and me and my boy did it together.

You can't fight a dog until he or she is at least eighteen months old and the first time he fights, I don't care what kind of dog it is, he's going to lose. But this is when you judge his heart. The dog doesn't have any abilities yet, so all you're looking to see is if he wants to keep fighting, if he's screaming and yelling to get more. That's how you'll know if you have a killer.

Throwing pit bulls together so they could fight "off the chain" was a pretty common pastime in the projects. I wasn't the only brother in Yonkers with a passion for pits (every now and then you would see a Rottweiler), so just like other illegal activity in the 'hood, dogfighting would go down all the time. My problem was that every time I fought one of my dogs, I would get hyped to the point that *I* would almost want to fight the other owner.

"Get that motherfucker, Boomer! Come on, boy . . . watch your legs . . . watch your legs!"

I'd be shouting and sweating, watching every move. I could feel my blood rush through my body. My heart would be pounding. My body probably wouldn't have reacted any differently if *I* was the one fighting. And I always had to make sure the other owner knew what was up.

"Don't touch 'em. Don't touch the dogs. I want to see my boy get out of this . . ."

Even if Boomer was getting beaten at that age, I always let him keep fighting. That let him know that I wasn't going to let him give up and was the best way for him to keep learning new skills. By the time he got his adult weight, Boomer would do whatever it took to win a fight.

One day, he had a battle with this big horse-looking pit called Lizm. The dog must have been three times Boomer's size, so while Boomer had a good bite on him, Lizm just kept swinging him in the air like he was a medallion around his neck. But Boomer didn't mind. He just held on and kept breathing out of the side of his mouth. I could see him thinking: *I'll wait, because I'm not going to let go. And when you get tired, you motherfucker, I got you.*

After about fifteen minutes of swinging, Lizm ran out of energy and Boomer grabbed his leg, flipped him over, and the fight was won. Nobody could fuck with me and my dog.

24

Buried in Paperwork

I HAD PUT THE DEAD BODY OF A CAT BOOMER HAD KILLED UP in a tree where he couldn't reach it to teach my boy how to jump. While my dog was going crazy, Jack walked over and suggested a management deal.

"I've got some new producers that I want you to meet and I've found some hot tracks that I want to get you to rhyme on," he said. "So I think it's time that you and I sign an agreement."

I liked Jack. I trusted him. He had hooked me up with a lot of shows and I really appreciated him giving me my own place to stay. He was more like an older brother to me than a manager, so I had no hesitation in signing his paperwork. But soon after I did, I realized that what I had just done was going to keep me broke for a long time.

See, now that I was officially "the artist," I was responsible for all of my expenses and studio costs and legally, managers don't have to pay for anything, they just make a percentage of the money that's coming in. Since Jack was managing me *and* promoting the majority of my shows, he saw most of the dough I was making, and since I was in the studio all the time, my artist bills were adding up. I went to the studio in White Plains almost *every* night. I went there to write and record, sometimes I even slept there, but what I didn't realize was that they were charging me for all of that time. Even when Jack hooked me up with producers who had their own studio, like Tony Dofat and his partner, Greg Troutman, I was still getting billed for engineering fees and lockouts.

That wasn't right. How could people who were supposed to be helping me tell me that I owed them something? They knew I didn't have that kind of money. That was the whole reason I was working with them in the studio to begin with! I mean, it would have been all right if I was close to getting some money for a record deal, but every time Jack went off to a label with my demo tape, he came back with a sorry look on his face. Either they didn't accept my demo at all or told him, "His voice is too rough." Or "He doesn't look marketable." One label executive suggested to Jack that I start dancing more. Another thought I should find a gimmicky outfit like the one rapper Kwame had with his polka-dot shirts.

"Maybe DMX can wear a polka-dot jumpsuit?"

Fuck that. I knew what I was and was not willing to do.

Wild Pitch and the house music label SBK Records were the only two companies that showed any interest in me, but they never followed through. It was like a lot of the labels just dismissed me automatically because of where I was from. Yonkers was a place they never heard of, so they felt that there couldn't be any talent there. To most of these A&R reps, if you weren't from one of the five boroughs, you weren't from New York, and if you weren't from New York then you had no vibe.

This artist shit is bullshit . . .

I started to get very frustrated. If everyone wants to bill me and nobody can get me any money of my own? Well then, listen, I'm just going to have to rely on my instincts . . .

```
Now who I am is who I'll be till I die
Either accept it or don't fuck with it
But if we're going to be dogs, then you stuck with it[23]
```

"I don't have your chain."

TQ looked at me, looked at Jack, then turned back to me again. The three of us were sitting in the living room watching television. TQ had gone to the bathroom and left his gold necklace on the table. Not a smart move.

"Come on, D. Stop playing."

"What? I don't have your chain. You probably dropped it some-where."

"Yo, D. For real. I left it right here."

"I don't have your fucking chain, TQ!"

TQ's faint smile slowly turned into a look of disbelief.

"Come on, D. Please," Jack chimed in. "I saw you take it. Let's keep this like a family."

Now the both of them were staring at me. But no matter what they said, they weren't going to win this one. I knew that neither one of them would try to fight me for the chain and I needed what I needed.

"Yo, I'm telling y'all motherfuckers I ain't got nothing, man. It wasn't me!"

I walked out.

Other times, when I was broke enough, *and the skies were dark enough*, I had to get even grimier:

"Give me back my tape, X."

"Nah, homeboy, you ain't acting right. I think I'm gonna hold on to this for a little while."

"But I just paid you for it!"

See, I could win battles, contests, be Unsigned Hype. I could be the baddest rapper in Yonkers, the Bronx, all over . . . but if I was still broke? I was going to get mine. Who said my own tapes were off limits? Fuck that. One DMX mix tape can produce a lot of ten-dollar bills . . . and you did hand it back to me. *Stupid.*

One dark summer night, this off-brand nigga walked into a house party on Ravine where me, Collie, Buzzy, and Kasun were chilling. He had a black ski mask pulled over his face and was rocking a huge gold chain around his neck with a horseshoe pendant on the end of it. He just waltzed to the front of the room and started profiling against the wall.

"Collie, do you know this nigga?"

Collie shook his head.

This was my man's party and I couldn't let a stranger just walk in all bold like that without doing something, not when he was wearing a motherfucking ski mask like he was hard.

One of Collie's friends noticed that I was getting anxious.

"X, I've seen him before. It's cool. That's so-and-so's boy."

"Who . . . ? "

My mind was made up. *I could get a lot for that piece . . .*

"Never heard of him . . . fuck him!"

The lights were out, the music was blaring, and the moment he turned his head I smacked him right in his chest and snatched it. Then I just turned and looked the other way.

When he didn't say anything, I knew he was a bitch. He just looked at me like I was crazy.

I was.

"What's the problem, money?"

Homeboy walked out without saying a word, but later, when I left the party, five guys were waiting for me downstairs.

"DMX, we heard you snatched my people's chain . . . "

"Yeah, whatever, homes. Your man is a bitch . . . this is my spot, nigga!"

In a fight, you don't feel it when someone hits you. The feeling comes later, but then it's different. Then you're sore and I could always deal with being sore. *Before* you get into a brawl is when you think it's going to make you hurt all over the place.

Ohmigod, he's going to pop my eye out!

But that doesn't happen. It's like how people believe the first beatdown you take is the hardest one to go through. To me, the first one is the *easiest* one because you don't know what's going on. By the time you wake up, it's all over. It's the second beatdown when your stomach starts fucking with you because then you know what's about to happen, then you have fear. Fear is the problem. But if whatever you're afraid of *does* happen, most of the time you will still be able to function properly. Your body will still follow your instructions, although that's never easy to remember. Then by the third or fourth fight, your body is just reacting. You have no control. It's all your subconscious working and even though we all say, "I'm a killer. *I'm the motherfucking man . . .* " we really don't know if that's true until it's on.

We would like to believe that we will jump on top of the car, pull a burner out, do a back flip, and bust two guys in the head. But we don't know that. We may hit the ground at the first punch and start shivering. It's only *after* a threatening situation that we find out what kind of person we are, and then your friends are the only people who can tell you about it because your instinct was running shit.

"Do you know what you did, dog? You jumped over that whole fence and kicked the shit out of money!"

"Word? I did? Get outta here . . ."

You don't remember it, but it happened. After my first couple of fights, I heard that I was a problem for real and realized that my inner self was worse than I thought. When the pressure was on, I turned into a monster, I was like the Incredible Hulk and I always got greasy. I never had a problem poking someone in the eye in a fight or digging in their nose—always with full force, hoping I had nails. I just felt my best bet was to go on the offense. Forget the defense.

Do you, and I'm going to do me, but best believe doing me is going to be stronger than you doing you.

(I was the same way when I had to fight a dog. Most brothers are scared of them, but ever since that hound came at me escaping from Industry, I knew that I could fuck a dog up. Kick him or punch him in the nose. Grab him by his nuts and hit him right in the stomach. The best tactic for a dog is to stick your hand down their throat. Then they can't bite you. Just wait for his mouth to open and make him choke. *Ackh!*)

But I've also learned that there is a cord your psyche is attached to, and you shouldn't ever try to go further than that cord lets you. If you've been doing pull-ups every night, then you know you can scale that wall. If you haven't, then don't try it. If you've been doing one hundred push-ups every morning for two years, then you know how strong you are. If you stay aware of your inner self, you will be good with any circumstance that comes up. Just be careful not to go further out than that cord allows and don't ever let it go.

That night on Ravine I handled my business, I slammed a few bigger-rep niggas up against cars and beat them down good. I knew all the details about the fight because I had a lot of time to hear about it since me, Collie, Buzzy, my uncle Buckeye, and my aunt Rhonda all got arrested that night when six police cars pulled in front of my grandmother's house.

"Yo, Jack, I'm in Valhalla."

"What are you doing up there, cuz?"

"I'm in jail."

25

X

I WAS USED TO BEING LOCKED UP. IT HAD ALMOST BECOME A comfortable place for me. I no longer feared or fought against the environment. I was used to sleeping on hard surfaces, used to eating rotten food. I just accepted the dirty loneliness of the life for what it was. I didn't want visits. I didn't want mail. Letters would just make me sick to go home. I'd get thirsty at the mail line waiting for something and have to flip on somebody the day I didn't get anything. So don't send me pictures, don't come see me, nothing. Just let me handle my bid. The jail was X's home.

See, DMX was the rapper. But X, X was someone different. X was hunger. X was rage. And when I found X locked up in that cell, I knew that I was losing Earl. X lived in a place within me that I knew a young boy could never survive. Almost like a monster. I could feel its force pulse through my veins. And when he showed himself, my music took on a whole new identity. I was still writing, but now my phrases were hostile and my stories were dark. Unconsciously, my words formed sentences that were loaded with the anger and frustration I carried with me every second of every day. I spit fire at anybody who came my way and slowly a new persona evolved out of the words of my own experience.

Look in the mirror, say my name five times
Turn out the lights, and I done took nine lives
Don't get scared now nigga, finish it 'cause you started it
Watched it grow out of control, now you want no part of it[24]

"Yo, X is battling someone on H-block!" inmates would cry out when they heard me starting to go at it with some clown who swore he was nice with the lyrics. Heads would put down their books, take off their headphones, stop whatever it was they were doing to bang on the metal bars of their cell gates. Twenty murderers banging in unison provides a loud, thundering beat and I would feed off the noise and just flow as hard as I could.

There was always one or two guys that couldn't stand the racket— "Yo, X, shut the fuck up!"—but I kept going and going until the officers came with their billy clubs out and would force us to break it up. Most of the time these jail battles went down on the late night, but if someone wanted to challenge me, I was ready to go at it anytime.

By now, "Spellbound" was by far my most popular rap. It had become the last song I performed at clubs and was the death blow I used in most of my battles. That's why the day one of my fellow inmates heard somebody spelling a rhyme on the radio, he thought it was me.

"Yo, X. You were on WBLS!" he told me.

At first I didn't believe him but after a few more guys told me that they heard it as well, I started thinking maybe Jack pulled a few strings and got "Spellbound" played somehow. It *was* on my demo tape. Then I saw the video.

It wasn't me.

K-Solo, the brother that I battled through the fence in Suffolk County, the brother who I beat in the hardest battle that I had ever had, the friend that I chilled and became cool with, had taken my style—and it was blowing up.

That biting motherfucker. I had explained to him how to do the style! Even though everyone in Yonkers and the Bronx and New Rochelle knew that the "Spellbound" style was mine, it didn't matter now, not when the record was getting national airplay. My talent was making a star out of somebody else and there was nothing I could do about it.

Crazy Earl would have been angry, but X? X got furious with it. I just sat in my cell for days and made so many songs dissing the bastard I renamed him "K-Stole It." And then I wrote something else, a song I called "Born Loser." It expressed exactly how I was feeling:

```
The born loser, not because I choose to be
But because all the bad shit happens to me . . .
No time for laughter, this shit's for real
Ribs are showing through my back 'cause I haven't had a meal
In about a week, you can see bones in my hands
The raccoons beat me to the garbage cans[25]
```

"Simmons, where are you from?" one of the corrections officers from my cell block asked me one night before lock-in. "How long have you been rapping?"

COs and I rarely shared any casual words. Most of the time our interactions dealt with discipline or disrespect.

"Because my partner and I make beats. And we were thinking maybe . . ."

"Huh? You're a CO, man, and I'm a prisoner. What are you talking to me about beats for?"

"Well, I was thinking maybe one day we could work together?"

"BORN LOSER," OTHER VERSES, AND A LIST OF FOLKS I WANTED TO BATTLE

This was crazy, but I could tell when a nigga was hungry for something. My man *had* been listening to me spit lyrics for months already up and down the cell blocks, so maybe he wanted to fuck with X?

"My manager, Jack MacNasty, handles all of my business," I told him. "You should talk to him and play him some of your tracks . . . But you know if you want me to rap over any of them, I can't do anything for you in here."

Two weeks later Jack came up to Valhalla to visit me and said that he had met with the two COs. It seems they wanted to be producers but they had no MC.

Well, let's see. I wanna be free, but I have no money.

"Let's make this happen."

That next Friday, my twenty-five-hundred-dollar bond was paid in full and I was out of jail within a few hours. The deal that Jack made was for me to go to their house in Mount Vernon where they had a keyboard and a four-track recorder set up and lay down some vocals. There was no contract, no nothing. When I asked Jack what their beats sounded like, he laughed and told me that he never heard them.

Chain-snatching was a pretty big "quality of life" crime in New York at the time; it was one of those random acts of violence that the public felt needed to be stomped out right away like car-jacking or "wilding," and when my trial came around I was nervous that the predominantly white jury would see me as a "threat to society" even though I hadn't been over to their side of the world in years. But witnesses tend to forget that when someone else is testifying you're forced to wait outside the courtroom so you can't hear what's going on. If you are trying to corroborate someone's story, you had better work out the details beforehand. The kid whose chain I snatched did none of that. His brother's story was different from his man's; his man's was different from his.

Jack was sitting behind me when, after a few hours of deliberation, the jury foreman read the not-guilty verdict. Now I was free for good.

26

Waah Rolls By

EVERYBODY TOLD ME I WASN'T GOING TO MAKE IT TO SEE twenty.

"Boy, you ain't never gonna make it to that old . . ."

So when I turned twenty, I was like, "Yeah, fuck you!"

Tashera had an apartment on Locust Hill in Yonkers. If I wasn't out in New Rochelle, that's where I would chill with her and her friend Nicole.

One night I was looking out the window and saw a burgundy Z28 with dark, black tints pull up on the block. It was late, almost midnight, and I didn't recognize the car. A good 'hood nigga should always be able to recognize all of the local vehicles, it's information that's as vital as the location of the weed spot or the name of a new shorty who recently moved into the projects, but I had never seen this Z before or the brother who got out of the driver's seat in a long, tan trench coat. When he walked up to the house and rang the doorbell, I told Tashera not to answer it.

The next night the same car pulled up again and this time I made sure that I had a burner tucked in my sweatpants and Boomer was ready by my side.

It was 3 A.M.

It was the same dude in the trench coat. He called out to me from the sidewalk.

"Yo, you know this nigga named DMX?"

"Why? What's up?" I answered, opening the door carefully.

"Are you X?" he asked me again.

Boomer started pulling. I started to reach for my waistband and then another dude jumped out of the passenger seat . . . But it was Tiny, this kid I knew from School Street. He had a smile on his face.

"Yo, D, what's up, dog? It's good. This is my man Joaquin."

Waah looked up and nodded his head.

"I've been looking for you, dog," Tiny said, "because we're trying to start some music shit and I told my man that you're the hottest rapper out here . . ."

Here I was thinking that someone was trying to come for me, when all they wanted to do was talk game.

"We're starting a company, yo, for real. We want to put some money in this shit and set if off. I was playing my man one of your tapes."

Tiny was a short muscle dude with broad shoulders. He spoke real fast.

"Yeah? That's good," I answered him, unimpressed.

See, I had heard this pitch before. Ever since the Castle, besides Jack and his partners, manager types were constantly stepping to me with some kind of music business proposition, as were all the random producers that I was meeting in studios who had "imprints" or independent labels of their own. But no one took it beyond talk.

"I'm looking for the best nigga out here," Waah interrupted, looking at me. "I just want the dude who knows how to get down and make some money."

Waah spoke carefully with a deep, gravelly voice. I could tell he was the hustling type.

"And my man said you got this whole area on lock with the music so you're the one I came to see."

"Well, it's nice to meet you," I said to him, heading back inside. "When you get it going, just let me know something."

"It's on now, D," Waah called out to me. "All we we're waitin' on is you, dog."

But I was already back in the house.

· · · · ·

The next morning, I heard someone banging on Tashera's side window.

"Yo, DMX!"

Waah was back again.

"X, it's Waah. Come outside, man. I want to talk to you."

He said he wanted me to roll with him, wanted me to hear more about where he was coming from and see what kind of nigga he was. I asked him if I could bring Boomer with me and that's when he told me he loved pits. He had two of them of his own and loved to roll with anybody that fucked with dogs.

I climbed in the Z.

Waah and his brother Darrin were raised in Mount Vernon and now called Harlem their main stomping ground. Hustling niggas, Waah had started to see how much money was being made in hip-hop while him and his peoples were losing lives in the street over much less dough. It didn't add up. So one day he made up his mind that music was going to be his new hustle, it was a way to make paper that didn't involve death or trips up north.

"How do we do this?" he asked me.

Waah wanted to learn everything about the music business he could. He knew that I wasn't a rookie anymore and he said if I showed him what I knew about the hip-hop game, he would give me what I needed to make it happen. If I was with it, the two of us could "walk these dogs together."

We ended up rolling together all week.

"D, do you got ends?"

It wasn't long after I met Waah that things suddenly started to look up financially.

"Here dog, take a couple of twenties . . . And yo, you need smoke, nigga?"

Yeah! This is what's up! This is the kind of treatment I deserve. Not only was I coming back on the block with bills in my pocket wearing a new pair of kicks, but I also had a bag of weed—and it wasn't the normal weed either, it was downtown smoke, the kind Y-O niggas didn't come across too regularly. This was a major step up from being broke in the studio, a major step up from Jack MacNasty.

· · · · ·

When I met Darrin, he was chilling by the phone booth on 125th Street and Lenox Avenue in Harlem with his partners Bishop and Skip. These were the pre-cell-phone days when the public phone on the corner was a hustler's money tree as long as you had a beeper and a lot of numbers in your head. Waah brought some of my tapes with us in his truck so he could play some of my songs for the crew. They weren't music niggas, but they were *hustling* niggas and a real hustling street nigga could always hear a banging hip-hop track.

"Yo, that shit is hard, D. Those lyrics are crazy!" they all said to me. "You need to get on, baby!"

Everyone who listened to my music on the street that day heard what I was capable of. They felt my music, *understood* my music, and I just got a real strong feeling that they were ready to do something about it.

"All you got to do is keep rapping like that, D," Waah said. "Just tell us what we need to do and we'll take care of the rest."

Jack and I started to spend less and less time together and it soon became clear to me that we were living in two different worlds. After he came home from his nine-to-five, he would usually just come home and go upstairs. Maybe his girlfriend would come over and the two of them would watch a movie, but that would be about the extent of his nighttime activities. Meanwhile, I needed to be hanging out. I needed to be in the streets, running, robbing, rapping. But I was twenty and he was thirty-five. He wore slacks and shoes; I wore sweats and Tims. That wasn't going to work. I couldn't go where he went and he surely didn't want to go where I was going. So when I told Jack that I wanted to roll with Waah and his brother to try and put a single out, he didn't object. He knew what I was drawn to; he understood the lifestyle that I needed to lead—and he knew they had the dough. He could see Waah and Darrin pull up in front of the house with the new trucks. He could figure out the reason I had new gear and money in my pocket and by this time, I was so frustrated working with people that were half with the money—the part-time hustlers, the working-at-the-garage type of dudes, that the decision to roll with Waah was an easy one. If I wanted to make five hundred tapes to sell on the street and someone had fifteen hundred dollars ready for me that same day? I was with it. I didn't want to wait until next Monday because you had to hit wifey off with some cash because she was beefing at you. If I wanted to record a new track? I wanted to pay whoever we needed to pay and get busy. I didn't want to owe a studio money, week after week falling into more debt that I was never going to pay.

Waah was always straight-up business. All I ever heard from him was "What? Tell me what we need . . . Okay, come on, let's go."

"Right now?" I always responded in shock, not believing that any-one could be built like I was, ready for war at a moment's notice. "Oh, shit. Bet. I like this!"

One night Waah was trying to think of a name for the operation, and I instantly thought of "rough riders." I just knew the type of nig-gas we were and how we were living in the streets and rough riders sounded perfect. I just thought that we should spell it differently because someone would probably be using it already and when the two of us went down to lower Manhattan to get the license for the company, Ruff Ryders was officially born.

AN EARLY PROMO T-SHIRT

27

"Born Loser"

THE PRODUCTION AGREEMENT THAT WAAH SIGNED WITH ME and Jack (who, based on his managerial contract with me, had the right to approve any deal that I wanted to make) was to put together an original single in six months time, so the first thing Waah and I had to do was learn what a hot beat was. Once I didn't need them to keep me out of jail anymore, I didn't deal with the COs too much. They were good guys and I had gone over to their spot a few times to spit some rhymes with them, but they just didn't have the tracks I wanted. So almost every night for the next few weeks me and Waah hunted down all the young producers in the city and listened to the tracks they had.

"Oh, so you have some ol' R&B material, huh?" I told a kid who had us thinking he was the rawest beatmaker in hip-hop while he only had a few Barry White loops. I already knew that I didn't want a beat that sounded good after two or three minutes. I needed something that grabbed me as soon as I heard it.

Chad "Dr. Seuss" Elliott was a producer that Waah had met who had been working with a group called Jodeci at Uptown Records. When he played us his material, I knew right away that I could match some of my rhymes to what he had. They were raw and sounded real hard. The first rhyme I wanted to use was "Born Loser." The second I called "Catchin' the Same Hell" and within a week Waah and I decided that those two songs should become the two sides of my first twelve-inch vinyl single. No more rhyming off of other artist's instrumentals, now I had my own shit.

I knew that if we pressed up five hundred copies of "Born Loser" on vinyl and gave them out to radio DJs and club promoters, we could get the song buzzing on the street. Once that happened, then record stores would take notice and we could start taking orders and selling copies to everyone. The science behind doing a single was the same as selling mix tapes, the payoff was just bigger.

Jack liked the record and when we received the first batch of vinyl, he printed up flyers promoting the song that listed all the request line numbers for the local radio stations on the back. He and his partners handed them out all through the projects, through School Street, Slow Bomb, and Ravine, hoping that all of the people that knew me in Y-O would call up WBLS or KISS-FM and ask for the song to be played.

His effort worked.

One night Ed Lover and Dr. Dre, who were the evening DJs on WBLS, announced that "Born Loser" was on their nightly countdown.

ONE OF MY FIRST POSTERS

The following week, two Long Island radio stations followed the lead of 'BLS and added the song to their own weekly rotation. "Born Loser," the first rhyme that I had ever put on wax, was getting airplay and I was amped.

Just like I thought, it wasn't long before Jack started getting purchase orders for the song from stores all over New York, so now we had to find a real distributor because up to this point, Jack had been sending the record out himself. I was with Waah the night Jack called me from Philadelphia and said not only had he found a company down there that wanted to manufacture "Born Loser," but DJ Ran, the main DJ on Philly's R&B station, Power 99, was a big fan of the song and had helped him schedule a meeting with Chris Shwarz, the head of Ruffhouse Records. Ran had said that Ruffhouse might want to distribute the song nationally.

Waah didn't like Jack. He felt he was a "clown-ass nigga" who wasn't capable of taking me to the next level and the more time I spent with Waah, the more I agreed with him. My music was hard, grimy street music because I was a grimy street nigga and that was the only way that I felt I should represent myself. If I was to succeed, I wanted it to be with 'hood niggas, 'hood niggas who shared a dream with me, 'hood niggas who knew how to handle their business. Jack was not that.

I didn't tell him that then, but he wasn't stupid. Jack knew he was losing me.

```
I wanna break bread with the cats that I starve with
I wanna hit the malls with the same dogs I rob with
Wanna be able to laugh with the niggas that I cried with
When it's over, be like, these are the niggas that I died with[26]
```

FLYER FOR THE "BORN LOSER" RELEASE PARTY   BACK OF FLYER

28

Tests of Strength & Faith

IT WAS 7:15 A.M. AND THE SKY WAS DARK IN NEW ROCHELLE.
I saw Jack walking his dog.

"Where you coming from, nigga?" he asked me.

"I was hanging out."

"Well, Tashera's going to be pissed . . ."

Jack looked curiously at my man I had with me, but he kept going.

When I got to the house I waited for Jack to come back and get ready to leave for work. Tashera asked me why I didn't want to go to sleep. At 7:55 A.M., once Jack was gone, I gave her her answer.

"Earl, you don't want to do this!"

The thirty-six-inch television that my manager had in his living room now belonged to me.

"Tashera, get out of the way and just leave me alone."

She actually tried to stop me from taking it.

"Earl, you can't just walk out with Jack's TV!"

She had her arms wrapped around one end of the set and was trying to pull it away from me. But she couldn't stop me, not in the darkness that I was in.

As I was walking away from the house, I heard her on the phone.

"Yo, Jack, I don't know what the fuck is wrong with Earl, but . . ."

• • • • •

I always got my weight back. Or as my uncle Pinky used to say, "I cleaned up well." I think that was part of how I was able to hide my struggle from people for as long as I did. After an episode, I could just stay somewhere for a few days and get myself back to looking normal. I could play it off, too, like the day Tashera wondered why I left her apartment wearing a purple leather jacket and came back a few hours later without it. A TV would be harder to explain.

"What? What did he do?"

"I didn't have nothing to do with it, Jack, I just wanted to call you and let you know, so when you come home tonight and see your shit missing . . ." Tashera tried her best. "I'm so sorry, Jack . . ."

Jack pressed charges. Waah tried to help the situation by finding who I sold the television to, but the damage had already been done.

That weekend, on the strength of "Born Loser," I performed at a new artist showcase at the Jack the Rapper music conference in Atlanta. When I saw Jack there, Waah urged me to apologize. It was the right thing to do, but that was the last time I would see or speak to my manager for many years.

A few weeks later, Waah and Darrin hired a lawyer to sever my management agreement with Jack MacNasty. A few days after that, in a meeting with Ruffhouse Records, I was offered a recording contract for "Born Loser."

"Those that don't have as much strength as the rest of us, we rely on things that we think make us stronger but actually make us weaker. And that's what this is, something that makes me weaker than I could be."

DMX speaks about the blunt he holds in his hand. Sitting in a swivel chair in the main recording room of Phoenix's Chaton Studios, it's part of a lesson about drugs and alcohol that he's been giving to producer Swizz Beatz's five-year-old little brother, who, for the past few hours, has been surrounded by a thick fog of weed smoke.

"This is something that takes away the strength that was given to me. It's like a crutch. I'm using something to help me be strong, because I'm not as strong as your brother."

Swizz has stopped smoking weed. X hasn't reached that place yet, but his dark days are far less dark today than they were in the past. I ask him about his own struggles.

"Struggles? That's putting it lightly, dog, 'cause yeah, I've had a lot of them. But what helped me a lot is the understanding that I got. I wouldn't have had the will to stop doing anything if it wasn't for my wife and my kids. I wouldn't have even given a fuck . . ."

X pauses for a few moments.

"I probably got about five more years, maybe four, before me and my son take a walk and twist one of these things," he says staring at his blunt. *"I know it's going to come up so I told him whenever you think about it, fuck with me. I can't stop Xavier from doing anything. That's like telling him don't fuck—Yeah, whatever, Pops—But I told him I'm your father, but I'm your nigga first. Whatever you need to know about life, I'll walk you through it and hold your hand. Not hold your hand like you can't do it yourself, but be right beside you when you walk. That way anytime you get nervous about walking, or don't want to walk anymore, or don't know where you're walking while you're walking, I'll be right there, for all of your questions, with all of your answers."*

X exhales a long drag.

"And then I'll probably ask him if he got any pussy yet!"

29

Before Light There Is Dark

IT WAS ONLY A DEAL FOR ONE SONG, BUT IT WAS STILL A deal. Ruffhouse was a division of Columbia Records, one of the biggest music labels in the world, and I was on it. Now everybody would get to hear my music, and now it was time to tell Tashera something.

I couldn't bear the thought of lying to her anymore. So one night I called her from a pay phone and asked her to meet me outside right away.

"What happened, Earl? Are you all right?"

"Tashera, I have something to tell you."

When she arrived, I gave it to her straight. I told her that I didn't want to mess with her anymore because she was a real good person and I had a problem. I told her it was something that I had to deal with on my own.

"No you don't, Earl."

"Tashera, you don't understand."

"I'm saying, so what, Earl? We could do this."

She was calm. I was getting hysterical.

"Do what? What are *we* going to do? Do you know how dark it gets? What it feels like to be in a place out of control with no light at all?"

"Earl, I can help you work through it."

She stopped me in my tracks with that one. I just couldn't believe it. Tashera was accepting what I was going through without a second thought. I never loved her more than at that moment. She was one in a million.

Then she told me that she was three months pregnant.

"What?"

She said she would have told me sooner, but she was nervous and didn't know how we were going to manage with a child—we had no money, we weren't married, I was running the streets.

"What are we going to do, Earl?"

"We're going to be all right. I don't know how, but I'm going to make it work. I promise you."

"But how are we going to take care of a baby?"

I didn't know yet, but I knew that I always worked better under pressure, when my back was against the wall. And I knew that I wanted this baby.

"It doesn't matter. I'll do whatever I have to do. I'll even get a job . . . Let's just do it, Tashera."

Tashera stood in front of me for a long minute. Then she silently nodded her head.

"I promise I'm going to try my hardest for you," I told her, my eyes wet with tears.

"I know you will, Earl. I love you."

"I love you, too, Boo Boo. I love you, too . . ."

I was in the room with Tashera while they were getting her ready to go into delivery. I was so excited to be with the woman I loved, having my first baby. It was a few days before my twenty-second birthday and I thought how beautiful it would be if my boy was born on the same day as me. But when they put her on the stretcher to take her down the hall and the nurse said that I couldn't go with her, all of my good thoughts vanished.

"Why can't I go?"

"Because you didn't go to the required Lamaze classes, sir."

"I don't give a fuck about Lamaze! That's my wife, lady. I want to see her give birth to my child!"

"Sir, I'm going to have to ask you to go to the waiting room now."

The nurse wasn't playing and Tashera was already halfway down the corridor.

Fuck this.

I tried to push past her, but the bitch had already called for security.

"Sir, now we're going to have to ask you to leave the building."

Then two short rent-a-cop dudes moved in front of me to block my way and things got hectic.

"Don't even touch me, you cocksucking motherfuckers . . ." I started yelling at them. Tashera said she could hear me going crazy the whole time she was giving birth.

They never let me pass, but a few hours later I didn't care anymore because I was holding my healthy baby boy.

Xavier. He was all wrinkled and peeling.

Me being DMX had a lot to do with calling my son Xavier. My name, for me, had become the label of an official motherfucker and since I knew that everyone would call him "Little X" anyway, as soon as I heard the name "Xavier," I knew that would be special.

The next day, while Tashera and the baby were still in the hospital, me and Tashera's sister Faatimah hopped cabs all around Yonkers shopping for my new baby. We went in and out of supermarkets and clothing stores. Neither of us had any money, so there was a lot of boosting going down. I just wanted my boy to come back to the best home that I could give him.

A few months earlier, Tashera and I had moved in with my sister Bonita. After the TV incident, Tashera lost her place with Nicole, too, so neither of us had a place to live. We stayed in my grandmother's house for a few weeks until it got too crowded with all of my uncles and aunts running around, then we stayed with Tashera's father for a minute. Over the years, he and Tashera had made peace, but when he started harassing me about all of the sins I was committing (and busted me for stealing shit from him), we had to leave and we had been in my sister's place ever since.

It was my birthday, December 18, 1992, when Tashera and I came back to the house with the baby. I was so happy to be holding my new son. He was so little and innocent, but not more than thirty minutes after I was sitting on Bonita's living room couch with Xavier in my arms, the buzzer rang. It was Waah. He said we had to go to the studio to remaster "Born Loser."

"Yo, but my baby just came home."

"Nah, dog. We got to go the studio tonight! If we don't do this tonight, we're going to miss the label's deadline."

"But I'm trying to chill with my son."

"Yeah, but we got to get this shit done, dog. This is business."

I was pissed, but Waah was right. There would always be time for me to spend with Xavier and I had committed myself to making my music happen no matter what. Five minutes later, I was gone.

30

0 for 2

DESPITE THE FACT THAT RUFFHOUSE RE-RELEASED THE SONG
as a proper 12-inch single, "Born Loser" never took off. It stayed on
the WBLS countdown for a few more weeks, but never made it to #1
and never caught heat anywhere outside of the Y-O or New York
area. The label said that it didn't have the kind of hook or club beat
it needed. I felt that Ruffhouse didn't put enough marketing power
behind it so not enough people heard the song in the first place. I
knew enough to know that you needed hype to sell records. Around
the way in Y-O, I was my own hype, but I couldn't help get myself
on the radio in Chicago or L.A. But after it died, with me having only
a one-song deal, it also became clear that Ruffhouse wasn't interested
in pursuing anything further with me or Waah or Ruff Ryders and
within a few months of me having my own major-label single and a
song on the radio, my professional recording career was over.

Waah was determined to keep going, though. He felt that we had
relied too much on Ruffhouse and we could do a better job on our
own.

Chad Elliott had introduced Waah to a young kid from Queens
named Irving Lorenzo. Chad had known him for a while and knew
that he was a DJ trying to become a producer who had a liking for the

same kind of grimy, hard-edged material that was becoming my trade-mark. Irv wasn't blown away by what he heard on "Born Loser" or "Catchin' the Same Hell," but when he heard me rhyme in person, he heard me move from one style to another and change flows without losing the beat. He saw how fearless I was about battling and how passionate I was about murdering any MC that crossed my path and he quickly changed his opinion. He said if I put the same kind of raw, street energy on wax that I put into my battles or on mix tapes, I would blow up. True street-bred hip-hop fans wanted something harder than the laid-back, more jazz-influenced hip-hop that was dominating the airwaves.

Irv's ideas were good, the only problem was that because he didn't have any production equipment, he didn't have any way of bringing them to life. "I can do this though, Waah. I promise. Your man is the nicest rapper out here, all I need is the stuff to make the music for him."

Waah believed.

So one afternoon, me, Waah, and Irv went down to a music store in Manhattan and Waah bought him a used MPC-60 sampler with two thousand dollars in cash. I thought two grand was a big invest-ment in a kid that we didn't know that well, but it wasn't my money and it *was* hard finding producers that wanted to dedicate their time to making beats for me. Chad Elliott always had other things going on. Anthony, this other producer kid I knew from Yonkers High School, had started to roll with us, and even though he had done a good remix of "Born Loser," he was busier throwing parties and put-ting his tag, "Pent One," up all over the neighborhood than he was laying tracks. But over the next few weeks Irv made good on his promise. Despite being rough and somewhat undeveloped, his beats were knocking. One of the best songs we made together was a joint called "Niggas Can't Touch Me Kid."

```
Funny how shit is before I shot the nigga
Should've seen how the bitch came up out the nigga
Now I got the nigga where I can run up in him
Made him say "daddy" before I put the gun up in him
One up in him
```

Two, three in the clip

Have his whole head looking like a busted lip . . .[27]

Waah and I decided to make that my next single so we pressed it up and made another batch of vinyl. Kasun's boy, a DJ named Superior, had helped come up with the beat for the track, so he took the twelve-inch to this record pool he was working with that most of the city's biggest DJs were a part of. We hoped that would take care of the clubs. Then one day me and Waah decided to take a trip downtown to HOT 97, New York's biggest and most influential hip-hop and R&B radio station.

We didn't know anybody at HOT 97 and hadn't planned how we were going to get the box of vinyl singles that Waah had in his trunk to the right person, but we did know the door that all of the DJs on the station went in and out of, so we parked the truck right in front of there and just waited around.

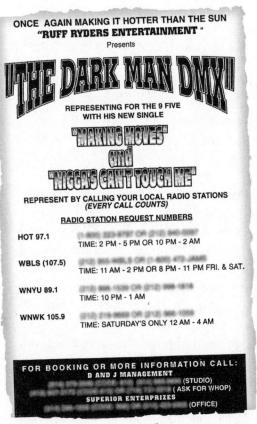

WE HANDED THESE OUT EVERYWHERE

Within a few minutes, we saw Ed Lover. He hosted HOT's popular morning show with his partner Dr. Dre.

"Yo, Ed. Yo, Ed!" Waah called out to him. "Me and my man got this hot single for you, we wanted to give you a few copies for your show."

"Hold on a second, guys," he answered. He was leaving the building and had stopped to say good-bye to a few people. After he finished, he walked over to us.

"What you got, fellas?"

"'Niggas Can't Touch Me Kid' by my man right here, DMX," Waah told him. "He's from Yonkers, baby. Y-O!"

Ed read the label and then handed the record back to Waah.

"Okay, cool. So why don't you bring it by my office in the morning? Right now I'm on my way to this party."

Waah was irritated.

"Yo, Ed! Come on, man."

"What? If it's good, I'll play it. I've heard of your man before. Just drop it off for me tomorrow . . . "

Waah was the aggressive type. He didn't even like to *think* someone was trying to play him out.

"I'm sayin', Ed, why can't you just take one now? You said you're going to a party and we got the shit right here. You can play our joint when you get there!"

Now Ed Lover was irritated.

"You know what? Y'all brothers are going to have to just come find me tomorrow." He turned and walked away.

Waah was pissed off. I thought he was going to chase Ed down and slap him in the back of the head, but before he could get the chance, I saw Wendy Williams walking out. Wendy was the biggest female personality on the station. She had a prime-time time slot and because of all of the Howard Stern–like gossiping she did about everybody in hip-hop, she was becoming one of the most-known—and most-hated—radio people on the East Coast. She had double-parked, but now the car that was next to the curb had pulled off, so she was running to get her joint out of the middle of the street.

"All right, all right. Give me one," she told Waah in a hurry. Wendy wasn't the best person to give "Can't Touch Me Kid" to, she wasn't Ed Lover or a mix-show DJ like Red Alert or Funkmaster Flex, but at least she would hear it and hopefully talk about it. As I watched her drive away, I felt like Waah had I had accomplished something. Then I saw something that I couldn't believe. There, lying on the ground, was the record Waah had just given her.

That fucking bitch dropped my single on the street!

I was crushed. Waah couldn't even say anything, he just started walking back to the truck. I really thought "Can't Touch Me Kid" was going to blow.

Years later, I considered that maybe it really *was* inconvenient for Ed Lover to carry a big record around in a club all night, and since she was rushing so fast, maybe there *was* a chance that Wendy could have accidentally dropped my joint. But then, standing there in that street, I just knew that both of them dissed me. I was 0 for 2 in this rap game and that hurt for a long time.

31

Slippin', Fallin'

COMPARED TO THE SCHOOL STREET PROJECTS, THERE WAS MORE
room on Ravine. While School Street was a self-contained set of high-
rises, Ravine's buildings were only a few stories high and they were
spread out along five blocks. Ravine also ran parallel to the Hudson
River so through the trees you could see the water and New Jersey
on the other side. You could watch the boats and barges pass by and,
at least for a second, take your mind off the struggles of the concrete.

There was a small basketball court behind building 55, down a set
of block steps, hidden by the trees. During the daytime, heads would
bring forties down there and play games of half court, but at night it
was empty and the court became a great place for me to go and chill
with Boomer, smoke a blunt and not be seen. I could relax back
there, behind the trees. Sometimes in the summer, it was a safe spot
for me to sleep or spend the night because I could hear anybody
coming from the top of the path—friend or foe. I wish I was down
there, though, the day these three motherfuckers tried to kill me.

I was standing in the street having a conversation with my man
Hip. He had just picked his daughter up from the baby-sitter. We
hadn't seen each other since I had got out of jail, so I was telling him
about everything that was going on with my music and the different
songs I was doing.

Then something made me look up and I saw three niggas walking down the middle of the street toward us.

They all had their hands in their pockets.

I recognized one of them from Slow Bombs but something wasn't right about the look in his eyes.

"Uhhh . . . A 'iight dog, I'm gonna holler at you later," I said to Hip, slowly backing up. My spider sense was tingling. Then the three of them called out to me.

"Yo, don't run."

Yeah, okay, motherfucker . . .

As soon as I heard "don't run," I was gone. I sprinted down that street as fast as I could and right away they pulled burners out and started busting. They were shooting for real. At least four shots rang out behind me before I made it to the end of the block. I saw Hip dive between two parked cars to protect his daughter. Then two more shots whizzed passed me by the time I hit the corner. Obviously, they weren't after him.

Awwwwww, man! It's going down. What is it about this time?

Around the corner I ducked through a backyard fence and just kept running and running. They never caught me. I needed all of my track skills for that one.

It didn't take me long to figure out what the deal was: Earlier that morning I did a robbery with this young kid who was stupid enough to let me hold his gun. It was a pretty black nine-millimeter and when the driver we stuck only had forty dollars on him, the skies were dark and I decided to sell the gun to get some more dough. *Fuck that.* The kid didn't know how to use it anyway. But of course it wasn't his piece in the first place and so he told the gun's real owner that I had stolen it from him. Now the owner wanted me dead. If the owner was a real nigga, though, he would have known that a nigga can only *lose* a gun; he can't get it *stolen* from him. But once a nigga shoots at you, there's no room for argument.

I was just glad that my instinct didn't let me down. I saw those bastards about one hundred yards away—just enough space for me to get gone. I didn't realize then that this was the second time the Lord put his hand on my life.

No, not this one . . .

• • • • •

Maybe it was because of all the robbing and stealing I had always done or the battles that I started—and won—with everyone everywhere I went, but over the years I had begun to feel some negativity coming my way in Y-O. More and more I started to catch people's hateful eyes and now that I had put out two singles that flopped, the 'hood started to take note of the darkness in my life and their judgments were no longer whispered. Soon hateful eyes turned into hateful stares and it was hard to stay unaffected. What I needed was support, but even the people who knew what I was going through didn't want to help me.

"You can't blame Mommy for your problems, Earl. It isn't her fault that you do the things you do."

Bonita never understood.

"But why can't you talk to her, sis . . . ? See, I knew you wouldn't have my back. You never gave a fuck about me!"

"Don't blame me either, Earl! I didn't make you do all of your robbing and smoking and sticking up people for their stuff, but you want me to put up with your mess."

It was six o'clock in the morning and my sister didn't want to open her door.

"No, Earl. I don't want that stuff around my kids."

"Come on, you fucking bitch. Open the door."

The sky had been dark for days.

"This is *my* apartment, brother, and I've already given you everything that I'm going to give you. Why don't you come back when you get yourself together!"

"You know what? Fuck you, Bonita!"

"Yeah, that's all good . . . but I'm still your sister and when you die, I'm not going to mourn you. I'm going to come to your funeral in a red dress . . . "

So much for that side of the family.

That spring, Waah set up a show for me to do at Drexel College. I was excited because I hadn't performed in a while and I figured there would be a lot of people there because he told me it was the weekend of a big track tournament. I just had never heard of the school before.

"Where is Drexel?" I asked him.

"Philadelphia."

Everything happens for a reason.

The last time I had seen my father was the last time he took me downtown with him to sell his paintings. That was almost fifteen years ago. My grandmother had always wanted me to call him. She had the phone number in Philly where he lived with his wife and three kids and always wrote it on a piece of paper that she put in my pocket any time she knew I was taking a trip. For years I didn't pay her any mind, but this time she was going to get her wish.

When me and Waah got to the hotel, the first thing I did was go to a pay phone.

"Who's this?" I asked as soon as I head a voice on the other end.

"This is Joe."

"Yeah? Well, *this is your son, motherfucker!*"

There was a long pause.

"Oh. You want to talk to my father. What's up, Earl?"

It was my brother Joe. Here I was taking out my anger on the wrong person. I felt like an asshole, but I hadn't seen my little brother in years so after we talked for a minute, I told him to come by the hotel.

I was standing in the middle of the lobby when my brother looked me in my face and walked right past me. He obviously didn't remember what I looked like.

"Joe . . . " I called out to him before he passed me again and made the same mistake twice.

"Oh shit, Earl."

"You don't remember what I look like?"

"Nah, I just didn't see you." (Later he did admit that he was looking for a guy closer to his more light-skinned complexion.)

Joe was a few years younger than me, and spending time with him I realized that we had many of the same mannerisms. Among other things, I couldn't help but notice that when either of us started to seriously think about something we had the habit of putting our hand to our face and chewing on the inside of our cheek. We had a good time together in Philly. That night, I taught my little brother how to smoke weed and, for the moment, I forgot about my father.

"Pass it back, man. What are you doing?" I asked him when he was still holding onto the blunt after two or three pulls.

"Sorry."

Later he got scared when he couldn't stop choking.

"You're okay, Joe. Your lungs just got to get used to it," I reassured him.

I was booked to open for this popular hip-hop group called Das EFX and even though that meant the performance would be full, I was more excited with the fact that meant there would probably be some good food backstage. After I ate up all the KFC that had been ordered for everyone, the promoter threatened to cancel my part of the show, but I didn't give a fuck. Das EFX was down with that bitch ass nigga, K-Solo, so fuck 'em. I was hungry.

My show only went over okay, though. I didn't get the same energy from the crowd that I was used to in New York or Westchester and during one of my songs a girl at the foot of the stage actually balled up this "Born Loser" poster that Waah had been giving out to everyone and threw it at me while I was rhyming. She was drunk, trying to show off to her girlfriends, and the poster hit me in the back.

I didn't stop rhyming but in the middle of one of my next lines I looked at her and threw in a " . . . saw you, bitch" remark real quick without missing a beat. She was embarrassed and her friends started laughing. She may not have known who DMX was when she came in, but I bet she knew who I was when she left. My brother had been watching the whole show from the side of the stage and when I looked over, I could tell he liked that move. Later that night, though, Joe did me greasy.

"You know your father would love to talk to you, Earl," he said all out of the blue.

"Yeah? Well, I'm not in the mood for another reunion."

"But he really wants to see you."

"I don't want to see that nigga, Joe. Damn. Leave me alone."

"Well, he's right downstairs."

Awww, man. I wanted to crack my brother's jaw open. He knew how long it had been. He knew that I wouldn't be able to resist this kind of opportunity. This was my father, the man I had wondered about my whole life. When I went downstairs a few minutes later, I wasn't prepared for what I saw.

"You?"

My father was standing in the lobby. He was wearing four different pairs of leg warmers.

"*You?*"

Red and white stripes, purple, green, and orange; all of them were different lengths. He also had on a pair of tan corduroy pants that were tucked inside the leg warmers, with a tan corduroy jacket with elbow patches—and he had dreadlocks.

Oh, no. I don't think so . . .

My father walked over to give me a hug.

"Hold on, hold on. Let me think for a minute . . ."

I couldn't believe what I was seeing. *This* was the man I had wondered about my whole life? *This* was the man who took me downtown as a boy and made me feel special? The man who left my moms for a white woman and skipped town? Four different pairs of leg warmers?

"What's up, Earl? How are you doing?"

He had a deep voice and spoke with an accent that I didn't recognize coming from any part of Yonkers that I knew.

"Are you taking care of yourself? You got a lawyer?"

Those were his first words to me after all these years. "Are you taking care of yourself?" How about "I love you" or "I miss you" or "You look good"? His cold, judgmental attitude cut through me. Scolding without even knowing, that was not what I wanted to hear.

"Are you getting things right?"

It didn't take me long not to like him. Now I know that I didn't try very hard, either, but I was the child. I was the one who had suffered for years from the choices he had made and I didn't feel like talking. I wasn't the one who left. Within five minutes, our conversation was over and after more than fifteen years being without him, my father was gone again.

Waah had witnessed the whole encounter. He looked over at me and laughed: "Damn, dog. That was *not* your father . . ."

I was traded the chance of being a child with a father
For a talent of being able to survive when it's harder
My balance on the high beams of life, keep my dreams in strife
That's why I hit these motherfucking streets tonight![28]

32

A Bark in the Dark

But you can't blame me for not wanting to be held
Locked down in a cell where the soul can't dwell[29]

SOON AFTER MY TRIP TO PHILADELPHIA, I WAS BACK IN
Valhalla Correctional Facility. My third day there, I spit in the face of
a captain and was sentenced to a year and a month of solitary confinement. They put me in Lockdown Block 3K. That was my home for
almost a year.

Ray Copeland was a social worker in Valhalla; he was also my
uncle. The youngest of my mother's siblings, Ray had grown up in
Mount Vernon and was close to his sister. They would speak to one
another on the phone a few times a week and see each other at family gatherings. I didn't know where I was during those family
reunions that he told me about, because I don't remember meeting
Ray until one night at a club Waah's girlfriend Keisha told me that
some guy had come up to her claiming to be my uncle. But when I
looked over at him, I knew we had to be related, since he looked
just like my aunt Vern. We didn't talk that night, just introduced ourselves and kept it moving, but a few months later, when one of the
prison guards told me that he wanted to visit me in my cell, I let
him in.

Ray wasn't assigned to my unit, but he said my mother had urged
him to come see me. She told him that she was scared for me always

being in and out of jail and felt she had no way of reaching me. Ray didn't know how true that was.

He didn't say much during those first couple of visits—which was a good thing because I wasn't trying to talk to him anyway—but he seemed to sense right away that I was losing my life.

"What do *you* know about me?" I asked him.

"Not much, but I know that jail isn't a place for any man, especially if he has a new son to take care of and a girlfriend at home that loves him."

He also told me that I was wasting my talent.

For the next few months, Uncle Ray came to see me almost three times a week. He said he wasn't there to judge me, he just wanted to help, give me some tips on how to improve my situation and bring some light into my life. Over the years, I refused to listen to anyone that kicked it to me that way. X would bark at them and bite their hand off before anyone could even begin to speak of upliftment or purpose or *light*. But months in solitary confinement gave me nothing but time to think. There was a freedom and a comfort there that I had felt many times before. Being alone day after day in the dark and the quiet allowed my mind to take me places that I had never gone before and one cold night I just closed my eyes and reached out, reached out for the sky.

> I come to you hungry and tired
> You give me food, let me sleep
> I come to you weak, you give me strength and that's deep

Grandma always said the Lord was with me. She said that all I needed was the faith, so I put her words to the test. Would He talk to me? Would He answer my call?

> You call me a sheep and lead me to green pastures
> Only asking that I keep the focus in between the chapters
> You give me the word and only ask that I interpret
> And give me the eyes that I may recognize the serpent
> You know I ain't perfect, but you'd like me to try
> Unlike the devil who just wants me to lie, until I die

E.A.R.L.

Lord, why is it that I go through so much pain?
All I saw was black, all I felt was rain
I come to you because it's you who knows
You showed me that everything was black because my eyes
    were closed . . .[30]

That night in Valhalla, in solitary confinement, I wrote my first prayer.

33

Home

A HOME IS WHAT YOU MAKE IT. GROWING UP, TASHERA NEVER lived in the projects but the only two options she had to find a place to live after we left Bonita's house were School Street and Mulford Gardens. She chose Mulford.

Mulford was an enclosed set of brown, three-story buildings that sat a few blocks above Warburton Avenue. It was a far less violent place than School Street, defined by more of a wanna-be player community than the you-better-not-come-up-in-here attitude you found in my 'hood, and $314 a month got her a two-bedroom ground-floor apartment with a living

MULFORD GARDENS

room, bathroom, and a large walk-in kitchen. When I came home from Valhalla, I moved in with her and Xavier and decided to make it as nice as I could.

Since he was born, Xavier had been my heart. I was so proud of him. My first, a boy! (One night when he was only three weeks old I brought him to the studio with me. There were a lot of other rappers in the lounge that night and they were going back and forth in a cipher. Two of the MCs in the group were pretty bad, though, and after a few minutes, anytime one of them started to rhyme, Xavier would let out a big yawn. Without fail, when they started spitting, my little wrinkled baby would start yawning in their face. *Yeah, that's my boy right there. He knows what's up!*)

As he got older, I brought him everywhere with me. I just wrapped him up in a carrier on my chest, grabbed his bottle, and we were out. Other kids always loved to play with him.

"When are you bringing Xavier back again?" they would ask me when it was time to take him home.

I didn't really know how to be a father, though. How would I? I never had one. But Tashera just kept telling me to spend time with him and do what comes naturally, so that's what I did.

Over the years, I had learned some painting skills from my uncle Pinky, and kind of liked doing it, so the first thing I did was buy some brushes and paint from the local hardware store and turn Xavier's room dark blue. Then I painted the living room walls of the apartment all black with a thick gray stripe across the top. I built a bench for Xavier in the kitchen where he could eat and a table for Tashera and me, and strung up a portable fan from one of the pipes to give us some air. We put blinds on the living room windows, a carpet on the bedroom floor that Faatimah and me stole from a store in Getty Square, and got the washing machine to work in the kitchen. When I burned some frankincense, you would have never thought that this apartment was in the projects.

But we were still broke.

I tried doing the job thing, but it never worked out. First I worked at the post office in White Plains, lifting big gray bags of mail on the conveyor belts in the back. I didn't last one week having to do nothing but sort shit out all day. Another time I got a demolition job in a warehouse and had to spend ten hours knocking down walls and breaking up stoves and radiators. That kept me in shape and I liked the work, but after three weeks the boss laid me off because I was the youngest guy in the crew. That was fucked up. I was the one who had to put up with his bullshit all day.

Whenever I was working, I gave Tashera whatever money I made. I would just keep thirty or forty dollars for myself and tell her to use the rest for the phone bill or food for Xavier. Whenever Waah or Darrin hit me off with dough, I would give her some of that, too. She was the one really busting her ass. Tashera always appreciated that.

Boo Boo always had a job and some of them were real crazy. For a few months she actually worked at this General Motors automotive plant in upstate New York. She had a spot on the assembly line. She used to wake up every morning at 5 A.M. so she could catch the bus upstate and make the 6:15 bell. Her job was to install the rearview mirror and the roof rack on all these different cars. The salary was huge—almost eight hundred dollars a week—but after a few weeks her back started hurting badly and when the plant left New York and moved out west, Boo Boo decided to put an end to her autoworker career.

Whatever jobs we had, though, we still had to buy groceries a whole month at a time and hope that they would last us a full thirty days. We never had the money for soda or juice; instead, we had to survive on nothing but water and iced tea. (I loved Kool-Aid, but iced tea was cheaper because you didn't have to add sugar.) Most of the time we would pull it off, but the last four or five days of the month we'd always be down to having no food in the house and the two of us would fight over who ate the last bit of cereal.

When it came down to it, though, I knew that I could get a meal with a dollar. A dollar would get me fifty cents' worth of turkey meat, a roll, and water for a quarter. If I had an extra twenty-five cents then I would buy a loose cigarette—but even that wasn't necessary because you could always find somebody with a spare one. So one dollar was all I needed. If I had five dollars, I was great.

Unless it was her sisters, Tashera rarely wanted anybody to come over to visit us in Mulford. She said she didn't want anyone in the projects in her business, always knocking on the door trying to borrow something. So she just went to work every day and stayed to herself. "Where your girlfriend be at, X? What? Is she too good to come outside?" chicks in Mulford used to always whine to me.

I was always out, though, and that's why I saw more of the dirt. As in most projects, people were always getting killed in Mulford. Every week you would hear about so-and-so's cousin getting shot or someone killing themselves in a car accident. It's just messed up when you knew the person who was killed *and* the person who did the killing, and they lived right next door to each other.

After my trip to Philly, my little brother, Joe, and I started talking more often and in the summer of '94, he came to live with me. He said him and our father were beefing and he needed to get away. I told him he was family and could stay with me as long as he needed to.

That spring, I had started selling mix tapes again to make some money. I wasn't fucking with any more jobs and I wanted to keep giving Tashera something. Her sisters were already whispering in her ear about how I wasn't helping out enough. So when Joe came, I got him to help me walk around Yonkers and sell my tapes—or at least I got him to carry the case. We had a good time together. When I only put two or three songs on a tape instead of the full sixty minutes because I couldn't stand to wait that long for the copying to finish, he wouldn't give me away, and he wouldn't start laughing when I sold someone a total blank until the coast was clear. (I had to make sure those victims weren't in a car or had a Walkman with them so they wouldn't notice until later that their ten dollars had bought them a bunch of dead air.) After we got rid of everything, then we'd go into School Street or Slow Bomb and hang out. I taught my brother how to gamble and shoot dice and since I saw that he had stayed smoking weed since that night in Philly, I taught him how to properly roll a blunt.

I hadn't had somebody that I could run with like that in a long time. Someone who knew how I got down but wouldn't judge the things that I did. I thought maybe that's what having a brother was for and that summer, even though nothing new was happening with my music, I actually stayed out of trouble. I also started going over to my grandmother's house again.

Grandma was proud of me when I showed her my "Born Loser" single, and smiled a lot when I told her about some of the songs that I had made and the shows I had done. I brought Xavier over to see her a lot and just like I was her first grandchild, Xavier became her first great-grandchild. She loved seeing me with him. She said she always knew that I would have a boy.

I loved my grandmother. For as long as I could remember she had always been there for me. She believed in me, protected me, loved me, and that summer I was happy to be able to show her the man and the father that I had become.

But the good feeling didn't last long.

In July of that year, my grandmother was admitted to the hospital for cancer treatment. I had known for a while that she was battling the disease because occasionally over the years she would get sick and have to check herself into the hospital, but she always came out in a few days so nobody in the family ever thought too much of it. My grandmother was a nurse. She could take care of herself.

This time was different.

"Do you need anything, Grandma?"

Every afternoon I would walk up the block to Yonkers General Hospital to keep her company. All she ever said she wanted was fruit, so I used to bring her all that I could find: apples, oranges, plums, watermelon. She loved purple seedless grapes. I brought her anything that she wanted.

"That's my grandbaby," she would say when I'd come back holding a big plastic bag from the store.

That was when she could still talk.

My grandmother had worked in New Rochelle Hospital for more than twenty years looking after other people and my entire life she had looked after me. Now it was my turn to return the favor.

Most afternoons, Joe would come with me and him and I would sit by her bedside for as long as the doctors would allow us. They never give you enough time.

On September 21, 1994, Mary Ella Hollaway passed away.

I wanted to die with her.

Oh, Lord, my God
In thee do I put my trust;
Save me from all them that persecute me,
And deliver me

215

Outside the studio, a woman in rags crouches beside an empty office building. Sitting on a piece of brown cardboard, with her head bent down between her knees, the woman didn't see the fleet of cars come to a stop in front of her or the wad of twenty-dollar bills that DMX placed in her blue-and-white coffee cup.

"You hungry?"

Startled, the woman looks up and sees a star standing over her.

"If you're hungry, then use this to get yourself something to eat."

The cash came out of his front jeans pocket, money he left the house with added to his winnings from the few minutes he spent playing pool. This wouldn't be the first time I had seen X give money on a whim to a hungry person that he happened to pass, and the reaction from the less fortunate one was always the same.

"Thank you," the woman mumbles, hesitantly fingering the bills. "Thank you so much."

"Don't thank me, thank Him," X whispers to her. "I didn't do it, I was just given it to give to you."

The woman's eyes fill with water and, as if on cue, a tear starts to fall down her cheek.

"And when your time comes—and it will come—remember not to be afraid to fulfill your purpose . . ."

"I like to give," X tells me later.

I think of the Thanksgiving celebrations that he sponsors every year at Nepperhan in the name of his grandmother or the time he and his wife spend every Christmas Day at the children's AIDS ward at Harlem Hospital, unadvertised and unreported.

"To see the smile on a child's face when you give them something that they've always wanted . . . I'll cry for that and not be ashamed."

"But what about you? When do you get given anything?"

"The Lord has blessed me. I have a true wife, beautiful kids, my dogs. I got cars, plenty of toys, so I don't need anything anymore. But, for real, dog, I don't want anybody to give me nothing, because you'll probably fuck around and give it to me and I won't be able to play with it!"

34

Make a Move

Stop, drop, shut 'em down, open up shop . . . That's how Ruff Ryders roll[31]

WHEN WAAH AND DARRIN TOLD ME THAT THEY HAD SET UP shop in Baltimore, Maryland, to get money, I didn't hesitate. I knew I wasn't the hustling type but I was willing to give it a shot. I was tired of being broke and I wanted to get out of Y-O.

We left on a Friday, and when I jumped in the back of the car that night to cross the George Washington Bridge and travel the two hundred miles south on I-95, I didn't realize that besides a few visits home, Baltimore would be the place where I would spend the next few years.

We had two different home bases set up on the west side of the city. At least eight of us at a time would work two twelve-hour shifts, and after a few weeks in Baltimore I confirmed to myself again that I wasn't with the hustling thing. Not that it wasn't a profitable operation. I mean I had never seen that many people in one place get high before. It felt like almost everyone in the city was lined up on one corner or another waiting on weed or dope or ready. But after six hours having to stand outside in the same spot, my feet would go completely numb and the cops always seemed to love to arrest me for just standing there. I couldn't take much of that.

"You know what? I think I'll be in the house. I'm the rapper, I'm gonna write something . . ."

It's two o'clock and I'm just about to hit the street
Till I knock off this rock I don't get to eat
Sometimes it's like that's the only reason why I hustle
Step on toes, strongarm and show a li'l muscle
Ain't no real dough, that's why a nigga feel so frustrated
I hate it, seeing crab niggas that made it
And I'm robbing cats just as broke as myself
Living foul and ain't looking out for my health, where's
    the wealth?[32]

So like I did as a kid in Yonkers, I quickly found myself walking all over Baltimore, from the west side to the east side, up North Avenue down to the Inner Harbor just soaking up all the different people and places and communities. That's what I loved to do and I ended up connecting the crew to so many people we would never have met if I wasn't out meeting people like that. I would just talk to folks I'd see walking on the street or brothers hanging on a block. We'd talk, smoke, and then I'd always hit 'em with some rhymes. Rapping was a universal language.

"Yo shorty, you're all right. Who you wit'?"

I don't think that kind of social interaction could have happened as fast in any other city. There was something about Baltimore. Sure there were a lot of cats who hated New York niggas but for the most part, brothers in B-more enjoyed meeting people they didn't know, and so did the sisters. If a chick heard that you were from out of town, you and your boys could probably work her hospitality to get a meal that same night.

There were also a lot of "ma's" in Baltimore to meet. A ma was the older woman on a block who had been there forever. She knew everyone, saw everything, and had everyone's respect.

"How you doing, Ma? You all right? Let me get that bag for you."

Brothers were always very polite to the neighborhood ma because she always threw down on the cooking tip or let you run through the back of her house to get away when the police were chasing. The word on the street was that if you took care of Ma, you took care of the 'hood, and if you took care of the 'hood, you were always good. (There were bullshit ma's, too, though, the nosy ones that you had to include in your hustle to avoid them ratting you out. They got different treatment: "Ma, just please fucking tell me what you need!")

Right away it felt refreshing to be in a place with new streets and new people. Nobody knew my rep and I had to learn a whole new set of rules. It was a thrill. It felt like I was invisible, like I was free to do what I wanted to do without the burdens of judgment or expectation. But because of the drug game, Baltimore's streets were always hectic. The city was filled with stickup boys who would pop their weapons at a moment's notice. It was crazy, far worse than New York. In B-more, kids would run up to someone in broad daylight, no problem. *Pop! Pop!* Whenever I came back to B-more after being home for a few days, invariably someone had been killed while I was away. It would be the cool niggas, too, never someone who was getting down in a way where death was a part of what they were doing. It was more like, "Why did they have to shoot Li'l Terry?"

But like Yonkers, B-more was a small world, everybody knew everybody, and after a couple of months being down there meeting different folks, I could walk anywhere without a problem.

Boomer may have had something to do with that. He stayed by my side every day that I was down there and quickly became the dog not to fuck with. I think he liked being in Baltimore more than I did. There were more fences to climb, more alleys to run through, and definitely more cats to kill. There were at least two or three stray cats in almost every alley in Baltimore, so Boomer was always on the hunt. Almost every time I turned around he had a dead animal in his mouth. One summer, he kept piling all of his kill in the corner of this one alley and by the middle of July there must have been about twenty or thirty dead cats thrown on top of each other. Boomer wouldn't let anybody touch them and it stank like crazy.

It felt good to get so much love in the city because technically I was the weakest nigga in the crew. Because I wasn't hustling, I was the lowest on the totem pole, which meant that while everyone else was making paper, I barely got twenty dollars a day from my mans and them. With that I would buy one bag of smoke, a forty-ounce, a pack of cigarettes, and try to eat with the rest. But not having a thick stack of bills in my pocket didn't bother me because folks knew that I was always game. Whatever was going down, whether it was rapping or scrapping, everyone knew X would be there first—me and Boomer.

. . . . .

But Baltimore had a dark side, too, and it started with the rats. There were rats *everywhere*. They were huge, ugly beasts that waddled around, up the streets and through the alleys, feeding off of everything in their path. Big piles of garbage, often higher than the fence to your house, marked the city's worst areas and rats would be all through them. When you walked past, you could see the whole pile move with the teams of rodents that were feasting inside.

That sucked, especially in the winter when it was too cold to go around and I had to walk straight through those alleys late at night. It made you want to kick yourself in the ass. *What the fuck am I doing here?* If I could have found a cab or a bus to jump in at those moments I would have gone right back to Yonkers.

There weren't many real cabs in Baltimore anyway, though, only "hacks." Hacks were people who used their own cars as cabs. They weren't licensed and didn't put any signs on their car; they just drove around in their old, beat-up Oldsmobile or Chevy four-doors waiting for people to flag them down. They wouldn't charge you very much if you needed a ride downtown, and if you needed some dough, well, you could bet they had fifty or sixty dollars on them at the end of a night.

Now you had to make sure you knew a place before you decided to cross the line in that place because you could fuck around and get left in an abandoned building somewhere where no one would ever find you. Home was one thing. You knew who lived where and who would or would not admit to seeing something. You knew who wasn't going to kill you anyway because he knew your mama and them. But being in another state was different. So I knew I was in deep in B-more when I started getting comfortable enough to rob hacks, and just like in Y-O, doing dirt became a way for me to get by.

Every few weeks, I would try to go home and see Tashera and Xavier. I missed them, missed our apartment, missed watching movies all night and drinking iced tea, but Baltimore was where I needed to be. This was where my peoples were; this was where I had any chance of making a living and this was where I started writing a bunch of rhymes again.

35

The Battle for New York

BALTIMORE INSPIRED ME FOR SOME REASON. EVERY NIGHT I would just sit in the crib and write. TV didn't distract me because we didn't have cable in the house where I was staying and with our bootleg antenna we barely even got the regular channels, so I could easily zone out into my music. Sometimes I would write a couple of songs in one night and often they were some of my best.

"Coming From," "Let Me Fly," and "X Is Coming" I wrote like that. I just finished one, listened to the next beat, then wrote the next one.

```
I sold my soul to the devil, and the price was cheap
Hey yo, it's cold on this level 'cause it's twice as deep
But you don't hear me, ignorance is bliss and so on
Sometimes it's better to be taught dumb, shall I go on?[33]
```

After "Niggas Can't Touch Me Kid" failed, Waah told me that we weren't trying to put any more singles out for a while, but I didn't care. There were so many thoughts and stories in my mind, the words just kept flowing. And I was still trying to battle as much as I could.

Most of the MCs in Baltimore were corny, but there was one dude named Nardo who was nice. One night, I went head to head with him for almost two hours straight. See, back then, I used to write ten-minute songs, so if I needed to give a nigga a forty-eight-bar rhyme or a fifty-six, it was no problem. Nardo was an exception, but most MCs ran out of things to say after a half hour or so, especially if they were just freestyling. Once I got older, I never liked to make up something on the spot or say a rhyme off the top of my head. Everything I said, I wrote. If I didn't write it, I wouldn't say it. Even though freestyling was thought of as the true test of a great MC, I felt differently. To me, making something up as you went along was meaningless; it had no point because once you put that rhyme in the air, it was gone. Even if it was the best thing you ever said in your life, you wouldn't remember it afterwards, and to me, that was a waste. I wanted my words to have permanence to them. I wanted listeners to know that I had thought carefully about what I was saying, my words and phrases weren't something hot that I just came up with. When I *did* think of a rhyme in my head—like when I took my walks through Yonkers—I always put it on paper as soon as I got home.

I'm glad I had enough ammunition for that Nardo battle. If I never lost a battle in New York, I wasn't trying to lose one out here, but my rhyme skills would be tested even more the night Darrin called me from Yonkers.

Over the years, Dee and Waah had put down a few other MCs with Ruff Ryders. One group was made up of some kids who called themselves Harlem Knights. They were young and needed a lot of work before they were ready to go into the studio and make songs, but they knew how to battle and Waah and Darrin loved to throw everybody into a rhyme fight.

The night Darrin called, he said that he needed me to come back to New York right away. Harlem Knights was going to battle a group called Original Flavor in a pool hall in the Bronx that night and he thought they might need a little help. Original Flavor had a lead MC named Jay-Z.

Jay was from Brooklyn. Him and his partner, Damon Dash, had started a company called Roc-A-Fella and, like us, were hustling to get a record deal. I had peeped some of his verses on different mix tapes and knew that he had built a rep on the street as one of the best rappers in New York, so when Darrin told me he was up there talking shit, I knew I had to go. I jumped in the first hack I saw and asked the driver if he would take the three-hour trip.

"You wanna go where? To do what?"

Luckily, the driver was a young dude from the neighborhood and saw how we were all getting down on the hustle tip. He also knew that I was the rapper of the crew, so he got excited about being able to take me to a big battle. He said he would even wait to bring me back afterwards.

The pool hall was on 145th Street in the South Bronx. When I walked in a few minutes after 1 A.M., the crowd was thick.

Jay and I weren't really supposed to battle. Darrin had wanted me there more like an insurance policy, to make sure that Roc-A-Fella didn't put their big gun in the mix. I think Jay's crew felt the same way about him because at the beginning we were both chilling on the side, but when things started getting nasty and Harlem Knights and Original Flavor started dissing each other, the crowd started eyeing the two of us. The people knew that we were the top dogs of our crews and they wanted us to go at it and after a few more rounds, I just couldn't stand to the side anymore. It was time to hold down the fam.

"I don't give a fuck. What?" I looked over at Jay. "Let's do it. Let's get it on, baby!"

We both climbed on top of the pool table and Jay stood in front of me and started it off right away. He did his thing with his first verse and the crowd started hollering like it was over.

Then it was my turn. I wasn't going out like that. In fact, I wasn't going out at all.

    This is the darkest shit, sparkest shit
    Hittin' with the hardest shit, 'cause I've always started shit

The two of us went back and forth for almost an hour, aggressively spitting rhymes in each other's face.

    It's about time to start another robbing spree
    'Cause, yo, my way is highway robbery

Everyone in spot had surrounded us on that pool table. Folks were hooping and hollering at the end of every line. It was like the Bill

Blass battle all over again, but this time there was more at stake, this was a battle for New York—and my opponent was much stronger. I brought all my heat.

> You bad, nigga?
> I'll be back to see if you'll still be here
> You know my style will put your fucking man in a wheelchair
> He'll never walk again, on the strength of me
> That's how I left him, G, scared to death of me[34]

I knew it was close. Jay had as many rhymes as I did, told stories, talked shit, flipped styles. I never liked my battles to be close because then you'd always get some clown to be like, "Fuck that. My man ate you!" when it wasn't even like that. I liked there to be no fucking way for anybody to say anything. But that didn't happen this time. That's why I started worrying: *some people are going to be thinking, maybe* . . .

Outside, after it was over, Damon Dash came over to Darrin and me. It was snowing, already early morning. Darrin and him knew each other from the streets, who brothers were, how brothers got down, so despite the fierce competition that just went down between Jay and me, there wasn't any beef. This was hip-hop. We all shook hands.

Then I heard some big words.

"Yo, your man did kinda get him," Damon said to Darrin.

What? What was that? I looked over to the two of them.

"Yo, your man did kinda get him . . ."

When I heard that, I knew my record was still intact. That was Jay's right-hand man.

Satisfied with my trip, I said peace to Darrin, got back in the hack, and went right back to Baltimore. I didn't even go home.

36

"Somebody's Gonna Die"

LATE ONE SUMMER AFTERNOON, I WAS WALKING BACK TO THE block with Boomer. I was walking in the street because I rarely walked on the sidewalk, there was more space and I wouldn't have to worry about bumping elbows with any B-more clowns that didn't want to give me my three feet. Boomer had just finished eating his lunch and was jogging beside me off the chain. I didn't hear the van coming behind us.

Bam!

When I turned my head, I saw Boomer in the air. The van hit him smack in his chest. He flipped over a couple of times and then landed ten feet in front of me. I knew right away. He was standing on his feet but I could see it in his eyes. THAT VAN HAD KILLED MY DOG.

For the first few moments, I couldn't even yell. I just stared at him. My boy's chest was split open and he was bleeding out of his nose. His legs were wobbling. He had no fight left. The impact had done more damage than he could bear. I watched Boomer take his last breaths and when he fell, I lost my mind.

"WHAT THE FUCK?!?" I yelled as loud as I possibly could.

Somebody's gonna die . . .

I wanted to murder everybody in that van. Boomer was my

motherfucking nigga and now my boy was gone. I didn't want to hear nothing. That whole family deserved to die.

I don't want to hear a fucking thing!

If I had had a burner on me, it would have happened, but when I looked up to find the bastards I saw that they had never stopped driving. That's what really hurt. They knew what they did, they just didn't care. My dog was lying dead in the street and that family was driving away like nothing happened, like my dog was a fucking alley cat or something. I couldn't understand. There was plenty of room. They didn't beep or nothing . . . but that was my boy, Boomer.

All I could do was cry.

37

Powerhouse

WHEN I CAME BACK TO YONKERS FOR GOOD, WAAH AND Darrin finished turning the upper half of this office building in downtown Yonkers into their own recording studio. The brothers understood that the first thing a production company needed to be successful was a place for its artists to write and record their music. Yonkers didn't have any full-fledged studios anywhere, so they couldn't rent someone else's spot like Jack had been doing in New Rochelle and Mount Vernon for all those years, and they also didn't want to pay studio costs. Their father, Mr. Dean, was a real estate broker, so they understood that the best way to do that was to be your own landlord. They called the spot Powerhouse and in the midnineties that became Ruff Ryders' home.

POWERHOUSE STUDIOS

Every night of the week, anyone that Waah or Darrin had put
down with double-R was in Powerhouse working on their skills. Producers stayed until morning time playing music on the different key-
boards and sample machines; young and wanna-be MCs sat on the
couches with their notebooks on their laps writing rhymes. The
lounge was always flooded with brothers from the neighborhood that
were trying to get into the "hip-hop game" in some way and then
there was always another bunch of random heads congregated outside arguing about what rapper was better then who. It didn't take
long for Powerhouse to become the most active hip-hop recording
studio in Westchester. But almost from the day we rolled in there, the
studio was defined more by the battles it hosted and I loved every
minute of it.

> When I creep through, niggas is see-through just like a
>   negligee
> And there ain't no talking because there ain't much that
>   the dead can say[35]

MCs traveled from all over—Brooklyn, Queens, Staten Island,
Jersey—to put their skills to the test. There would always be a banging beat playing in the studio room so it could go down as soon as a
stranger showed up, but sometimes battles would just erupt in the
lounge or the reception area. It didn't matter.

> Get the mayor on the horn
> Time for shit to go down
> Strapped for the showdown, wet up the crib, kick your
>   door down
> I know you scheming so I gots to get you first
> Put you right up in a brand-new hearse
> Could be worse[36]

I never cared where an MC was from or how far he came, I just
jumped all over them and made sure they left with a loss. Just like I
had been doing on the street since I was fifteen, my style wasn't win
by a little bit, it was *beat the shit out of him*. Finish him—and after he

doesn't want to rhyme anymore, then hit him with two more verses just because he came up.

Motherfucker, what made you think you could . . .

I wasn't the only one representing Ruff Ryders in these battles, though. The younger MCs always gave me some help. Harlem Knights wasn't around much anymore, but these three Yonkers kids I had introduced to Waah who called themselves the Warlox (Jadakiss, Sheek, and Styles) and their man K-Sino were always there, as was rapper Murder Mase from Harlem, Drag-On, this Newark MC called Loose, and even Nardo, the brother that I battled in Baltimore. So with all of them around, the idea whenever a challenger showed up was to first "put the pups on 'em" and then they would go at it for a few rounds and represent double-R. Then, if it looked like the battle was stalling or I needed to get us the win, I'd step in and knock out whoever was left standing. The strategy made us a pretty dangerous home team.

```
Sat money down, told him how much his peeps missed him
Boom!
One shot through his respiratory system
Kissed him good night, put him to bed
with four more to the head
So I know he understood what I said. Red
was all over the place and it didn't look good
So I did what a crook would, searched the crib and took
    goods 37
```

One night I wasn't there, some group from Queens came in and almost set it on us. 'Kiss did his best to hold it down—he would always catch a nigga with his first two bars—but once I heard that the group got the better of him, I made sure that they were brought back to the studio as soon as possible. When they showed up the second time, I murdered those strangers one by one. I just stood in the middle of all three of them for two hours, flowing nonstop. When it was over, my jeans and my sweatshirt were soaked in sweat. It felt like I had lost ten pounds but our win-lost record was intact.

As more and more MCs found their way to Powerhouse, more and more MCs left as losers. Rappers learned to be wary of showing up in Y-O without their best material because we would tell them everything they needed to know about their wack rhymes. It didn't take us long to build a rep, and with each win, the word on the street kept getting louder and louder.

While I was away, Irv Lorenzo had been making moves. Now he was "Irv Gotti," a big-time producer, and had got this Queens MC called Mic Geronimo a record deal with a small New York–based label called TVT Records. He had also put together a group called the Cash Money Click that TVT was close to signing as well. So when Gotti invited me to do a verse on one of Mic Geronimo's singles, a track called "Time to Build" that he also had a kid named Ja Rule on, a young nigga from the Cash Money Click, I jumped at the opportunity to flex on all of these new artists that he was working with. Maybe my old friend needed to be reminded of how I got down.

    I'm peeling niggas caps like oranges
    Hit 'em in the head with two-by-four inches
    I'm a grimy nigga so I like my bitches cruddy
    My clothes dirty, dick shitty and my knife bloody[38]

It was a good verse and I was going to be the last MC to spit on the song, but then Gotti did me dirty. A few days after I laid my vocals, he told me that he decided to put Jay-Z on the track as well. There wasn't any beef between Jay and I, we hadn't seen or even spoken to each other since the battle in the pool hall, but knowing that he would be on the song, I wanted to do my verse over.

"Come on, X. Don't do me like that," Gotti complained. "We got to get the song out."

But my instincts were right. See, when Jay went to the studio, he got upset when Gotti told him that I was going to close the record over him, so he listened to my verse and took some shots at me.

    So when I'm browsing through your housing projects
    Niggas get five thousand, shit is rough . . .

That was fucked up.

"If you were going to put him on the song, why didn't you put him on the song like you put me on the song?" I yelled at Gotti. "You let him hear my shit so he knew how to counteract what I said. That gave me a disadvantage. If I knew there was going to be a battle on wax, I would have finished him."

"But both of y'all are my niggas and I didn't know with how crazy you can get if I could safely put you two in the same room together," Gotti answered.

That was a weak excuse.

A few weeks later, Gotti made up for the move by taking my demo tape to TVT, to see if he could get me signed there like he did with his other artists, but the president of the label didn't like my material. He claimed that I sounded too much like the group Onyx (who were known for rowdy anthems like "Throw Ya Gunz" and "Slam"). I knew that was some bullshit, but when Waah had brought my material to Sean "Puffy" Combs, who had blown up with my Y-O girl, Mary J. Blige, and now had his own label, Bad Boy Entertainment, he had pretty much said the same thing. I wasn't marketable, I cursed too much and the public wasn't ready to hear "that kind of anger right now." I finally started to sense a pattern. I knew what these check writers really wanted to say. They wanted to say I wasn't a stable investment, that I was running the street and in and out of jail. They wanted to say I was a problem, a risk . . . but that wouldn't have been the first time I heard that. Try School 18 or Andrus or living with my mother in School Street. I just wished someone had the guts to come to a motherfucker real, like "we know what your struggles are, but we see your talent."

Trust. That was all I wanted. I was reckless because I didn't give a fuck. I robbed niggas because I was starving and I was broke every fucking day! Couldn't anyone ever understand that?

In 1994, the biggest label in the world was Death Row Records. Fueled by producer Dr. Dre and his G-funk sound and artist Snoop Doggy Dogg, Death Row had brought a West Coast gangsta aesthetic of "chronic" and "gin and juice" to the music and started selling millions of records in the process. On the wave of that success, the label's CEO, Suge Knight, had thoughts of creating a "Death Row East," a New York–based affiliate of his company that would expand his empire and attempt to mirror the success he had with local artists in Compton and Long Beach with East Coast MCs. One night on the word of Kurupt, one of his artists, Suge came looking for me.

It was the night Snoop had a show in Manhattan at Trafalgar Square. Suge brought Kurupt, Snoop, and some of his other Death Row artists up to Powerhouse to hear me rhyme. I had heard of these niggas; I knew that Snoop and Tha Dogg Pound were the biggest rappers in the game at the time, but I didn't care. They were in my house and I was going to do what I do.

```
Y'all motherfuckers talking about it ain't nothing but a
    G thing . . .
But nigga I'm still living
So hollow tips must be the only thing I'm still giving
You fuck with me they'll be a ribbon
around your tree. How did your mother put it?
Oh, yeah, "in love and memory . . ."
```

Gotti was there that night and by this time he knew how to set me off, how to spark my fire and get me to spit my most aggressive rhymes. All he had to do was look at me and shrug like he knew I could do better.

```
I like to laugh and first play it off like I'm cool with him
Then wet him up like a fucking pool hit him
Let the pit bull get him
Break y'all niggas down to nothing
That's what y'all faggots get for bluffing
Who's next?[39]
```

All eyes were on Snoop, Daz, and Kurupt. They were supposed to be the hottest niggas in the world, but they stayed seated. Waah and Darrin stood next to me with this ugly, confident look on their faces and we all just looked at Suge. He was standing in the back smiling, loving every minute of it.

A week later, Suge flew me, Waah, Darrin, Gotti, and six other Ruff Ryders out to L.A. to talk business. It was my first time to the West Coast. Suge said that he never saw an MC who kept it as raw as I did and he wanted to sign me as soon as possible. I would be a perfect fit for the loud, arrogant, fuck-you ghetto attitude that he wanted Death Row to

ME AND RUFF RYDERS WITH DR. DRE

have. But when Waah, Darrin, and Gotti came out of the meeting they told me the deal wasn't right and after less than an hour of negotiation, it was clear that I was not going to join the Row.

38

Niggas Done Started Something

GOTTI ALWAYS TOLD ME HIS PASSION WASN'T WITH MIC
Geronimo, but he couldn't front on how well he worked with Jay-Z.
Later that year, even though he was still spending time with me in
Powerhouse making tracks, even though he still drove his MPV to the
crib every once in a while to say what's up to Tashera and me, Gotti
got down with Jay's Roc-A-Fella label and helped Jay put out his first
album, *Reasonable Doubt*. I wasn't mad at him, I just couldn't understand how everybody was doing their thing and I was still living in
Mulford. I couldn't understand why I wasn't a dime richer than I was
before I did "Born Loser," opened for Leaders of the New School,
battled K-Solo, Lord Finesse, Andre the Giant, Bill Blass. It didn't
make sense. Nobody anywhere I went could ever fuck with me on the
rap tip and yet I was the one broke. I was the one without a deal. I
didn't give up but I was so tired of being disappointed, so tired of
being turned down and watching other niggas blow up, that in 1995,
I just decided to do what I did best . . . hit the streets.

Swizz was Waah's nephew. He grew up in the Bronx but a couple
of years after I met Waah he moved in with his uncle in Mount Vernon. That's when we started hanging together. Swizz was much
younger than I was but he was a good brother to roll with because

every night the two of us went out, we were game to get into any dirt we could. Whether it was running pockets, knocking deliverymen off their bikes or just leaving everybody broke in a game of dice, Swizz and I were always out on the street looking for that next thrill. One of our favorite pastimes was hopping cabs.

See, the key to hopping a cab is to make a few stops before you get to your final destination. Tell the driver where you're going when you first get in, then along the way, ask him to stop in a store somewhere for a few minutes, come back, then ask him to stop again a few more blocks up. By the second or third time you get out of the car, the driver will be comfortable with you getting out, so then the next time, you just don't come back.

Or you can take the more direct approach:

"We're hopping you, homeboy. Just take it easy and go with the flow."

You normally saved that move for when you needed a cab to join you on a robbery. An unmarked cab could make for a good getaway car, although drivers often got nervous.

"No, I'm not going to do that!" they would yell from behind the wheel. Then you'd have to put a lot of pressure on them and hit them in the back of the head a few times but you still had to be careful that when you went to make your move, they didn't pull off on you and leave you stranded in the middle of nowhere with a victim up the street.

One time, though, Swizz and I happened to come across this African dude who was as gangsta as we were.

"Give me thirty dollars and I'll take you anywhere . . ." he said.

He heard shit going down, he heard the shots and everything, but he never budged, he just stayed right on that corner as calmly as a professional. The problem was that when it was time for me and Swizz to get out of there we realized that we had asked him to park behind us on a one-way street. So once we got in his car we had to drive right past the scene of the crime. That wasn't smart. Thankfully, our game was much tighter the night we went to war.

There had been a party at School 12 and as usual, everyone was hanging out in front of the building after it was over not trying to go home. I was posted in the front when Tashera told me that she had noticed some young guys from her old block eyeing me, like they were scheming. She said she heard one of them mumbling about how I had robbed their man or something.

Now Y-O had been my spot for years already. I was twenty-five years old and had been robbing cats in the city since I came back from group home in '85. So when Boo Boo put me on to what she thought was going on, I caught an attitude real quick.

Y'all niggas ain't gonna creep me! I done raised y'all. Don't try that bullshit!

Then I noticed one of the dudes she was talking about staring at me.

Come on, man, don't play me like that. You're a kid. Don't stare me in my face like I'm a bitch. I've seen you and your older brother pull your pants down before, you bitch-ass nigga . . .

Then another kid walked by me pulling the tuck-and-show move with his shirt, flashing the gun that he had in his waistband.

Oh! Y'all got balls like that? Okay. I'm going to have to kill one of you motherfuckers tonight . . .

"Yo, Swizz. Go get that."

Mulford was right around the corner from School 12 and Swizz made the round trip in less than five minutes. It was funny, though, because it was summertime, no less than seventy degrees outside, and he came back wearing this big, brown, goose-feathered vest. If we weren't in this kind of situation, I would have clowned him. *What, are you cold? You trying to match with something, dog?* But the coat served its purpose because Swizz had a fully loaded Glock and a baby shotgun hidden underneath it.

Now, common street sense should tell you that if you see someone walking down the street, as hot as it was, with that kind of oversize jacket on, you should probably get the fuck out of the way—especially if you don't really know the person. But those young boys really wanted to get hurt that night because as soon as they saw Swizz, instead of moving away, they stayed there and waited for us to get fully loaded. They really thought they were going to put us down.

Don't get your dicks hard now, motherfuckers!

Swizz and I just got back to back, guns in hand.

What? What!

We were outnumbered and this was also Swizz's first time in a gun battle so he didn't know much. But even though he didn't do exactly what he was *supposed* to do, he showed the heart to do whatever he *had* to do, and that's always the most important thing. No matter how dangerous a situation is, if you have heart, you'll learn the rules to any street game in two tries. The first time you will struggle, but then the next time out the gate, a nigga with heart will always say "I got this . . ." Swizz learned fast.

I didn't see him amidst the commotion, but my man, a DJ named Cool C, also had my back that night. I had been trying to buy a nine-millimeter from him earlier at the party and he didn't want to sell it to me. I was glad when he saw what was going down and decided instead to put the gun to use on my behalf. While me and Swizz kept moving forward, he came over my shoulder shooting, and the three of us kept busting at those bitches back to back. After a few rounds it was over.

I will rob and steal witcha, dog nigga, what
Ride till we die, on till it's up[40]

39

Harlem

DARRIN AND WAAH OFTEN HELD COURT IN FRONT OF THE Mart on 125th Street in Harlem. Sometimes they would pick me up in Yonkers and drive me downtown, but most often I just jumped on the Metro North commuter train to Manhattan and then took the local subway to get to 2–5th because besides hopping cabs, I still didn't have any way of getting myself around. (Now that I wasn't a juvenile anymore, stealing cars was a less attractive activity because with the record I had, one auto theft conviction would have easily sent me up north for a few years.)

Once you regularly start coming to a block, you begin to see the social dynamics of that block: who the hustlers are versus who is trying to do something legit, who has a valid beef with who and who is on some bullshit. That's important because if you don't know the players in the 'hood you're rolling in, you are vulnerable to getting caught out there.

One day, Waah took me up to 129th Street and introduced me to a producer cat named Grease. Him and his man, Big Stan, had put together a rap crew called NIB (Niggas in Black). They threw a lot of parties in Harlem and ran around the streets battling cats like I did in Y-O.

When I went through his block, him and Big Stan always had the card game going or they would just be chilling, smoking and playing music. Often I would join them for a few passes of the blunt and soon there began to grow a quiet acknowledgment between the three of us that we probably could become friends. It was just because of the kind of guys we were, we all knew it would take a minute. See, relationships are a delicate thing in the street; you have to be careful of who you got close to—if anybody—because there are many ways a person could betray you when the game is survival. So for months, me, Grease, and Big Stan were just cool.

One summer, Waah asked Grease to get down with Ruff Ryders.

"No thanks," Grease replied.

Not to be turned down, Waah let him think about it for a few days and then rolled up on him again.

"Nah, I'm good."

Grease was only a block nigga, but he knew what he wanted. He couldn't deny the money Waah and Darrin were clocking in the neighborhood on the hustle tip, or the plans that they had for Ruff Ryders, he just didn't want to be tied down to anyone. When Waah offered to manage him instead of asking him to sign the more encompassing production agreement that he was talking about before, then Grease agreed.

After that, Grease would troop to Powerhouse every day and bang out his music. He'd leave Harlem late in the afternoon—jeans pocket loaded with a bag of weed—and stay in Yonkers until three or four in the morning. Grease used to rhyme, but after an asthma condition made it difficult for him to flow the way he wanted to, he concentrated on making the music. ("All those words back to back, I'm not with all that. I'm not trying to pass the fuck out," he used to say.) When I heard his beats I was surprised by how many different styles he had. Some of his tracks were laid back, others were more street, but they all had this grimy, almost eerie quality about them—and they were always very musical. Right away I could hear that there was more going on in one of Grease's beats than the simple loops and samples that I was used to. We did a lot of songs together those early nights in Powerhouse (joints called "Final Call" and "Against the Grain" were two of the best), then Waah would always give him a ride back to Harlem and he'd sleep and do it again the next day.

Whether you were a producer or an MC, soon that day-and-night routine became the schedule for everyone down with Ruff Ryders. Pent One, who was now going by the producer name PK, finally gave up his tagging career and followed a similar late-evening-to-early-morning routine. Swizz bought himself a pair of mismatched turntables and had started coming to Powerhouse all the time to teach himself how to make beats. And of course the pups were always there. There wasn't any punishment if you weren't at the studio every night, your absence just proved that you weren't as hungry as the next man, and at least among the young niggas, competition was the defining element of being in the Ruff Ryders family.

For the first few years that I knew Darrin, he concentrated on his hustle game and let his brother handle most of the music business, but since we came back from Baltimore he had started spending more and more hours in the studio and quickly developed an ear for the music. Whatever kind of beat it was, Darrin had a knack for coming up with the perfect chorus and, like Grease, PK, and the other producers, always had an instinct for what rappers and what flows best matched what beats. Darrin always believed in me and he also knew that Ruff Ryders had too much talent in one place not to be able to make something happen, we just had to keep working at it.

After a few months, Darrin was right; Ruff Ryders' discipline paid off . . . just not for me.

40

Let Me Fly

IN THE SPRING OF 1996, RUFF RYDERS PUT OURSELVES officially on the map by signing Jadakiss, Sheek, and Styles (now called the LOX) to a recording contract with Puff Daddy's Bad Boy Entertainment. Grease was to produce their first single, "If You Think I'm Jiggy," and Puff wanted the album fast-tracked for a summer release so that his new group could share in the celebrity spotlight enjoyed at the time by his other artists: the Notorious B.I.G., Mase, Faith Evans, and 112.

I didn't need any more hints that my dream wasn't meant to be.

"This shit ain't gonna happen, Gotti," I said to him one night sitting outside of the studio. "I can feel it. This shit ain't gonna happen."

It was late, the streets were cold and quiet, and the reality of my twelve-year journey was hitting me in the face.

Either let me fly or give me death

"X, don't worry about it, these label dudes are assholes. They don't know what's up. We just got to keep banging these niggas."

"Did you know this rapping shit was all I ever wanted, dog? This is what I was blessed with. This is the only thing that I'm fucking good at . . ."

There was a long pause.

"Yo, I think they're going to make me an A&R over at Def Jam, so as soon as I get in there, I'm gonna—"

"I DON'T WANNA HEAR THAT SHIT. I don't give a fuck anymore, Gotti! I've been doing this shit for *twelve years!*"

"Dog, you know you're the nicest nigga out here. It's gonna happen."

Gotti meant well. Everybody meant well. I just couldn't keep doing it. It was getting too hard to hold on to the strength and the patience and the faith that I needed to go on.

"Nothing with me ever matters, dog. Nothing . . ."

I thought of Tashera. I thought of Xavier and Boomer. I thought of all those nights I spent alone on those rooftops staring at the sky.

```
Either let me fly or give me death
Let my soul rest, take my breath
If I don't fly, I'm gonna die anyway
I'ma live on, but I'll be gone any day[41]
```

41

Payback on Ravine

I ALREADY THOUGHT THAT RAVINE WAS THE DEVIL BLOCK. IT was my darkest place, the place where I committed most of my sins, and I never imagined that it would ever get worse for me there, but it did.

RAVINE

I was sitting in front of one of the buildings a few feet away from a bunch of young niggas who started panicking when they saw a police car come down the block flashing its lights. It wasn't a rare sight to see the police roll up on a block looking for somebody. Every few days, around the way, brothers were getting arrested for something they did or fit the description of doing. But these kids ran into the building like they had a murder warrant out for them, obviously not understanding how much guiltier their scrambling made them look.

"Why y'all running like that?" I yelled after them. For some reason, the police didn't seem to give a fuck that day and after they finished their drive-by and did nothing, I walked into the building, too. That's when I saw the chain. It was a nice gold herringbone. *Yes! Just what I need.* I was broke and a nice little chain could get me a few dollars so I scooped it off the floor and put it in my sock.

A few minutes later, the young bucks, who now that the police were gone had their brave 'hood faces on again, walked over to me.

"Yo, I lost my chain."

Now lost property is always fair game, so I didn't have anything to say. Neither did my man Percel, who had since walked over to chill with me.

"Are you sure one of y'all niggas ain't got it?"

The young boy was getting heated at me. He probably knew my rep for being the robbery nigga, but I simply ignored him and told Percel to give me a ride home. But instead of going to Mulford, I asked him to drop me off at Slow Bomb, where I got out and sold the chain for forty dollars. As I left the building, folks on the block had a warning for me: "Yo, X. Niggas is looking for you. They say you robbed some kid for his chain and his leather coat."

"What? I didn't rob nobody for no coat . . ."

"They said you stuck up a sixteen-year-old for his herringbone and his Avirex."

An Avirex? That was one of the nicest leather jackets a person could have in the 'hood. It *would* have been nice to take that off somebody, but I hadn't seen an Avi on a potential victim in a while—and I did not rob kids.

"They said they're coming back around to look for you, dog."

"I don't care. I didn't do nothing, man. Watch. I'm just going to sit and wait for them right here."

The boy whose chain it was must have had a lot of family because a little while later his father and three of his older cousins came back to Slow Bomb looking for me. I told them that I hadn't done any robberies.

"I *found* that chain, man. I didn't rob nobody. I can even take you to where I got it from."

Pops didn't seem to care.

"My son said you robbed him."

"Well, it wasn't me."

The only reason I followed him back to where his son was waiting was because I knew I wasn't guilty of anything. I didn't steal anybody's chain. This time, though, the truth didn't matter.

"Yeah Dad, that's him." Just like Che had done so many years before, the kid looked me right in my face. "He's wearing the same jacket."

I had found the coat that I was wearing earlier that day in someone's front yard. Either this was a fucked-up coincidence or the kid was totally lying, but there was no time to explain. Before I knew it, two guys grabbed me from behind and the father punched me dead in my chest. I tried to release my arms but I had no chance. He kept punching and punching me and soon all I could feel were his fists smashing against my nose and my eyes and my open jaw.

Boom, boom, boom . . .

I felt the blows against my face and when I fell to the ground, that's when everyone started kicking me. Over and over, heavy Timberland boots crashed against my body. I curled up to protect my ribs, but it was no use.

I didn't do it.

The kicks kept coming, harder and harder, slamming against my spine and the back of my legs.

I didn't do it . . . I didn't do it . . .

One guy wouldn't stop kicking me in the head.

Then I heard someone say they should take me into the park and three guys started dragging me up the street by my shoulders. My body was too beaten to resist and as they pulled me up the street, the mob grew. Niggas who didn't even know what had happened with the chain came over to help administer the beatdown and then I realized what was going on. For all the times I had robbed someone and ran up on them with the dog; for all the times I had left someone in an alley, broke and embarrassed with their pants down and their girl watching, this was their payback. This was their chance for vengeance.

They brought me to the park, and there, out of the corner of my eye, I saw one of my attackers pick up a brick.

No, Lord. No. I'm not going to let them kill me . . .

Somehow I summoned all of the strength I had left and made it to my feet. I heard sirens and I stumbled away as fast as I could. I don't know why that guy never caught me with that brick.

A few minutes later an ambulance found me a few blocks away, laid out on the street in a pool of blood. But whoever called the paramedics must have also told them what had happened, because they weren't just there to help. They were also there to comment.

"So you wanna rob kids, huh? Well, this is what you get," the bastards said to me with a greasy attitude.

My head and face were numb. My ribs felt like they were crushed against my lungs. I was having an asthma attack and I couldn't get enough air. I thought I was going to die.

"I c . . . an't . . . br . . . ea . . . the," I told them.

"You'll be fine. Shut up and get in the ambulance."

Once they took me away, someone ran to Tashera's apartment and told her that I had been beaten up. At first Boo Boo hesitated about coming to the hospital because she feared that I was beaten up too badly and didn't want to see me like that. But when she arrived at Yonkers General, she felt better because the doctors in the emergency room told her that I was going to be okay. They had taken a bunch of X rays and said that I hadn't broken anything.

Tashera called Uncle Ray and asked him to come to the hospital. Ever since Valhalla, him and Boo Boo had become close friends, and just six hours after I got to the emergency room, the doctors told my uncle that they were sending me home.

"He's all right," they said.

Later, Tashera told me how deformed my face looked that night, how swollen and inflamed it was. The hospital had barely cleaned all of the wounds on my body when they discharged me and I wasn't wearing any clothes because they had been torn off during the beating. But Boo Boo took care of me. She washed me up, applied some extra bandages, and made a fresh bed for me in the living room. Then she watched me go to sleep.

Three days later, I felt like I was getting worse. It was getting harder and harder to breathe and every time I woke up there would be blood all over my pillow.

"You need to go back to the hospital," Tashera said to me.

At first I didn't listen to her—until I looked at myself in the mirror and saw that the whole right side of my neck had swollen out past my face. One side of my jaw appeared to be hanging lower than the other side and the front of my chin was loose. I couldn't stop drooling blood.

Ray still worked at Valhalla so he said that he could take me to the hospital at the prison. We thought anything would be better than Yonkers General and we were right.

The doctors in Valhalla told me that my neck was swollen because I had a huge abscess in my throat that was filled with pus. They told me that if I had stayed home for one more day without treatment, all of the infected liquid in my face would have begun to choke me to death. They also said that my nose and my upper and lower jaw were badly broken. They were going to bring me into surgery right away to reset my jaws and remove all of the pus and then they were going to have to wire my mouth closed.

How could Yonkers General have sent me home like that? Was it because I didn't have any ID on me? Because I didn't have any money or insurance? How could they just tell me I was all right? That was crazy. If I had been able to breathe properly I would have gone back to that hospital and killed every single one of those doctors.

After the surgery, Valhalla kept me for three days under observation. Tashera and Ray came to see me and sat with me for most of the time. I never saw anyone else in my family, although one day Ray told me that they had actually seen my mother on their way up to the hospital. They were leaving the supermarket downtown in Getty Square and saw her leaning out of her apartment window. I hadn't seen or spoken to her since she had moved out of School Street a few years before.

"Hey sis, what's up?" Ray had called out to her.

"How are you doing, baby?" Arnett still spoke to her youngest brother at least once a week.

"We're going to see Earl. He's in the hospital."

My mother paused for a second.

"Oh yeah. I heard he got jumped."

That was all she said. Ray looked up at her waiting for more of a response, but nothing came. He didn't feel comfortable asking a mother if she wanted to come visit her own son.

"So I guess I'll talk to you later, then."

"Okay, baby."

My mother left the window.

My jaw was wired closed for three months. I couldn't eat any solid food. I couldn't chew. I couldn't drink anything that I wasn't able to sip through a straw, and then it couldn't be too hot or too cold or it would inflame the nerve endings in my mouth. I couldn't talk, instead I was forced to make the sounds of words through my clenched teeth and hope that people could understand me. It was a living nightmare.

Tashera looked after me every day, making all different kinds of soups and shakes. Ray gave me a blender and every week I came up with a different concoction. A mix of hard-boiled eggs was nasty but Farina was always good, and when I blended up the mashed potatoes from Kentucky Fried Chicken with the gravy that came with it, I figured out that the proportions were just right to make a perfect liquid.

I still didn't get any visitors. I didn't see Collie, Buzzy, or any of my other aunts or uncles, didn't see my sisters, and definitely not my mother. I didn't see Waah or Darrin. A friend of mine, Denardo, would ride his bike over every few days from School Street to come say what's up, and Butler, a friend of Darrin's who I was locked up with in Valhalla and had started rolling with Ruff Ryders, came by every now and then to bring me soup from the store. And, of course, Ray. But that was it. So laying in that bed made me realize who cared about me and who didn't. Everybody on the music tip was running with the LOX and it was obvious that most of my family had written me off. I knew that they heard what happened and how bad it was—the story of DMX getting beaten up was all over Yonkers by that next afternoon—but that didn't seem to motivate any of them to knock on the door or even pick up the phone. Fuck it, I said to myself, at least I had Boo Boo.

I had been robbing niggas my whole life and I never had this kind of dirt thrown back at me until now, *until the one time that I didn't rob the nigga.* That was crazy, and I couldn't help to wonder if my beatdown was some kind of spiritual payback. Had I earned it? Had the fifteen years that I had spent robbing and stealing with no mask and no gun finally come back to haunt me?

The more I thought about it, the more it made sense, the more I began to believe that the beatdown had been my Day of Judgment. I was hurt. I was fucked up. I almost died, but God was doing nothing but teaching me a lesson.

You wanna piss in the bed, Earl? Huh? Then sleep in it.

It was like when the kid said later that the person who robbed him was wearing a ski mask, everyone in the street knew that meant I couldn't have done it because they all knew that whenever I did my dirt, I rolled with a bare face. That's why they hated me so much, because I was always bold enough not to give a fuck about who saw me. But no one cared that I was wrongly accused. *You do dirt, you get dirt.* And if my robbing and stealing was all they knew about me, why should they care? *Everybody knew Earl, but there was another Earl.*[42] So lying on that bed with my face still swollen and all these fucking metal wires cutting my mouth up, I convinced myself that if this was a lesson, then I didn't deserve to feel sorry for myself either.

Did you think life was that fucking sweet? I let you slide for a minute because I love you. But when it was time, you knew I had to smack the shit out of you . . .

I was alive. I should have been dead but I was still breathing, and that was the fact that I couldn't let myself forget. I was still breathing and there must be a reason for that. There must be a reason that He kept me alive . . .

As the days wore on, I also became more and more glad that I was smacked that hard *literally,* instead of *figuratively.* I already knew how to deal with a physical lesson. It didn't matter how vicious or violent the lesson was, I had experience with physical shit. I had beatings my whole life.

What's that? Steak and eggs? Oh, yeah. I know what that tastes like.

But since I always thought so much, since my mind and my thoughts were the most sensitive parts of myself, I knew that an emotional lesson of that size would have probably fucked my head up for real.

I can't front. Before I came to terms with it, I did want them niggas dead. Driven by the same feelings of anger and payback that they used against me, I wanted to kill all of my attackers one by one and wouldn't have felt any remorse for it. It would have been easy enough because I knew that they all lived around the way. But the more I kept thinking about who I was and the lesson that I needed to learn, those vengeful feelings began to fade. The dirt that I had done in the streets had now been returned, and this would give me the opportunity I needed to move on. A few weeks later, Darrin found out how much the kid's chain and jacket cost and gave him the money for what he had lost, and when I saw some of the guys outside on the block a few weeks later, I didn't say nothing to them.

After what I just saw, I'm riding with the Lord
'Cause I really can't afford to lose my head by the sword
And now that I've seen what I need to see
Please take me where I need to be[43]

42

One More Road to Cross

IT'S HARD TO TALK WHEN YOUR UPPER AND LOWER JAWS ARE wired together by metal braces that are glued onto your teeth. You have to move your lips as much as possible to make up for the fact that your tongue has nowhere to go. You drool a lot and have to breathe through your nose. It's difficult to fully pronounce words that have more than two or three syllables and you can't talk very loud.

But if it was hard to talk, it was almost impossible to rap, although, after about two weeks being in that bed, that's exactly what I did. I stalked around the house rapping as passionately with my jaws wired closed as when my mouth was wide open. I just pressed my upper and lower jaws together and forced the lines through my clenched teeth, spitting out each word like it had a rotten taste, like I was like a pit trying to break out of a muzzle. The restriction in my mouth made me more intense, angrier. I was at war with my own body and while the pain in my jaw was immense, the agony served me well. Now my first priority wasn't getting put on or getting a deal, it was an injury I had to overcome and I was going to prove to everybody that no matter what the circumstances, I was the best that ever did it. Nothing would hold me back. I was a dog possessed.

The effect was pretty scary. When Tashera saw me wilding in the living room she would wonder aloud if I was doing my face more damage by talking and rapping and yelling so much, but I didn't care. I was still thin and shaky from not being able to eat solid foods, but I wasn't going to let anything get in the way of me saying what I wanted to say. Rapping was what I did. It was my gift, and no matter if I had a deal or not, no matter if my jaws were wired together or not, I was going to make sure niggas heard me.

A few weeks before the beatdown, I had spit a few rhymes for a mixtape DJ named Ron G. Along with Kid Capri, who had blown up as a DJ since his days at the Castle, Ron G had built a career around selling tapes of hip-hop freestyles. Every few weeks, Ron would invite the best MCs, signed or unsigned, to his studio to lay a few verses that he would put together and sell on the street for five or seven dollars. It was a good business. Folks would often prefer to buy a mix tape on the street that was filled with a bunch of different rappers than buy a whole album of one artist in a store for twice the price. You just had to recognize the names of the MCs that were on the mix tape or trust the guy that was making it. Ron was already famous for his "blends"—where he would lay R&B vocals by Luther Vandross or Michael Jackson over contemporary hip-hop beats—so whenever one of his tapes hit the streets, most of New York would be rocking to his latest jams.

When Darrin told me that he had contacted Ron G through his man, Black Fred, and had set it up for me to go to Ron's apartment on Riverside Drive in Manhattan to lay a rhyme, I was amped.

Mix tapes demanded a certain kind of rapper because real hip-hop heads bought them and listened to the *lyrics*. Every MC knew that they had to represent because if you said a bullshit rhyme, you could bet that you wouldn't be able to sell any of your own stuff in the 'hood. So for a new MC, mix tapes were an intense trial by fire and since I knew that Ron hadn't ever heard me rhyme before, when I walked in and he asked me to kick something, I knew I had to kill it.

> Niggas say I'm buggin', and ask me what's the shit I'm on
> 'Cause I did them wrong
> Carry 'em greasy and get 'em gone

Ron started nodding his head.

When I'm on, it's some real fuck the world shit—

"Okay. Okay. That's enough," Ron interrupted me, open off my delivery. "You're dope. Just spit that again and I'll press record."

The hook was hot: *Everybody knows you can talk all day, but when it's on whatcha gonna do, walk away?* and "Watcha Gonna Do?" became the opening song of *Ron G's Mix Tape #23.*

"Yo, who the fuck is DMX?"

The streets started talking. Everyone loved the song but few people knew who I was.

Typically, Ron G sold two to three thousand copies of every tape he dropped. Add to that the small deals he had with distributors to move the tapes out of state and the African vendors that would dupe another few thousand of their own, and it wasn't uncommon for a Ron G tape to be in the hands of ten thousand people. So it was safe to say that "Whatcha Gonna Do?" gave me my first real buzz in and around New York City since the "Born Loser" single four years before.

While my mouth was still wired shut, Gotti came to Mulford and told me that Ron G's mix tape had helped him finally get the attention of Lyor Cohen, the president of Def Jam Records. On the strength of Jay-Z's *Reasonable Doubt* album, Gotti had got his A&R gig at Def Jam. From the minute he got there he had been pressuring his bosses to sign me, but for months the execs had been ignoring him, telling him to focus his attention instead on the new acts they already had in-house like Trigga and this Brooklyn chick called Foxy Brown. Gotti answered back that Def Jam was being grossly outsold by Death Row and Bad Boy because the identity of the label was lame. I was the perfect person to change it up for them. Once his peoples heard the Ron G tape, they finally listened.

"So dog, tell me when you're going to get your wires off and I'll set a date for all the check writers to come to Powerhouse," Gotti said to me one night while I was watching an episode of *The Simpsons.*

"It doesn't matter, man. They can come whenever they want," I said to him through my clenched teeth, still focused on the TV.

"Yeah, but, X, we want them to see you at your best. This will probably be the only time they'll come up here. I'm going to bring

Lyor Cohen with me, who's the president, and the brother they got up there, Kevin Liles."

"Irv, I don't give a fuck," I said, finally looking up at him. "They can come whenever the hell they want . . . I'm gonna do what I do."

"X, your jaw is wired shut . . ."

"It doesn't matter, dog. Don't you understand? That shit doesn't matter to me. BRING THEM UP HERE!"

Gotti looked at me for a moment without speaking. Then he gave in.

"Okay. Fuck it. Then I'll let them know it's on tomorrow."

"Whatever, man. It's on tomorrow then . . ."

That night Powerhouse was packed. Not only were all the pups there: Jadakiss, Sheek, Styles, and this other Yonkers MC called Jinx, but Big Stan was there with Grease, PK was working the mixing board, and Waah and Darrin were downstairs handling the night's business. Add that to the usual dozen or so wanna-be MCs from the neighborhood for whom the studio was a regular hangout and there were about thirty niggas inside—and everybody was battling.

With that many hungry MCs, it doesn't take long for a battle to get disrespectful, but when everyone's together in one tight, little studio room, then things can get ugly. When I arrived, Darrin told me that folks had been going at each other's throat for almost an hour already.

"Gotti here yet?" I asked him.

"Yeah, he's in there with his peoples."

Six feet four inches tall, broad-shouldered with a conspicuous accent, Lyor Cohen was easily the most recognizable executive in hip-hop—that is, of course, if you knew who he was. I had seen him once but no one else besides Waah and Darrin knew that the guy standing in the back was the president of the biggest hip-hop label in the world. "Yo, who's the big, tall white dude?"

"I don't know."

That kept everyone honest.

I wore the clothes I had on that day: sneakers, jeans, a black hooded sweatshirt. I wasn't shaven; my head wasn't cut. My mouth hurt. But I knew this was my time.

Either let me fly or give me death

I walked into the studio room alone.

As soon as he saw me, the kid who was rhyming at the time turned his head and looked my way. The beat was blasting but then it stopped and brothers got quiet. I moved into the center of the room and the crowd of MCs that had filled almost every inch of that studio moved to the side. They parted like the Red Sea. They knew what was about to go down.

"Yo, throw that beat back on!"

First I had to shut everyone else down.

"What? Do y'all niggas want war?"

> . . . how do brains taste when they're mixed with
>   gunpowder?
> Send me the fully automatic because it makes the gun
>   louder . . .[44]

Then I let them know who I was and gave them all that I had.

> You tell me that there's love here
> But to me it's blatant
> What's with all the blood here?
> I'm dealing with Satan
> Plus with all the hating, it's hard to keep peace,
> Thou shall not steal, but I will to eat

Not focusing on anyone or anything, I just said what I had to say.

> I tried doing good, but good's not too good for me
> Misunderstood. Why you chose the 'hood for me?
> Me? I'm all right. I just had to work hard at it
> Went to Grandma for the answer and she told me that
>   God had it

I called it "The Convo." It was a new rhyme, a dialogue I had composed between myself and the Lord. I played both parts and meant every word.

> But when the funds are low, the guns will blow
> Looking for that one that owe, make 'em run that dough
> [Lord:] No! Put down the guns and write a new rhyme
> > You'll get it all in due time
> > You'll do fine, just have faith 'cause you mine
> > And when you shine, it's going to be a sight to behold
> > So don't fight to be old or lose sight when it's cold
> > See that light down the road? It's going to guide you
> > > there
> > Two sets of footsteps, I was right beside you there[45]

I started sweating. I could feel the wires in my mouth pulling, straining to keep my jaws together. But no matter what I had been through, no matter what I had done, I had to prove that I could still rhyme better than anyone in the world so I hit 'em with "Let Me Fly." There was no better song.

> I'm a flow regardless because I'm an artist until I'm
> > trapped
> I continue to hit the hardest, whether I scrap or rap
> You give me dap, but you ain't my friend
> I see it in your eyes, you contemplate my end

Lyor kept nodding, tapping his hand against his knee. Kevin Liles kept looking at Waah and Darrin and Gotti in disbelief. All the pups were paying attention.

I knew that I had made my point. I felt it in the air. Then I kept going:

> You're waiting for that
> bend in the road, where you were told that you would go
> > when you were old . . .
> And if you died young, it was cold
> Sold! Not for nearly what it was worth
> Think back twenty-six years, be like, what if his birth
> was a miscarriage and I never existed?
> Have I given something that if taken away, you would've
> > missed it?

Didn't know, but I persisted
It was the call of the wild
I merely say what's in my heart, and you call it a style
Don't put it in a cage; don't mistreat it
You say you hunger for knowledge? Here it is, eat it!
Another song completed is another thought captured
Let me do my thing, I got it locked with this rap shit

"That's it! He's the man!" Lyor jumped up. "DMX IS THE MAN!"
"What? Who want it? What?" I looked around growling. I felt like
I could rhyme forever. But they had heard all they needed to hear.
The night was over. My new life had just begun.

It's a few hours after midnight and now we're racing furiously down a long stretch of desert highway toward home, in the middle of another of the artist's frantic and unpredictable dashes into the unknown. His entourage appreciated his need for space and let him leave the studio without a hassle, likely accepting the fact that their boss has far more reckless navigational skills than they do and if they tried to give chase they'd probably get lost anyway—or even end up dead.

"I get beatings from so many angles," X tells me, banging his fist against the steering wheel at ninety miles per hour, an open bottle of Heineken sitting next to him in the cupholder. "Just put me in the woods with three of my dogs, some bullets, and a gun, and leave me the fuck alone for a couple of months. That would help me retrieve what's left of my sanity . . .

"There are so many different extremities in my heart. So much turmoil, animosity, anger. But that is not my heart. My heart is gold. My heart is pure. But because of the fleshly things that I go through, my heart and my spirit get compromised. Nothing will ever kill my spirit, but things sure can fuck it up good."

With his foot heavy on the accelerator, X pushes the car to one hundred miles per hour.

"It's like the better person you are, the more you come in conflict with yourself, the more life's realities eat away at your own soul."

One hundred ten miles per hour.

"Do you know what happened when this spiritual advisor lady I started meeting with first saw me? It was 1998, I was doing a show for my first album and when I came offstage she told me that she saw a 'dead man walking.'"

One hundred twenty miles per hour.

"And the crazy thing was, dog, that she was right."

X flies past a police car parked on the side of the highway. He doesn't slow down.

"I know that I've done a lot of dirt in my life. You do dirt, you get dirt.

"But the truth about a thug is that a real thug has a golden heart. A real thug will shoot somebody right in their face but then turn around and give a couple of dollars to a kid on the street who's hungry. He understands that if you're in the game, you're susceptible to the rules of the game, but that child is not a part of that game. See, there's a difference between doing wrong and being wrong and if your heart is good, it will steer your bad in a certain way."

Trying hard not to think about the cops that must be behind us, I attempt to unravel the complexities of his argument.

"But isn't it easier to be ugly? To just say fuck the world?" I ask him, trying not to notice that we're now going ten miles an hour faster than we were before.

"Yeah, but even though a real nigga may get a lifetime of suffering, I believe that he's rewarded in the end. Like one time in the club this drunk nigga spilled his drink on my sleeve. It was my first time wearing that silver-and-black Ruff Ryders jersey, so I was chillin'. But it was some fruity drink so my shit got all colored and sticky and when I turned around, the dude was looking at me with the screw face, like he wanted to start something!"

A Benz truly becomes a Benz at seventy miles an hour over the speed limit.

"Come on, I thought. Don't do me like that. You could be dead in four seconds, you fucking bitch. You know who you spilled your drink on!

"But do I tell myself he could lose his life right now in this club? Or say, Lord forgive him for he knows not what he does?

"See, even though I was just disrespected, it was up to me to look after his life because he didn't know what he was doing. You can't whip a baby's ass for throwing up. Until they understand what you're saying, you can't fault them. He was drunk, and I prayed for him, because I know that the next man may not be as gracious as me . . ."

"Will the streets ever respect that kind of move?"

"First of all, it's not easy to keep it real like that. Second, I don't care what motherfuckers think because I don't have to be real with anybody else but Him. All that fake shit doesn't matter to me because when I wake up, I crack that Bible and say what I have to say to get on with my day, and then before I go to bed, no matter how drunk I am, I crack that Bible again and pray. I pray for forgiveness every night, dog."

Cruising at 125 miles per hour, with no police in sight, DMX reaches for the CD player. The artist rarely listens to music that is currently on the radio; instead the stereos in his cars are filled with old-school R&B compilations and his own CDs. Occasionally a Scarface or a Nas album will slip its way into the rotation, but only for a few select songs, so the music *that DMX rides to is normally a soundtrack to years past. Tonight's mood calls for Atlantic Starr's "Silver Shadow."*

```
I remember gazing on those quiet nights
The stars were as bright as they could be
Wondering if things would ever go right
And if there was a spot up there for me
```

The song eases his mind.
"I didn't know why I liked this song in 1985, but something drew me to it. Now I listen to the words and realize that the words applied to me then, I just didn't know it."

```
Then one star got brighter by the minute
Strange that it seemed to have my name written in it
```

"In 1985, I didn't have any reason to thank my lucky stars," he says, relaxing back into his seat. "But that's when I was given the shadow and I think that I've been growing ever since. My life didn't get better and better since '85, but my talent developed, and that's the one part of me that no one can ever take away . . ."
DMX hangs a left and safely pulls into his driveway.

PART III

43

Taking It Back to the Streets

I can feel it coming in the air
Yeah, it's getting closer [46]

I WASN'T DOWN WITH ALL THAT PRETTY, HAPPY-GO-LUCKY SHIT.
In March of 1997, Puff Daddy suffered through the murder of his
man, the Notorious B.I.G., and then went straight to the top of the
music charts. Suge Knight and Death Row had stepped the game up
the year before when 2Pac sold a couple million copies of a double
album and proved to everyone that a real hip-hop artist could sell like
crazy (before 'Pac, it was thought that you had to be MC Hammer to
sell that many units), but then Puff did even better than that. That
summer he released his own album that had everyone in the fucking
world singing and dancing. (I guess not far from a Hammer move anyway.) My man had the radio on lock, the clubs on fire, had people
thinking that hip-hop was all about bright lights and shiny suits and
smiled all the way to the bank.

X, on the other hand, still lived in the dark. I never saw any bright
lights around me, nothing about my Tims and hoody was shiny. I
couldn't hate on what Puff was doing, but I wasn't with it. It just
wasn't me—but I also wasn't stupid. I knew that I needed a deal. I
had a kid. It felt like every fucking label in the world had already
dissed me. All the pups were already in the game and I was still
broke. But I needed to make sure that Lyor and Def Jam were committed to taking hip-hop back to the streets where it belonged. If they

wanted to do some other shit, then well, they could give me some money, but I made a promise to myself that I would not take my audience to the wrong place. I didn't wait all this time to get put on to sell myself out now.

So when Lyor said that he didn't want to change anything about me, that all he wanted to do was find me as large of an audience as possible for my music and, in fact, "taking it back to the streets" was going to be the idea behind how they wanted to market and promote me, he said all the right things. DMX, Ruff Ryders, Def Jam—*just let me do my motherfucking thing* . . .

44

"Who Is That *Last* Guy?"

Niggas will never win, this whole rap game is mine
As hot as you've ever been, I was that in '89 [47]

TOWARD THE END OF 1997, SOME OF THE SONGS THAT I HAD
done guest verses on were starting to get played on the radio. There
was the LOX's "Money, Power, Respect," LL Cool J's "4, 3, 2, 1,"
Cam'ron's "Pull It," and Mase's "24 Hours to Live."

"You can do better than that!" Puff said to me when I was in the
studio laying the vocals to the closing verse of "24 Hours." That made
me mad as a motherfucker, but he wanted a rap without too many
curses, so I wrote another one for him right there.

```
Twenty-four left, until my death
So I'm gon' waste a lot of lives but I'll cherish every
    breath
I know exactly where I'm going, but I'ma send you there
    first
And with the shit that I'll be doing, I'ma send you there
    worse⁴⁸
```

"Who is that *last* guy?" Angie Martinez, the afternoon DJ on HOT
97, said on the air when she first heard the song.

At the time, Puff was actually trying to sign me to his label. He kept telling Waah that he would offer me double whatever Def Jam's money was and give me some more dough for myself. I guess he didn't think that I was "too hard" anymore, probably because he saw the reaction of his own crowd.

It was Puffy's No Way Out tour at Madison Square Garden in Manhattan. Mase had asked me to do my "24 Hours to Live" verse onstage with him and the LOX. I only had twelve bars to do, but the Garden was sold out and I wanted to try to show everybody in that audience exactly what X was about. So I put on a green army fatigue outfit that had all these grenades hanging off the coat, a pair of black boots, and fit this ill gas mask on top of my head—DMX was ready for war.

See, people had heard me spit on a couple of songs by now, but they hadn't seen me yet, so it was only natural for them to wonder: "Well, we like what you're saying, homey, but how are you going to move onstage?"

When I got out there and felt the energy of twenty-thousand people, it was like nothing I had ever felt before. The audience loved every word that I said and cheered for me when I was done like *I was the star of the show! Awww, man. I can get used to this!*

> I've been living with a curse and now it's all about to end
> But before I go, say hello to my little friend
> But I gots to make it right, reconcile with my mother
> Try to explain to my son, tell my girl I love her[49]

The next night I was riding in a van on my way to the Garden for the second show and I heard HOT 97 give me more love on the radio.

"Yo, that new guy DMX did his thing onstage last night!"

I was amped.

"Yeah, baby. We're about to blow up," I started screaming to Tashera when I got back home. "It's about to go down!"

Boo Boo couldn't stop smiling.

45

"Where My Dogs At?"

THE BIGGEST SONG OF MY LIFE STARTED OFF AS A FREESTYLE. It was called "Get at Me Dog."

Like Ron G, DJ Clue was a mix-tape DJ who had a huge following in the streets. He had gotten a good response from putting this song I did with the LOX called "Niggas Done Started Something" on a few of his tapes, but was talking shit to Waah one day about why I always rhymed last on every song that I was on. Just like Gotti knew better with me and Jay-Z on "Time to Build," producers *still* couldn't put me in the middle of a song. I was so aggressive and rhymed so hard that it would have been detrimental to whoever came after me. It was a given that if I was on a joint, I was the closer. But Clue wanted to be hardheaded.

"I think I wanna hear your boy rhyme first," he used to tell Waah. "Let's see what he can do then . . ."

Waah knew all he had to do was tell me that someone was doubting me and I would get pumped.

Okay, Clue thinks I'm a fucking joke, huh?

I wrote the "Get at Me Dog" freestyle the day I went to Valhalla Hospital to get the wires taken off of my jaw. I had brought a pen and a pad with me to write in and was glad that I did because when the nurse told me that after four months of suffering, they couldn't take my appliances off that day because my doctor was on vacation, I suddenly had a lot of frustration to unload:

```
I'm the type to sit back and look at shit because crooked
    shit gets me amped . . .
```

Grease did the beat a few days later. He chopped up this old BT Express record that he got from PK and turned it into a wailing, bass-heavy track that just made me want to flow for days.

```
Bring all them pretty niggas thinking they gritty to one
    city
Let me show them niggas shitty
It's a pity, but for fifty
A motherfucker can get a bullet to hum to him
Put the gun to him
Hit 'em with something that come to 'em
But it run through 'em
Look what I done to 'em?
No more smiles
Got the whole top half of his head running wild . . .
But you don't hear me though, so I turn off the lights
We can take it to the streets, dog, turn off the mics . . .⁵⁰
```

The rhyme showed Clue exactly what I was made of but, more importantly, the "Get at Me Dog" freestyle marked the first time that I ever growled and barked on a record.

```
If you want war then you want more then you can stand
and this .44 will leave you with your dick in the sand
Who's the man?
Now you cats know for real
Get at me dog
[growl] [bark] What's the deal?
```

I didn't plan to bark like it, I didn't even really think about it before it came out of my mouth. I just identified so much with my pits, what they stood for and how they got down, that the sound came out of me naturally. It wasn't a gimmick. That growl and bark was a form of expression for me; it communicated how I was feeling. Little did I know that it was about to be a bark heard around the world.

The Clue freestyle hit the streets hard and once Def Jam heard what I did, they immediately had an idea for a first single. They thought I should turn the "get at me dog" phrase into the hook for a whole song. The LOX were on the freestyle as well (Gotti's boy Ja Rule was supposed to have done a part but couldn't get his lyrics ready in time) but Def Jam wanted me to do three whole verses on my own. If I could make that happen, I would have a first single that they just knew would go crazy in the clubs and blow up on radio.

I didn't want to do the record. I thought it would be meaningless. Why would my new label want to put out a song with me talking shit when I had so many other songs that actually said something?

Didn't they realize that I've talked shit for ten years already!

But Gotti helped convince me ("Dog, it's only one song!") and one night me, him, and Grease went to the studio, got Sheek from the LOX to do the hook, and flipped "Get at Me Dog" into a full-length single.

```
What must I go through to show you shit is real?
and I really never gave a fuck how niggas feel
I rob and steal
Not 'cause I want to, 'cause I have to . . .
Y'all niggas wanna be killers?
Get at me dog51
```

The record exploded. The song was instantly the rawest cut on radio.

DJ Funkmaster Flex broke the joint nationally. He played it over and over every night on HOT 97. One time, folks told me that he played it six or seven times in a row for a half hour straight! Gotti said that he never saw a song take off that fast, never felt the sound of hip-hop change so completely overnight, but he just knew that hip-hop kids had been yearning for an underdog. Street niggas from coast to coast were starving for someone whose music was talking to them on *their own* level, not from miles away in a million-dollar house, driving a fancy car.

Where my dogs at?

That was the call. It was in the street, it was in clubs; everywhere I went I heard it blaring. I actually didn't realize just how crazy folks were getting over the record until I did a show in the Bronx and when that beat came on there was complete pandemonium. Everybody got me so wild that night, I actually jumped into the crowd and got mobbed by a few hundred people (serves me right for watching too many white-boy concerts on TV thinking that's what you do when fans are going crazy over you in a club). Then some chick scratched a hole in my back with one of her nails, and the club's security rushed me out the back door thinking that I got stabbed when they saw me bleeding so much. Of course, I ran right back inside.

"Get at Me Dog" was the new anthem.

Where my dogs at?
We right here, dog . . .

46

Official Member of Society

THE SUCCESS OF MY RECORDING CAREER WASN'T REAL FOR me until I got my first check. Having "Get at Me Dog" be a big record wasn't enough to kill all of my doubts about what was happening, because I had had hit records in the street before and I knew I could still get jerked. But when I saw that first money, then I believed at least *something* was different this time. Checks are usually small, green pieces of paper, but when I got my first check from Def Jam, it was a huge monster joint about three times the size that I was used to! I didn't think it was real.

"How are they going to have me go into a bank with this bozo-looking check?"

Luckily, Uncle Ray had already hooked me up with the driver's license and the social security card so I didn't have to cash a fifteen-thousand-dollar check in a check-cashing place. I remember we had to run back and forth from City Hall to Motor Vehicles a few times just to get me all of the paperwork I needed to become an official member of society. I never gave a fuck about ID before, but I guess that's what you needed in this world to be considered human.

The first thing I did with the money was *buy* a little gold chain for myself and a brand-new pair of the Reebok DMXs that had just come out. Then I bought a twenty-five-hundred-dollar used Honda Civic from this guy on Ravine (it was only worth about half that, but I was just so open over having money and not having to steal the car that I paid him what he wanted) and brought the rest of the dough back home to Tashera.

When "Get at Me Dog" came out, Tashera and I were still living in Mulford. It was a fun time, though, because everybody in the projects was happy for me that I finally had a hit song on the radio and they were very eager to be friendly and show me love. Every night, folks would crowd around me on the front steps of the building to hear about all the things that I was doing.

"Yo spark, shark," folks would call over to my window to see if I was home and wanted to smoke a blunt.

I was still writing in the apartment every day and the night I wrote "Look Thru My Eyes" there were actually about five or six people chilling outside my window watching me come up with every line. When I finished, everybody let out a collective cheer.

But after about a month of smiles, Tashera and I started to recognize how phony and extra everyone was being. It bothered me that most of the people that were becoming so friendly with us now, never cared about us before. None of these niggas had ever asked to smoke with me *before* I got a big record deal, no one was stopping by the crib "just to say hi" *before* Flex was blowing me up on the radio.

"Hey, D, why don't you come upstairs for a minute?" random chicks started to ask me all the time on my way home.

Bitch, you weren't inviting me upstairs a month ago!

I couldn't ride with that one.

So shortly after I got that first bit of money, Tashera and I left the projects and moved to New Jersey. I was sad because I learned almost everything I knew from Yonkers. And for that, even though I didn't know everyone in Y-O, I loved everyone in Y-O from the bottom of my heart. They saw me grow. They saw me change, and that was some special shit. But folks were getting too ridiculous, so late one night Tashera and Ray just got all of our clothes together and got out of dodge. They didn't need a van because I told them to leave as many things as possible. Tashera wasn't so thrilled with that idea ("Earl, I paid for all this furniture!") but if we were going to leave my home for good, I wanted us to get a clean start.

"I see you!" an old lady called out to the two of them as they drove away. And after twenty-seven years, my time as a resident of Yonkers, New York, was over.

47

In the Lab

AFTER THE "GET AT ME DOG" FREESTYLE, IT DIDN'T TAKE
long for the streets to start anticipating a whole album from me, so it
was good that ever since Lyor's night at Powerhouse, me and Grease
had become more connected. I would see him there all the time and
we'd lay tracks down together. There was never a lot of extra bullshit
involved. It was always just "What's up, my nigga? You ready?" Then
we'd get in and get dirty—and make some memorable songs. I liked
his beats because they were never just beats. There were layers to his
tracks; he threw different instruments and sounds into the mix to say
different things. Even the joints that I didn't want to fuck with, the
ones that weren't my style, were still good, quality music.

The two of us had actually gone down to Atlanta together for a little while to record. I didn't have any Def Jam money at the time, so
me and Grease just turned the basement where we were staying into
our own private studio with an MP sampler, a pair of headphones,
some little speakers, and an amp, and banged out a bunch of ideas. No
engineers, no nothing. At the time, Waah and everybody else were
busy with the LOX, so even though it felt like niggas dropped us on
some stranded shit when we were down there having to call back
home and beg for dough, as usual I kind of liked the isolation and

after a couple of weeks I had written most of the lyrics that I ended up using on my first album.

Back in Yonkers, PK had also been spending a lot of hours in Powerhouse coming up with hot tracks. I was always very possessive about the music that I felt I could rhyme best to and I knew that there was always a lot of competition among the pups for PK's beats, so I made sure that if I went in the studio and heard him playing something that I liked, he put my name on it right away. PK always held me down by making sure that no one else tried to write to it. Checking on what PK was up to a couple of times in Powerhouse was how I ended up with the beats for "Stop Being Greedy" and "How's It Goin' Down."

I always came up with the hook before the lyrics. Songs were just much easier to write when I had a chorus in my head because once I knew what the theme was and the meaning of the whole piece was, then I just had to tell the story—and I had stories for days.

So with Grease and PK both giving me crazy tracks and Gotti helping me put everything together as an album, I felt that I was ready to make it happen whenever Def Jam was. There was just one more place I had to take it. One particular story that I really needed to tell . . .

I needed to talk about the devil.

Why is it every move I make turns out to be a bad one?
Where's my guardian angel? Need one, wish I had one.[52]

I called him Damien.

[Damien:] I'm right here, shorty / and I'ma hold you down.
[Damien:] You trying to fuck all these bitches? / I'ma
    show you how
But who?
[Damien:] Name's D like you / but my friends call me Damien
[Damien:] And I'm a put you into something / about this
    game we in.
[Damien:] You'll need to take it there, then you'll be

[Damien:] the hottest nigga ever living.
That's a given?
[Damien:] You'll see . . .

I didn't know how I could bring him across in the song, didn't know how to articulate his presence. Then I just opened the door to my soul and he was right there. He was right fucking there . . .

[Damien:] I got some weed . . . Go ahead, smoke it.
   Go ahead, drink it!
[Damien:] Go ahead and fuck shorty, you know I can keep
   a secret

He came out in a garbled, slightly high-pitched voice and as I expected, he was up to no good.

[Damien:] I'm about to have you driving, probably a Benz.
[Damien:] But we got to stay friends. Blood out, blood in

A deal with the dark was one that I had made many times. Whether it was something that I *needed* to get out of hunger, or something that I *wanted* to get out of temptation, throughout my life I agreed to do dirt and suffer the consequences. Even though I was beginning to understand the difference between *doing* wrong and *being* wrong, the repercussions of rolling with the devil were always severe:

Now I'm ready to chill, but you still want me to kill
[Damien:] Look at what I did for you, dog. Come on, keep
   it real
All right, fuck it, I'ma do it. Who is it this time?
[Damien:] Hey yo, remember that kid Shawn you used to be
   with in '89?
Nah, that's my man.
[Damien:] I thought I was your man?
But yo, that's my nigga!
[Damien:] Hey, who's your biggest fan?

[Damien:] You can do it, or give me your right hand,
    that's what you said.
I see now there's nothing but trouble ahead.

Earl wrote that song. Not D or X, but Earl. This was *his* battle with the devil, a battle that each and every day I tried so desperately to help him win. Earl was winning, I felt it, but I couldn't ever stop fighting.

That night I decided to call my album *It's Dark & Hell Is Hot*. It was the perfect title. The darkness described my biggest challenges; hell described the reality of the world that I was living in. After all these years, was the world finally ready to hear what I was trying to say? I was starting to see some signs, but I really didn't know yet. I just knew that I was trying my best to pour twenty-seven years of my life into the words of sixteen songs and a prayer.

48

Belly Up

ONE NIGHT, GOTTI BROUGHT ME TO MEET A FRIEND OF HIS named Al Monday. Gotti said a video director he knew named Hype Williams was making a film loosely based on Monday's life and wanted me to talk with him for a minute to see if I had a feel for the guy. After a few minutes, I told Gotti that while I didn't know his friend personally, he was like one of the many characters that I crossed paths with in the 'hood and because of that I *knew* who he was. I could read his behavior and understand why he did the things he did. I didn't know that Hype was stuck without anyone to play this role in his film or that it was a couple of weeks before filming was supposed to begin, but after Gotti's recommendation and a subsequent audition, I was cast in the lead role in *Belly*. It was the first time that I had ever thought about acting.

I liked being in front of the camera and even though Hype had us rehearse too many fucking times (and the baby oil he had us shining ourselves up with got real aggravating after a few days), I enjoyed it. Uncle Ray still had his job in the prison, but had slowly taken on the role of my manager and so it became his responsibility to get me up in the mornings to go to set. Hype always had a 7 A.M. call and that was never easy. Ray had to fight with me all the time to get out of bed. But *Belly* allowed me to lose myself for a minute and think about someone else's life struggles and hanging out with Nas and Method Man all day was a lot of fun. They were successful rappers but they were also real niggas and that was still the most important thing to me.

Hype did do me dirty one time, though. For my sex scene, he cleared the set but put monitors all over the house that we were filming in. Everywhere I looked there were girls sitting up in front of the screens watching. Even the woman who owned the place showed up on set that day. I couldn't do anything about it, so I just told Hype to keep the room that I was in real warm so that my balls wouldn't shrivel up.

"Keep this motherfucker hot, Hype! Don't have me looking like li'l man on film!"

I didn't like shorty's body double too much, either. The scene called for me to pretend to have sex with her from behind and I told her beforehand how I was going to do it.

"Aight. I'ma throw your legs up, pump you a couple of times, then flip you over dumb fast and hit it from the back—"

"Well, just don't put your tongue in my mouth," she answered.

Now that was stupid. *What are you, the fucking Exorcist or something?* How am I going to put my tongue in your mouth from behind?

After the scene, there was a lot of blushing going down from a lot of the women that were watching. My time spent in jail didn't make me self-conscious at all about being naked in front of people, but I was glad Tashera stayed home that day because I wouldn't have wanted Boo Boo to get mad.

During the final week of filming the movie, I got a "One Love Boomer" tattoo on my back in memory of my dog. I had thought about doing it ever since he died. People asked me why I made it so big, why I had the design stretch from shoulder to shoulder, but I just knew whoever asked me that didn't understand the relationship I had with that dog. They didn't understand the relationship I had with *all* of my dogs, and they definitely didn't know Boomer. Boomer was nothing less than the greatest friend I ever had, and the tattoo was my way of paying him permanent tribute.

I wanted the "Get at Me Dog" video to look as different as possible. Everyone agreed that it should have the exact opposite feeling of the superclean, grass is so green, sky is so blue, multicolored look that Puffy and others had made the norm with the Biggie and Mase joints. If I was serious about "taking it back to the streets" then my first video needed to look as dirty and grimy as possible. There would be no iced-out watches on my side of the world. So first we decided to film it at the Tunnel during a regular party night. The Tunnel was Funkmaster Flex's home base infamous for attracting the most street, ghetto hip-hop crowd in New York, and when Hype took his cameras in there that Sunday to do the video, the whole club went nuts. Folks were everywhere wilding out; it felt like a riot was about to jump off, but it was all about the music. I had to perform the song about twelve fucking times and every single time the crowd rocked with me! It was hectic, I was sweating like crazy, it was hard to breathe, but this was my element. To rock a club like the Tunnel, with my own song, with my own people in the audience? This is what I had waited for my whole life. Waah, Darrin, Grease, Gotti, everybody was in full dog mode because it was going down. We could feel it. I was actually about to fly . . .

When Hype put a black-and-white strobe effect over the final cut of the video, "Get at Me Dog" looked even more ridiculous. There was nothing else like it on TV. It had a realness, a recklessness to it that fit the aggression of the song and represented what I was about. I loved it.

But when MTV refused to play the video, "Get at Me Dog" also gave me my first lesson in big music politics. MTV said that the song was too violent and would incite a riot. The phrase "Where my dogs at" was an example of how the lyrics were gang related.

Huh? When you got a song called "Smack My Bitch Up" in heavy rotation at that same time? "Smack my bitch up" is a direct and disrespectful threat, but I'm the artist you're scared of?

MTV said they would only play "Get at Me Dog" if I rerecorded a clean version of the song. Gotti tried to get me to do it one night in the studio, but I didn't care about the "larger" audience that I could get from being on MTV and I refused to let anyone try to get me to compromise my music. I played pool all night instead and never redid it. Needless to say, MTV never played the video. I'm glad all the other stations held me down.

49

Def Jam #1

MY SECOND LESSON ABOUT THE MUSIC BUSINESS CAME WHEN the first ads for *It's Dark & Hell Is Hot* started to appear in magazines. I liked the image, especially how it was tinted that bloodred color, but was curious as to why Def Jam's logo wasn't on the ad. Ruff Ryders was listed underneath my profile along with "333 526 #1."

See, what Gotti had told me about Def Jam was right: They had sold sixty million dollars' worth of music the year Lyor came to see me at Powerhouse. The problem was that they spent over one hundred million dollars to make that sixty. While they had big artists down with them like Method Man, Redman, and Onyx, they weren't selling that many records. So Lyor and Russell Simmons, the founder of Def Jam, were under a lot of pressure at the time from Polygram, Def Jam's parent company, to increase profits. Polygram was unhappy with the label being outsold and around the time Lyor signed me was threatening to write him and Russell a good-bye check. But if that ever happened, Lyor had a plan: "333 526," the spelling of Def Jam on a phone keypad, was the name of a new company Lyor came up with that he hoped to form with his top people from Def Jam if Polygram decided to lower the boom. He thought he could negotiate with Polygram for them to let him have me (along with Gotti and Ja Rule), and I would be his new label's first artist. So running my ads with

"333 526 #1" and not the Def Jam logo was a way for him to present the new label to the industry, a slick kind of insurance policy against being fired. Knowing about this fear of losing his job explained to me why the man started going so crazy a few weeks later once he saw how well "Get at Me Dog" was doing.

"DMX is going to save the company!" Lyor used to run up and down Def Jam's hallways screaming. "He is going to save us all because Def Jam is a company that was *born* in the streets, and now, thanks to the Darkman X, we are going *back* to our roots!"

I didn't give a fuck who I was saving or what label I was going to be on, I just wanted to be heard.

50

The Final Call

Take away hate, now I'm supposed to love the one that cursed me
The one that wouldn't give me a cup of water when I was thirsty
It was always him versus me, but now I gotta teach him
Personal feelings put aside 'cause now I gotta reach him[53]

SOMEBODY TRIED TO DRUG ME THAT NIGHT.

Tashera and I were in a bar in Yonkers having a drink. Since we had moved to Jersey, I was hanging out a lot in Y-O, it was still home, the only place I really knew, and wifey and I were in there chilling with a few folks. A few minutes before I wanted to leave, I went outside to back up my truck from where I had parked to the front door so that Boo Boo wouldn't have to walk up the whole block. When I walked out, I left my drink on the bar. When I came back a few minutes later, I went to pick my drink back up but the bartender, a nigga I knew from School Street, told me not to worry about it.

"Forget that small shit, X," he said, handing me a bottle of Hennessey instead. "Here you go, dog."

The bottle was open and there was a tissue stuck in the top, but it looked brand new because I could see the liquor still in the neck of it. Now this was my throw-back-a-bottle-of-Hennessey-a-day-time so I didn't wait to get to drinking.

When Tashera and I left, I saw my man Karate Kato outside. He was the bouncer at the bar and I had known him for years. He must have seen how much I had been drinking because when I went to my truck he offered to follow me home.

"I just wanna make sure you all right, dog," he said to me. He was with my other man Hip.

Then I saw this Mulford nigga standing outside. I didn't know his name but I recognized him because I had robbed him a few times and I noticed that he looked like he had had too much to drink himself.

"Yo, where you going, dog?" I called out to him. "Come on, I'll give you a ride."

Kato and Hip looked at me like I was crazy when I said that, but I was trying to help the brother out so me, him, and Tashera climbed into my truck and drove off.

The next thing I remember is trying to make a left-hand turn and almost falling over into the passenger's seat. I lost my grip on the steering wheel, lost control of the truck, and almost hit a couple of people who were trying to cross the street in front of me.

"WATCH WHERE YOU'RE GOING!!"

The next thing I knew I was in Mulford Projects.

How the hell did I get here?

Tashera told me as soon as he saw me losing my bearings the nigga I had given a ride to started yelling about how I had robbed him and that he wasn't going to let me do him dirty no more. He was going on and on about how I "needed to pay for something." Then when I pulled up in front of his building he started wilding and tried to grab the steering wheel from me.

"Yo, fuck that, X! I wanna drive!"

Everything was still a blur but somehow I was able to push him off of me. He ran into the building and then Kato and Hip got out of their car and dragged me out of my truck onto the pavement. Then they carried me inside after him.

My man was there waiting. He was wearing a long gray coat and underneath I could see that he had on a bulletproof vest.

Immediately, he started talking greasy to Tashera. "Your boyfriend robbed me, girl.

"And I ain't trying to let that shit slide. . . ."

Words like that directed to Boo Boo must have triggered something in me.

That's when I remember waking up.

"Yo, that's my fucking wife, nigga. You can't be serious. I'll fucking kill you!"

I was the man of this house.

That's when he pulled out. It was a nice-size gun, black with a long barrel. I think it was a .357 and he had it pointed right at me.

Now Karate Kato was given that name that for a reason, so anybody who knew what they were doing with a piece would have shot him first, and Hip was a thorough nigga but not a killer, so I knew that this was not a good situation. But as soon as that coward pointed that piece at me, without thinking about what I was doing, I just grabbed the gun right out of his hand. Before he had a chance to say a word, I just snatched it from him and got an attitude. He didn't get off a shot.

"What the fuck is you doing? I robbed you already, nigga, you're a bitch!"

I was offended. Here I was, in a better place than I had ever been in my entire life, about to fulfill a dream that I had struggled twelve years to achieve, standing next to the woman that I would die for and this motherfucker was about to try to take it all from me?

NO!

My instinct refused to let that happen. Twisted, or in whatever state I was put in by that poisoned bottle of Hennessey, my second nature took over and saved my life.

"Get the fuck outta here!"

Later, Tashera and I thought that niggas in the bar had probably been scheming on me the whole night. They knew it was just me and her together and I would probably drink anything that was given to me. So with a quick exchange of glances, the bartender and his man outside thought they got me where they wanted me, just like that day when ten niggas jumped me, just like that night when three niggas shot at me, just like when the old man swung that aluminum bat at my head and I . . . *slipped*.

But did I slip that day in the parking lot or did I *trip*? Slipping you do on your own but when you trip, something, somewhere, has gotten in your way. Was there something on my feet the night I flew around that corner and avoided those bullets? Something in my brain that made me wake up in that project hallway with enough time to grab a loaded gun? All of these times my life was spared . . .

51

May 19, 1998

ON MAY 19, 1998, DEF JAM RELEASED MY FIRST ALBUM, *It's Dark & Hell Is Hot.* It debuted at #1 on the *Billboard* albums chart and sold more than a quarter of a million copies in its first week in the stores. Like the way "Get at Me Dog," "Fuckin' Wit' D," and "Stop Being Greedy" became big hits in the clubs, Faith Evans added vocals to a remix of "How's It Goin' Down" that helped turn a laid-back groove into a top ten single and "Ruff Ryders Anthem," the first track that my man Swizz Beatz ever produced, became the monster jam of the summer.

```
Stop, drop, shut 'em down, open up shop . . . that's how
    Ruff Ryders roll
```

"Let Me Fly" was on the album, as was "Damien," but the devil's presence was balanced by "The Convo," my conversation with the Lord. And while I got a lot of heat for my lyrics on "X Is Coming" ("if you got a daughter older than fifteen, I'ma rape her"), those critics seemed to forget that I had a prayer on the album as well.

(Ironically, a woman actually did charge me with rape that summer. Purely a case of mistaken identity, I wasn't even at the party where the alleged assault took place. The case made its way to trial and my lawyer, Murray Richman, used DNA evidence to help clear me of all charges.)

Later that summer, Def Jam challenged me, Waah, and Darrin to deliver another album right away, and when *Flesh of My Flesh, Blood of My Blood* was released on December 22 of that same year, it sold more than seven hundred thousand copies, again debuting as the #1 album in the country. That was the first time in history that an artist released two albums in the same year that both debuted at the top of the *Billboard* charts. Safe to say, Lyor never lost his job.

I loved every song on my first two albums, my soul said what it needed to say and found many ears. I kept it as honest to my life and my spirit as I knew how, and because of that, I also knew that whoever chose to ride with me would not be taken to the wrong place. Now I just had to take care of my own heart.

"Earl, I'm letting you know that we're getting married when you come home," Tashera said to me before I went on tour for my second

album. "I'll take care of all the arrangements while you're working, but we're getting married."

I didn't even have to answer her. Boo Boo knew me and loved me more than anyone in this world and in my mind and in my heart I had already been married to her for years.

Tashera didn't ask me to wear a suit for the ceremony, but I knew she'd be rocking the dress and heels so I wanted to step my game up. Ray took me to this store in Harlem and Darrin, who was one of my seven best men, along with Waah, Ray, my uncles Pinky and Buzzy, and my brother Joe, bought me my Versace suit as a gift. When I looked at myself in the mirror, in that beautiful white three-piece, I had to admit that I looked damn good.

Those suit-and-tie motherfuckers ain't got nothing on me!

Tashera was the most beautiful girl in the world that day. My angel in the blue-and-white robe. She would always be a source of light in my life and where there's light, darkness can never take over. The gifts of love and understanding are what she gave me, and for that, I would never be able to repay her.

And to my boo, who, stuck with a nigga through
All the bullshit, you'll get yours, because it's due[54]

Epilogue

Look within and you will know
Where you're coming from, and where you gotta go[55]

"I WOULDN'T CHANGE A THING ABOUT MY WHOLE LIFE, DOG," DMX says, walking in the house. "Not one fucking thing."

It's 4 A.M. The sky is large and black and quiet. The thermostat reads eighty-five degrees. Sports highlights flicker on the muted television and the radio is on. X is in for the night.

"It's like I wouldn't be where I'm at. Not just *physically* where I'm at, but *mentally* where I'm at. It's like I've gone to see my father again. He still lives with his family in Philadelphia and art is still his passion. He actually painted a picture of me one time when I went to his studio. Philly has become the seeing place for me, the knowing place, and out there I learned that in terms of how the situation went down, my father wasn't the bad guy for leaving me. It was more just some circumstance shit . . . My mother wasn't the bad guy in my life, either. I love her. She just wasn't ready for what she had, and life with her, for whatever it's worth, made me a little deeper."

There have been thirty-one years of chaos, struggle, and survival for Earl Simmons, thirty-one years of a life too real, and now, perhaps, some truths have been found.

"Do you know what it is, dog? Now I know that the Lord has always been taking care of me. He was taking care of me *before* I even came out the pussy. Before I spoke my first word or shed my first tear He was there with me. I was just never able to see or trust that until now."

I never knew a love like this before
Messin' with the thug life, I missed it all

You opened the doors and let me in
I'm down for the cause, so let's begin
Prayers that you give to me, I give to them
Same way you live in me, I live in them
Life is a blessing now
You got me smiling from inside of my heart, when inside
    it was dark
And it doesn't rain anymore, only sunshine
No pain anymore, I really love my
You washed away the tears with the fears
I'm happier than I've ever been in my life, the whole
    thirty years . . .[56]

"You've been very lucky."

"Nah, it ain't luck. Luck lasts for a few hours, sometimes a day or two, but not a lifetime. I'm not alive because I'm lucky—*with as much dirt as I've done and pain that I've caused*—I'm alive because I'm blessed."

His point is hard to argue with, but "what about all the pain?"

To live is to suffer . . .

"I think the chosen ones are the ones that struggle more. The Lord's children always start from the dirt up. If you only start from halfway up, then you're going to know less and you're going to be worth less to Him, but there was something that I had to see, *that He wanted me to see*, so I could be what He wanted me to be."

"And what does He want you to be?"

"The greatest gift the Lord has given me is the gift of the word, the ability to communicate with, and I know now that I'm here to share everything that I have learned. That's why I've always said I don't want *sales*, I want *souls*. Fuck a sale, a sale is eleven dollars, thirteen dollars. But if you give me a soul, I've got that for life and I'm going to try my best to bring it to the right place."

```
Now if I take what he gave me and I use it right
In other words, if I listen and use the light
Then what I say will remain here after I'm gone
Still here, on the strength of a song, I live on⁵⁷
```

"Folks miss so much because they've been blinded by the diamonds and the fat asses and the fucking cars. That's all they've been trained to focus on, so that's all they see. But this music is not just a bunch of fucking words, it means something, it stands for something."

```
But to survive, well, that's to find the meaning in the
    suffering
```

Earl gets up and walks over to the window.

"I don't think I'm gonna be in this rap game long, dog. Five years, that's it, and I've got three and a half in now." DMX turns around to look me in my eyes. "There's a higher calling for me and I'm no longer afraid or ashamed of it."

```
[To God:] You know that one day I'll speak the Word
You know that when I do I will be heard
You know that you gave me a permanent smile
You know this, Father, because I am your child⁵⁸
```

"You sound like a preacher."

"Maybe. If it comes like that, I will embrace it with open arms, but it's not so much *where* I think I'm going, it's what I speak to and how I *feel* about what I speak to. Sometimes I get skeptical about saying shit because it might sound stupid to some niggas, but then I get to the point where it doesn't matter and you always gotta walk through to talk to. If I've never been on Franklin Avenue, I can't tell you a motherfucking thing about Franklin Avenue. A preacher can't tell me to put down a gun, if a preacher never had a gun, never bust a gun. 'Nigga, you ever did it? All right, then. Shut the fuck up . . . ' But if you *have* done it, then you get their ear for a little longer.

"That's why I start off all of my shows with 'fuck you,' 'suck my dick,' 'where my niggas at,' but then at the end I hit you with the 'Prayer.' I have to say, 'fuck that bitch' to get you to listen, or 'smoke that blunt' or 'I robbed this nigga' to get your attention. I talk to you like you expect me to talk to you, like a nigga *should* talk to you, but then I bring you somewhere else. Okay, you listening now? Then check this out; come over here for a minute. I wanna show you something.

"Pain is a lot easier to deal with when it's ours, not just yours."

```
When it rains it pours
Now my pains are yours, as yours were once mine
Divine
Revolving doors⁵⁹
```

"So now that you've told your story and there are so many more listeners, what do you say?"

"I didn't feel like I was worth anything for a long time, dog, but I did everything that I could to hold on to my dream and you can't ever be afraid of doing that."

```
Shit wasn't right and it was all blamed on me
Didn't know I was special till this rap shit came to be
Gave me a way out . . .⁶⁰
```

"It's like a lot of folks like to draw, but when they pop up on the block on some drawing shit, niggas look at them like they're crazy.

But you gotta say, 'Fuck that. *This is what I like to do,*' because that's your real shit. If you don't get a chance to fulfill it, after a while you forget that your dream exists. You close the door on it, like forget it, I'm about getting money and fucking bitches. But God didn't make hustlers or robbery niggas or dope fiends—you just have to allow yourself to consider more than that."

> Places that I have been, things that I have seen
> What you call a nightmare, are what I have as dreams[61]

DMX made history again in 2001 when his fourth album, *The Great Depression*, debuted at #1 on the *Billboard* albums chart, making that a string of four in a row. He has sold over fifteen million albums, headlined a few national tours, and has now become a worldwide star at the box office. He has connected with generations of young people who are sparked by the aggression that he never tries to hide, and become a hero for those who relate to the pain that he is so willing to share. For someone that "just wanted to be heard," he has gone way beyond his goal.

But there is a psychic toll that is often charged to an artist when they achieve this level of super-success, the frustrating ironies of being adored by millions of people that you don't know—and definitely don't know you. And when you've chosen to take this time to ask yourself the most difficult questions, to *look inside the deepest, darkest corners of your life*, it's not hard to imagine conflict, or nightmares.

"I ain't gonna front, I kinda like X. X keeps me good, 'hood to the wood, and I kinda miss robbing and stealing. That rush, it kept a nigga hungry. So I think I need him for now . . . but I'm also trying to develop the different parts of myself and learn how to control the anger. It's like I don't wanna see nobody die no more . . . I'll still take it there if I have to, but I don't want to see the results of that. It hurts too much."

DMX finishes the last bottle of Heineken.

"One day I hope to turn around and say, 'X has left the building.'"

"And would that be Earl talking?"

"Yeah, probably."

· · · · ·

"Phoenix!" Earl calls out to his dog. "Come here, girl."

Awakened by our conversation, the puppy eagerly jumps on her owner's lap.

"I love the shit out of my family, dog, I really do. My kids are the best things that could have ever happened to me and I love my wife to death. She knows that I can't see life without her . . . but sometimes I wish that it was just me and I had no one to love because then I would have no one to be concerned about. It's like on one level, I love people, because I see their hurt and feel their pain. For that, I'm here to be taken advantage of."

Don't let me go to waste; let not my life be in vain.

"But on another level I don't even like people collectively because people don't show, because they don't know, unconditional love. It's always I love you . . . *unless you fuck my girlfriend*. Or, I love you . . . *unless you steal something from me*. I don't want that.

"I've been a loner my whole life and alone is still where I feel most comfortable. Now that I don't feel confined by anything anymore but the will of my spirit; I wish I could be a person and just . . . fly . . . fly with the sun in my face and not worry about crashing."

The thought closes his eyes.

"Fault me for wanting that, but that's what I want," he says, opening them again after a pause, "and if I have to pay with my life to get it, I will . . . but my life will be poetic."

It's 7 A.M. The dawn of another desert day is on its way. The TV still flickers, but outside the sky is large and quiet. The faint colors of sunrise begin to paint a new picture.

At the end of this part of his journey, DMX doesn't pretend to have found all of life's meaning. He may, like the rest of us, never find it all, but there is a commitment there to keep working. And, although so much of what he is has come out of his isolation, today he is not alone. There are folks in the desert who will go wherever he goes, a dog who will lie by his side, and a woman he loves who will stay next to her cell phone.

X may or may not have left the building. Who knows? But at least for today, Earl Simmons will get a good night's sleep.

"I'm tired, dog," he says. "Time to take it in."

Appendix (Song Lyrics)

"SLIPPIN'"
Flesh of My Flesh, Blood of My Blood

See to live is to suffer but to survive, well
that's to find meaning in the suffering.

Chorus
Hey yo I'm slippin', I'm fallin', I can't get up
Hey yo I'm slippin', I'm fallin', I can't get up
Hey yo I'm slippin', I'm fallin', I gots to get up
Get me back on my feet so I can tear shit up!
(Repeat)

I been through mad different phases, like mazes, to find my way
And now I know that happy days are not far away
If I'm strong enough I'll live long enough to see my kids
Doing something more constructive with their time than bids
I know because I been there, now I'm in there
Sit back & look at what it took for me to get there
First came the [Howl!] the drama with my mama
She got on some fly shit [What!] till I split
And said that I'ma be that seed that doesn't need much to succeed
Strapped with mad greed and a heart that doesn't bleed
I'm ready for the world or at least I thought I was
Baggin' [Uhh!] when I caught a buzz for thinking about how short I was
Going too fast it wouldn't last but yo I couldn't tell
Group homes & institutions, prepared my ass for jail
They put me in a situation forcing me to be a man
When I was just learning to stand without a helping hand
Damn! Was it my fault, something I did
To make a father leave his first kid? At seven doing my first bid
Back on the scene at fourteen with a scheme
To get more cream than I'd ever seen in a dream
And by all means I will be living high off the hog
And I never gave a [What!] about much but my dog
That's my only [Howl!] I would hit off with my last
Just another little [Come on!] headed nowhere fast

Chorus

That ain't the half, life gets worse as I get older
Actions become bolder, heart got colder
Chip on my shoulder that I dared a nigga to touch
Didn't need a click 'cause I scared a nigga that much
One deep went to <edited> startin' <edited> for kicks
Catchin' vicks, throwin' bricks, gettin by bein' slick
Used to get high just to get by
Used to have to [Howl!] in the morning before I get fly
I ate something. A couple of forties made me hate somethin'
I did some [Arf!] now I'm ready to take something
Three years later showing signs of stress
Didn't keep my hair cut or give a fuck how I dressed
I'm possessed by the darker side, livin' the cruddy life
Shit like this kept a nigga with a bloody knife
Wanna make records but I'm all fucked up
I'm slippin' I'm fallin' I can't get up

Chorus

Wasn't long before I hit rock bottom
[Howl!] was like, "Damn!" look how that <edited> got him
Open like a window, no more Indo, look at a video
Sayin' to myself that could've been yo <edited> on the TV
Believe me it could be done
Somethin's got to give. It's got to change 'cause now I've got a son
I've got to do the right thing for shorty
And that means no more getting high, drinking forties
So I get back lookin' type slick again
Fake niggas jump back on my dick again
Nothin' but love for those that know how it feel
And much respect to all my niggas that kept it real
Be strong kept a nigga from doing wrong
[Uhh!] who they is and this is your fucking song
And to my Boo who stuck with a nigga through
All the bullshit you'll get yours because it's due

"COMING FROM"
Flesh of My Flesh, Blood of My Blood

Believe me, when I say
Before light, there was dark

Chorus [Mary J. Blige]
If I don't know where I'm coming from, where would I go?
If I don't know where I'm coming from, where would I go?
(Got to keep it real with me)
If I don't know where I'm coming from, where would I go?
(So the hell with you)
If I don't know where I'm coming from, where would I go?
(I think I'm going to the top)

Places that I've been, things that I have seen
What you call a nightmare, are what I have as dreams
Bad as that may seem, I know it's only going to get worse
Love, a slug, which one am I gonna get first?
My journey's been a rough one, I'm not sure when it began
But the way it's looking, I kind of know when it's gonna end
Spread love, hold me down baby, it's gonna be a rough ride
Niggas give us plenty of room, 'cause I guess enough died
Let me travel, 'cause my intentions are to travel in peace
Fuck around I lay you down, you hit the gravel and cease
I could be a beast, or I could be a gentleman
But if you ain't my dog, you gonna be like 'Oh, it's him again'
Niggas will never win, this whole rap game is mine
Hot as you ever been, I was that in '89
Seek and you shall find, look within and you will know
Where you're coming from, and where you gotta go

Chorus

I will spend mad time in one spot, plotting my next move
Trying to figure out why is it, that X do what X do
Some questions go unanswered, that's what I'm afraid of
Sometimes I can't show, but I know what I'm made of
They made love, or should I say they made lust
Found there didn't have to be love there, 'cause they made us
I got quite a few sisters. I was the only boy
But being with my dog, was my only joy
Like a kid with a new toy, I forgot about the grime

297

Escaped the misery, didn't think about the crime
Lost all track of time, was in another world
Everybody knew Earl, but there was another Earl
Lighter side of the dark, fight in the park but wouldn't wanna
Stayed too far but when they jumped me, became a good runner
One by one they all went under, so I had the last laugh
They all thought it all was a joke, but I had the last laugh

Chorus

I feel the ghost from within, coming back to haunt me
Stay loving my peoples, even though they don't want me
When I was bad, I was forgotten, like I was dead and rotten
Should've been getting love, but instead was plotting
Shit wasn't right, and it was all blamed on me
Didn't know that I was special till this rap shit came to be
Gave me a way out, showed me it was better to teach
Than bust niggas with the .44 leave 'em dead in the streets
Over beef that was worth less than the cost of the slugs
That I bought to kill them
And that's because I thought I ought to kill them
Little did I know, death wasn't right
Didn't always show every breath was a life
That was to be captured in suspended animation
To be felt by all, understood by every nation
What's the sense of hating, when I can show love?
What's the sense of faking, when I can show blood?

Chorus

"DOGS FOR LIFE"
Flesh of My Flesh, Blood of My Blood

Chorus
I will rob and steal with ya, dog nigga what
Ride till we die, on till it's up
Thick black blood, where's my dogs?
Uh, there's my dogs

Now who I am is who I'll be until I die

Either accept it or don't fuck with it
But if we gon' be dogs then you stuck with it.
Let me go my way but walk with me
See what I see, watch me, then talk with me
Share my pain, make it a little easier to deal with
'Cause despite all the fame, *you*, I'm a keep it real with
Rob and steal with. Dog nigga what
Ride till we die, on till it's up.
Love is love and I enjoy the love,
But when it's conflict then it destroys the love.
You can't toy with love. Niggas take it to the heart
You ain't gon' find too many niggas willing to bark in the dark
Keep your head from the start, don't fuck it up now,
Later on don't even hit me like, 'Fuck it up how?'
You my dog and I die for you, let's keep it like that,
Give me unconditional love, and I give it right back.

Chorus

Most niggas make movies, but niggas like us make it happen
The shit we used to do never thought that we would make it rappin'
But now we here, at the same place at the same time,
And got jokes 'cause now niggas get it, with the same rhyme
Yeah niggas is living comfortable, 'cause life is all good
But one thing we must remember, is that life is all 'hood
And the casket's all wood and we all take there one day
Shit today is Sunday we both could be there on Monday
Life is funny like that. What? Bug the fuck out
Sometimes I take it to the church, sometimes I thug the fuck out
Niggas get dropped the fuck out they boots, violating family rules
Motherfucker, stay in your shoes!
Now see what you need to do, is chill shorty
Somebody please come and get him before I kill shorty
I will do for my niggas as they would do for me
Bust a faggot like you for free, wanna see?
Come on!

Chorus

I'm always surrounded by dogs, for the love
The only niggas I fuck with is thugs, nigga what!
Blood in blood out, vatos locos homes, there's nosotros homes
When we smoke them chromes, and how we broke them bones.
While the last niggas is ass niggas,

The ski mask niggas to trash niggas they ass niggas. Pussy.
And half you cats can't even flow
And when I hear y'all niggas around my way all I hear is, 'Well, you know.'
But that's a whole 'nother issue, right now we on this
We keep spittin' like this, how the fuck we gonna miss?
'Cause the camp is strong, and the stamp is strong
Double-R motherfucker, keep the caskets flowing
You done got yourself caught up in some shit you can't handle
And you, know I can't stand you, your man, too!
This one time I'ma let a dog be a dog
But I'ma see you in the ring and when it's on then it's on

Chorus

"LET ME FLY"

It's Dark & Hell is Hot

If you love something let it go, if it comes back to you it's yours.
If it doesn't, it never was.
Hold me down, baby

Chorus
Either let me fly, or give me death
Let my soul rest, take my breath
If I don't fly, I'ma die anyway.
I'ma live on but I'll be gone any day
(repeat)

Hold me down.
Niggas wanna know me now
Didn't want to play with me, wanted to show me how
No meow
It's all about the bark
Let the dog loose, baby. It's about to spark
Light up the night, like the 4th of July
Niggas know, when I let go, niggas die
If it's why and you don't know, you slow
Like Baltimore, if you ain't trying to go, you blow
I soak up all the pain and accept it in silence

When I let go it's violence, 'cause the wildest
is the dog barking up the tree for the cat
In the fog but all y'all niggas see is the bat
Flappin' away, but I'm blind like Stevie
Niggas don't hear me, still tryin' to see me
Stop being greedy, ya heard what I said
Let me go, let me flow, or I'm dead

Chorus

I sold my soul to the devil, and the price was cheap
And yo, it's cold on this level, 'cause it's twice as deep
But you don't hear me, ignorance is bliss and so on
Sometimes it's better to be thought dumb
Shall I go on?
You on the real, what the deal? It's a mystery
How is it I can live and make history?
If you don't see it, then it wasn't meant for you to see
If you wasn't born with it, it wasn't meant for you to be
But you can't blame me for not wanting to be held
Locked down in a cell where the soul can't dwell
If this is hell, call me the devil and give me the key
For it can't be worse than the curse that was given to me
It's what I live for, you take away that and I'm gone
There's a difference between doing wrong and being wrong
And that ain't right
Just keep it fair, baby
Put me in the air and I'll take it there, baby

Chorus

I'ma flow regardless because I'm an artist until I'm trapped
I'ma continue to hit the hardest whether I scrap or rap
Give me death but you ain't my friend
I see it in your eyes, you contemplate my end
You waitin' for that bend in the road, where you were told
That you would go, when you were old
And if you died young, it was cold
Sold!
Not for nearly what it was worth
Think back twenty-six years, be like what in his birth
Was a miscarriage and I never existed?
Have I given something that if taken away you would've missed it?

301

Didn't know, but I persisted
It was the call of the wild
I merely say what's in my heart, and you call it a style
Don't put it in a cage.
Don't mistreat it
You say you hunger for knowledge?
Here it is, eat it
Another song completed is another thought captured
Let me do my thing I got it locked wit' this rap shit

"HEAT"

Flesh of My Flesh, Blood of My Blood

Chorus
The heat is on. Are y'all really ready to fly?
The heat is on. Are y'all really ready to die?
The heat is ooooon.
Have your mother ready to cry
The heat is on, huh
The heat is on, you know

The heat is on what's my next move
Do I stick with the score, or get with the door?
Feds got the drop in the back of the U-Haul
Snipers on the roof. Chance of getting away? Too small
Tell 'em like this, 'Look, it's gon' be a shoot-out
Whoever make it out meet back at the new house. Good luck
If I don't see you again. Peace
Let's handle our business with these government police
You and you go out the front. You take the back
You cover the first two and I'll take the sack'
Boomer didn't make it, neither did Stan
Now it's three niggas, splitting four hundred grand
We all feel the loss but enjoy the profit,
The game is the same and nothing gonna stop it
Most times you make it, one time you won't
All a nigga could really do is have the vest under the coat

Chorus

Me and my two mans gave money twenty grand
For a scam they don't get that condo in the sand
And chances of gettin' caught slim, next to none
Now we like three deep and need that extra gun
Bump into my man I remember from up north
I remember he had principles and wasn't nothing soft
Off with discuss just what's going dizzy
Everybody got it. All right let's get busy
Run up in the bank. Bitch, hit the deck!
Yo bust money and get the keys off his neck
We on the clock, three minutes until we finished
Feds are on the way, but I'm tryin' to see spinach
In and out duffle bag across the back
Extra large sports coat to cover up the mack
Feds they attack, I spit lead out, niggas spread out
Run up on a civilian in his car, make him get out

Chorus

High speed chasing, racing through the streets
Death's in the air, I can taste it through the heat
My partner's goin' fast. I don't think he's gonna last
And if he don't, I'ma hit his wife with his half
But that's the type of nigga I am this ain't just rappin'
I made it, he didn't, but hey, shit happens
What can I do, but go on livin'?
Fleein' from the condo, I go on a ribbon
Life goes on, that may sound wrong but hey
We all live by the rules of the game we play
Day to day, death is a possibility
The way I play is a vest stops you from killin' me
It's too hot to be in the heat 'cause it's on
Too hot to be in the street, so I'm gone
Go back to being discreet live long
Till one day, either me or the heat is gone
Come on!

Chorus 2x

"WHAT THESE BITCHES WANT" featuring Sisqo
And Then There Was X

Hey, yo!
Dog, I meet bitches, discreet bitches
Street bitches, slash, Cocoa Puff sweet bitches
Make you wanna eat bitches, but not me
Y'all niggas eat off the plate all you want but not D
I fuck with these hoes from a distance
The instant they start to catch feelings
I start to stealing they shit
then I'm out just like a thief in the night
I sink my teeth in to bite
You thinking life, I'm thinking more like—wassup tonight?
Come on ma, you know I got a wife
And even though that pussy tight I'm not gon' jeopardize my life
So what is it you want from a nigga?
I gave you, you gave me—BITCH, I blazed you, you blazed me
Nothing more, nothing less, but you at my door
Willing to confess that it's the best you ever tested
Better than all the rest, I'm like, "Aight girlfriend, hold up
I gave you what you gave me Boo, a nut!

Chorus [SISQO]
What these bitches want from a nigga?
What you want (what you want)
     What these bitches want from a nigga?
Really want
     What these bitches want from a nigga?
     I've been keepin' you up on it
     Bling bling'n, all that jewelry girl I bought it
What these bitches want from a nigga?
     Aiyyo, tell me what you want from me
     Baby tell me what you want from me!

There was Brenda, LaTisha, Linda, Felicia
Dawn, LeShaun, Ines, and Alicia
Teresa, Monica, Sharon, Nicki
Lisa, Veronica, Karen, Vicky
Cookies, well I met her in a ice cream parlor
Tonya, Diane, Lori, and Carla
Marina, Selena, Katrina, Sabrina
About three Kims. LaToya and Tina

Shelley, Bridget, Cathy, Rasheeda
Kelly, Nicole, Angel, Juanita
Stacy, Tracie, Rohna, and Rhonda
Donna, Ulanda, Tawana, and Wanda
Were all treated fairly but yet and still
Bitches is on some other shit now that I'm fuckin wit' Dru Hill
But I'ma keep it real
What the fuck you want from a nigga?
What the fuck you want from a nigga?

Chorus

Aiyyo, I think about when a nigga didn't have
And a nigga told a joke, and the bitches didn't laugh
See now I do the math, I see if you got this
And this and this to some cats, that nigga's the shit
And that's all they fuckin' with, but see these bitches don't know
If these bitches ain't for real, these bitches don't go
Knock on the door, no show, I'm sleep trying to creep
With yo' best friend, put it in, dig deep

"THE FUTURE," Dame Grease featuring DMX, Big Stan, and Meeno
Live on Lenox soundtrack

Running through niggas is how I do niggas
And two niggas got nothing for me
When they saw me, they looked the other way and tried to ignore me
I put holes, like foot holes, in niggas buttholes
Stomp a mudhole, when I cut hoes, the fucking blood flows
That was bustin' niggas wide, I was ten when I died
Now I'm walking dead with the infrared by my side
Keepin' niggas in line like a parade
Then they scatter like roaches when they get sprayed with Raid
Like a grenade, playing with spades is the plan
Now what part of 'suck my dick' don't you understand?
Better act like you know or get smacked like your ho
When you strapped, toe to toe, but can't strap with the flow
And I gets down for mine, with the crime

And if I gots to do time, fuck it
I don't mind
I handle my business and I shoot snitches
'Cause I know nowadays niggas is more ass than loose bitches
It's all good, I'm still out
Knock on wood, robbin' niggas like my last name is Hood
'Cause I could, go with that mob that goes out to rob
That mad scheme to get cream without the job
I house more niggas than a shelter
And if a nigga ever felt a heltah skeltah
It would melt away, 'cause the pain is too much to bear
Let the dead be dark while the dark is here

"COMIN' FOR YA"
And Then There Was X

Chorus
X is comin' for ya, can't do nothin' for ya
'Cause X is comin' for ya
Run, hide, duck, duck
We don't give a fuck, fuck
(repeat)

Look in the mirror, say my name five times
Turn out the lights and I done took nine lives
Don't get scared now nigga, finish it 'cause you started it
Watched it grow out of control, now you want no part of it
Nigga, where you heart at? Tell me what you made of
Already lost a stripe 'cause I know what you afraid of
We both know you pussy, but I ain't gonna say nuttin'
Just hit a nigga off and you can stay frontin'
I gotcha back for now, till I cased the joint
Plus, give the feds a real good place to point
We laced the joint, I ain't gonna front I had my hands full
Glad to be alive, but you like, 'That's that bull'
But now you know, what you get, when you fucking wit'
'Cause you shoulda left alone, now you stuck in shit

Duckin' shit, till that headpiece gets blazed
Screamin' this, ahh, cease to the grave
It's over, at least for you it is
It don't take the coroner to see how true it is
I knew these kids, but did that stop me from getting 'em screamin'
It was all for the money, while I'm hittin' and splittin' him down
From his nose to his nuts
Fire department coming to put the hose to his guts
Washed away, just like dirt when it rain
And now because of you, I hurt when it rains

Chorus

My real name is Damien and my girl's name is Carrie
That Poltergeist bitch is hot, but too young to marry
That nigga Satan be fakin' mad jacks so I taxed his ass
Every chance I get, is just another hit
Another nigga split; there go white meat—another nigga
Taking up room in the morgue under a white sheet
That's what you get for trying to take it there
But with this Desert Eagle in your mouth
You cryin 'bout let's make it fair
Sometimes it takes pain to make the brain a little smarter
When I think the rain will stop, it only starts to rain harder
Part of the game is niggas wanna become famous
And doing the same shit I do, remain nameless
I want house money, Jag money so I gots to bag money
I ain't laughing, but yo it's mad funny
I used to talk about that shit you got
But you ain't never got that shit when that shit get hot!
Runnin' up in the spot with two niggas from Israel
'Cause it is-real, you did squeal, now how you think you kids feel?
Knowin' you died a snitch, I look in yo' eyes and see a bitch
Wasn't surprised to see a switch
Let's make it quick, I got a flight at six going to Pakistan
So let this nigga know, I know he pussy, I'ma smack his man
Fuckin Willie niggas and silly niggas
I'd rather be eating off a plate
With all them Baltimore and Philly niggas
'Cause I done took about as much I can stand
A nigga smilin' in my face like they my motherfuckin' man
Aiyyo, it gets a lot worse, 'cause there's a curse
That says, the reward for being real is a hearse
Before you turn thirty, 'cause the dirty shit you did

Catches up and gets you right when you thought you slid
It's getting dark, and with the cold to the heart
You realize, you ain't gonna see your shorty
Old enough to walk, for real

Chorus

"BORN LOSER"
12" single

The born loser, not because I choose to be
But because all the bad shit happens to me
I got kids, but their mothers don't want them to know me
Sisters used to like me but now they call me "homey"
Used to have a family, now I'm out on my own
Had to scrap with a pit because I tried to take his bone
Bitches don't like me, they don't kiss me or hug me
They call me "kill pretty" because I'm mad ugly
I used to get pussy, but I busted off quick
Now I gets none so I gotta beat my dick
Times are hard in the ghetto, I gotta steal for a living
Eating turkey-flavored Now & Laters for Thanksgiving
If that ain't enough, life is rough I swear
I don't have an address so I can't get welfare
They kicked me out the shelter because they said I smelled a
Little like the living dead and looked like Helter Skelter
My clothes are so funky, they're bad for my health
Sometimes at night my pants go to the bathroom by themself
Even when I was little nothing went my way
I got beat up and chased home from school every day
And despite the fact I won all the spelling bees
On my report card, I didn't get A's, I got C's
But for those who choose to snooze
'Cause I was born with no hope, I got nothing to lose

The born loser, a title I was branded with
Went to Liberty Island, and got stranded with
The Statue of Liberty, but they didn't really have to

Leave my black ass there until the day after
No time for laughter, this shit's for real
Ribs are showing through my back 'cause I haven't had a meal
In a week, you can see bones in my hands
The raccoons beat me to the garbage cans
I'm starving Marvin, and it shouldn't be like that
The only thing that I'm carving is an alley cat
But sometimes in the daytime I dream of a Manwich
But all I'm really eating is an oxygen sandwich
For those that don't know, that's two pieces of bread strapped together
Or I'll have a rain sandwich, depending on the weather
Born loser caught up in the game
And I ain't even got nobody to blame

The born loser, yeah, that used to be my M-O
When I couldn't get a soul to listen to my demo
Doors shut in my face until I started jamming them
I'm behind the doors now and I'm the one slamming them
I did what I had to to get where I got
Though I'll admit what I had to do was a lot
I gave it a shot, and sometimes I had to shoot
Catching vics just to get a little loot
I thought it was cute and didn't care who knew
Mess around, get in my way and I'll bag you, too
'Cause I was born to lose straight from the beginning
In the dugout because I struck out the first inning
Winning was everything, that's why I had to
Ask my man to find the loot, and he said "I'd be glad to"
Now who needs a major label? We got our own
I'm the Divine Master of the Unknown
Ain't nothing changed, I'm the same as before
When opportunity knocked I just answered the door
Criminal at heart even though I don't show it
I was always a winner but I just didn't know it

"FUCKIN' WIT' D"

It's Dark & Hell Is Hot

What's on y'all niggas minds fuckin' wit' me?
Y'all know somebody has told you about fuckin' wit' D
Stuck in a tree is what you will be, like a cat
And I'm the dog at the bottom, lookin' up. Now what's that?
Your worst nightmare 'cause I take it right there,
You got niggas comin' where they at, right where?
I make 'em like air, floatin' away
Wouldn't tell me what he was thinkin' so I opened a way,
Went from broken away, you know he hurt before he died,
And you wonder if he lost his shirt before he died
Only two knew the answer and one of us is dead
So anyone who seeks the truth can get it straight to the head
Then you and him can discuss what I did
Yeah it was wrong, dog, but I slid
I'll repent one day, just not right now
You hear my shit all on the street, I'm kinda hot right now!
Come on!

Chorus
I don't give a fuck about y'all niggas
'cause y'all . . . ain't killing nothin'!
(repeat)

I wanna break bread wit' the cats that I starve with
Wanna hit the malls with the same dogs I rob wit'
Wanna be able to laugh with the nigga that I cried with
When it's over be like these is the niggas that I died wit'
What do you do when you find out in the hall there's a rat?
What do you do when you find out that your dog is a cat?
Shit! On niggas back, can't hold but two
So while you gettin' more gats I'm puttin' holes in you
The snubnose will do break 'em off real proper
Need to keep it spittin' and I ain't gonna stoppa'
Cock her, unlock her, let her go
Give it to his man just to let him know,
All things considered it was real for a minute
Got what was yours and tried to steal something with it
Now feel something hit it, your chest that is,
The best that is, is possibly the best that slid,
Yo, stress that kid!

Chorus

When niggas hear that dog bark, they better run
When police hear that dog bark, they better come
They expect the same in their lives and their lives will be lost
There is a price to pay, how many lives will it cost?
Since I run with the devil I'm one with the devil
And I stay doin' dirt so I'm gonna come with the shovel,
Hit you on a level of a madman whose mind's twisted
Mad niggas dreams caught the last train, mines missed it,
Listed as a manic depressive with extreme paranoia!
And dog, I got somethin' for ya!
Hear my name, feel my pain
Niggas wanna steal my fame, but first feel my reign
Know what it's like to suffer, never
Have enough of shit, starting off hard than only gettin' rougher
Tougher, but then came the grease
So if you wanna say peace, tame the beast!...

"I CAN FEEL IT"
It's Dark & Hell Is Hot

Sometimes, sometimes you just know, you just know, that's all

Chorus
I can feel it coming in the air tonight, hold on
I've been waitin' for this moment for all my life, hold on

The best of y'all niggas remind me of myself when I was younger
When it was hunger that stopped the nigga from goin' under
And you wonder, why I pat you on your head and smile
Look in your eyes and thank the Lord for my child
Meanwhile, there's something I gotta show you and I hope you can take it
Gonna leave you in the desert, and I hope that you make it
Gotta put you on your ass to see what it does to you
When you stand up and see that I'm just showing love to you
Other niggas would put a slug through you, over your ends
Cats I fucked with are real, but hey, those are your friends
It's just what you got coming sometimes you don't know

What you asking for, yet you ask for more
Shut the casket door. This one here, it is done
You thought you was a killer, you swore you'd never run
Nigga died with his gun still up in the holster
It's coming in the air. Yeah. It's gettin' closer

Chorus

I see life through many shades of grays and blacks
I could take that and hit 'em with the blazing tracks
When I make that you fake cats have violent dreams
Takes another dog to be able to hear my silent screams
The devil got a hold on me and he won't let go
I can feel the Lord pulling but he moving dead slow
Let 'em know that amidst all this confusion
Some of us may do the winning
But we all do the losin' it's just who does the choosin'
Easy goin' up or down.
What have you been proving, just that you a fuckin' clown?
Been seen through the bullshit, but never spoke on it
'Cause I know that deep down you really don't want it
I was traded the chance of being a child with a father
For a talent of being able to survive when it's harder
My balance on the high beams of life, keep my dreams in strife
That's why I hit these motherfuckin' streets tonight
Come on!

Chorus

There's a lot of shit that I let slide, 'cause it's outta my hands
A lot of niggas I let ride, but it's not in my plans
And a lot of my mans is not seein' through the fog
Families by the truckloads, fleein' to the morgue
Full moon, [arooooo], the howlin'
[grrrrrrr] the growlin', [shhhhh] the prowlin'
Don't know love, can't show love
That means you gon' need more love than an old thug, but hold up, roll up
Talkin' out the side of your mouth is what's gonna let niggas know
Why you died in your house
When they lied to your spouse told her it was suicide,
But you and I both knew the truth will never die.
Listen nigga, if you scared, get a dog, but be prepared for the morgue
'Cause you dead up in the fog, and that's your head by the log

I can smell it in the air, I can tell when it's there
This is hell and we both here
Can you feel it? Tell me yeah

Chorus

"RUFF RYDERS ANTHEM"
It's Dark & Hell Is Hot

Chorus
Stop, drop, shut 'em down, open up shop
Oooh, nooo
That's how Ruff Ryders roll

Niggas wanna try, niggas wanna lie
Then niggas wonder why niggas wanna die
All I know is pain, all I feel is rain
How can I maintain, with mad shit on my brain?
I resort to violence, my niggas move in silence
Like you don't know what our style is
New York niggas the wildest
My niggas is wit' it
You want it? Come and get it
Took it then we split it
You fuckin' right we did it
What the fuck you gon' do, when we run up on you?
Fuckin' wit' the wrong crew, don't know what we goin' thru
I'ma have to show niggas how easily we blow niggas,
Let me find out there's some more niggas, that's runnin' with your niggas
Nothin' we can't handle, break it up and dismantle
Light it up like a candle, just 'cause I can't stand you
Put my shit on tapes, like you busting grapes
Think you holdin' weight? Then you haven't met the apes

Chorus

Is y'all niggas crazy?
I'll bust you and be swazy

Stop actin' like a baby, mind your business lady
Nosy people get it too, when you see me spit at you
You know I'm tryin' to get rid of you
Yeah, I know it's pitiful
That's how niggas get down
Watch how niggas spit rounds
Make y'all niggas kiss ground, just for talkin' shit clown
Oh you think it's funny? Then you don't know me, money
It's about to get ugly, fuck it dog I'm hungry
I guess you know what that mean, come up off that green
Wild niggas on Ravine, don't make it a murder scene
Give a dog a bone, leave a dog alone
Let a dog roam and he'll find his way home
Home of the brave, my home is a cage
And yo, I'ma slave till my home is the grave
I'ma pull paper, it's all about the papers
Bitches caught the vapors and now they wanna rape us

Chorus

Look what you done started
Asked for it, and you got it
Had it, should have shot it
Now you're dearly departed
Get at me dog, did I rip shit?
With this one here I flip shit
Niggas know when I kick shit
It's gon' be some slick shit
What was that look for, when I walked in the door?
Oh, you thought you was raw? [Boom] not anymore
'Cause now you on the floor
Wishin' you never saw me walk through that door, with that .44
Now it's time for bed, two more to the head
Got the floor red. Yeah, that nigga's dead
Another unsolved mystery, it's goin' down in history
Niggas ain't never did shit to me
Bitch-ass niggas can't get to me
Gots to make the move, got a point to prove
Got a make 'em groove, got 'em all like oooh!
So to the next time you hear this nigga ryhme
Try to keep your mind on gettin pussy and crime

Chorus

314

"MAKE A MOVE"
And Then There Was X

Chorus
I gots to make a move and make it soon
I gots to take a block and make it boom
I take the car and hit it with this boom
Now come on, let's get that money!

It's two o'clock and I'm just about to hit the street
Till I knock off this rock I don't get to eat
Sometimes that's like that's the only reason why I hustle
Step on toes, strong-arm and show a li'l muscle
Ain't no real dough, that's why a nigga feel so frustrated
I hate it, seeing crab niggas that made it
And I'm robbin' cats just as broke as myself
Living foul and ain't lookin' out for my health. Where's the wealth?
Not in New York, 'cause niggas talk about going out of state
Money got an eighth, coming back coping a lot of weight
Where's my plate nigga? I'm hungry, too
So I'ma do like hungry do, and get a hungry crew
Niggas that ain't never had, and doing bad
Won't be mad to get up off that stoop looking sad
Grab your bags, it's about to go down
We going to this hick town, let's get the lowdown on how they get
    down

Chorus

I gots to make a move and make it soon
Gots to take a block and make it boom
We comin through so make some room,
Found somethin' that could be somethin' if I pump it up
This kid Black is the only thing that could fuck it up
The purple top? Thirty-five smalls a ring of games?
But I'ma crush him with the black 40 double-L's
I send two niggas back up top, and come back
We chop up rock, by midnight, we open up shop
It's four in the morning, we on the block creepin'
Killin' the cash, while yo' ass is sleepin'
Look here, I'm what they call a true hustler
'Cause nigga if I ain't know you since I was like six then I don't trust ya

And we'll bust you over something petty like a few dollars
Put something hot up in that ass and watch you holla
You think I'm here for the ho flow? I want the dough flow
And fuck the po'-po', nigga keep a .44

Chorus

I spend my money on niggas 'cause niggas get me rich
And a bitch ain't doin' shit but suckin' my dick
Niggas is family now, and we stand strong
Thirty niggas on six blocks, making the cash long
Shit is good, because niggas getting what they been wanting
And we see the same shit, other New York niggas frontin'
Stick up kids hunting but I ain't got no love for 'em
I keep the burner in the Dumpster with the glove for 'em
Them motherfucking knockers come at us and chop us
And I know they really trying to stop us and wanna drop us
So we pump, from the alley and the last house we use as a cash house
It's holdin 'em strong, it's a stash house
I got runners that work for twelve-hour shifts
And when them niggas keep they count correct, I don't riff
But I ain't tryin' to hear that nigga took your pack shit
Ain't tryin' to hear jack shit, fuckin' black bitch
I ain't a greedy nigga, all I want is a five-year run
If I don't make it, then fuck it, let me die near a gun
Got bitches to transport without an escort
I'm makin moves from D.C. up to Westport
Local police ain't a problem 'cause they don't even stress us
It be them ATF niggas that have you under pressure
Just so you know, ain't gon' never put my Glock down
'Cause I'm a hustling motherfucker, and I'm holdin' my block down

Chorus

"SCENARIO 2000 (JIGGA MY NIGGA REMIX)"
Eve, *Ruff Ryders' First Lady*

[DMX]
This is the darkest shit, sparkest shit
Hittin' wit' the hardest shit, 'cause I've always started shit
With kids I knew my fucking friends all turned against me
Said fuck it, bought me a dog ever since me and my dog has been like this
He got my back I got his, schemin' on mad niggas
That's how we do biz
It's about time to start another robbing spree
'Cause yo, my way is highway robbery
When I was up north, in Sing-Sing,
I was sending niggas home in a coffin livin' like a orphan
You bad nigga? I'll be back to see if you'll be still here
You know my style will put your fucking man in a wheelchair
He'll never walk again, on the strength of me
That's how I left him G, scared to death of me
Niggas cannot run, hit wit' the hot one
From the shotgun, caskets close, wondered how we got done

"WHO'S NEXT"
DJ Clue, *The Professional, Pt. 2*

When I creep through
Niggas is see through
Just like negligee
Ain't no talkin' 'cause there ain't much that the dead can say
Long as I'm walking I be strappin' my dogs
Rackin' the hogs
Desert Eagle packin' the morgues
Metal slabs with yellow tags on toes it's
What happens to those that
Chose to be foes and
Bet his man knows
But yo, we only get stronger
And the amount of time we're facing is only gettin' longer
Get the mayor on the horn!

317

It's time for shit to go down
Strapped for the show down
Wet up yo crib, kick the door down
Know you schemin' so I gots to get you first
Put you right up in a brand new hearse
Could be worse
Shoulda seen what I gave this nigga
Two vests couldn't save this nigga
The way I laid this nigga
Played this nigga
But that's what I'm good at
Layin' niggas out fightin' pits and fuckin' hoodrats
Where's my fuckin' 'hood at?
Cripple niggas like switches
Rip on niggas like bitches
Then pour niggas in ditches
They ain't found half the bodies that a nigga caught
Or should I say a nigga bought?
'Cause ain't nothing like gettin' paid for a nigga sport
Triple what a nigga thought
But that's just how shit be
I know that one day they gon' try that shit wit' me
But just as long as I'm on top of shit
You ain't stoppin' shit
And ain't a motherfucker droppin' shit

Chorus
If it ain't ruff it ain't me
If it ain't ruff it ain't D
M to the X
Most y'all niggas is straight sex
[Click] [Click] [Boom] [Boom] [Flat line]
Next?!

Chorus

Plenty of niggas know dirty is how I do 'em
Put buck shots from a thirty right through 'em
'Cause ain't none of y'all muh'fuckers built for war
And I lay down the law
When I spray down the door
Fuck around on my name will be 95-B-64-11
On a three-and-a-half to seven
When even up north I put niggas to waste

318

So you wanna stop the violence?
Get the fuck out my face!
Parole before peeps hit the board off
Bitches is fuckin' but I sleep with the sawed off
I got shit to do, rules to break, crew to break
Before the news to break, I got dudes to take
I don't joke 'cause Jokers is cards
And cards are what I pull
Infrared with the clip full
No leash on the pitbull
That shit is hot like the wax off a candle stick
But how I handle shit
Is to dismantle shit
De-de-de-de-de-de
Like Popeye when it's spinach time
Runnin' through two niggas like the tape at the finish line
What's your crew, gonna do when I put the pressure on?
And it hurts, wannabe gangstas in skirts
And the bitches comin' all out them niggas
One false move and their moms'll read about them niggas
And they wives'll be without them niggas
Matter of fact, I'm tired of talkin' money
Throw your joints up, scrap, bitch!

"TIME TO BUILD"

Mic Geronimo featuring Ja Rule, Jay-Z, and DMX, *The Natural*

[DMX]
I'm peeling niggas caps like oranges
Hittin' 'em in the head with two-by-four inches
I'm a grimy nigga so I like my bitches cruddy
My clothes dirty, dick shitty, and my knife bloody
I did too much dirt to turn back now
I'm the reason my li'l sister's smoking crack now
I'd feel guilty if I had a heart but I don't
To live a carefree life if I stop killing but I won't
It's in my blood to destroy mankind
With every murder I lose a little more of my damn mind
And I ain't got much left to lose, nigga, so don't snooze, nigga

I'm killing crews nigga, just pay your dues nigga
Respect my motherfucking style of rap
Murder your mic and your unborn child
This ain't wild just how niggas living on the street
A little something that can't be beat

"READY TO MEET HIM"
Flesh of My Flesh, Blood of My Blood

We each walk the path that you've chosen
Yes...

Chorus
I'm ready to meet him 'cause where I'm livin' ain't right
Black hate white, white hate black, it's right back to the same fight
They got us suspecting a war
But the real war is to follow the law of the Lord

Lord, you left me stranded, and I don't know why
Told me to live my life, now I'm ready to die
Ready to fly, I cry, but I shed no tears
You told me you would dread those fears, it's been years
Snakes still coming at me—just missing
Sometimes I think all you do with me is just listen
I thought that I was special—that's what you told me
Hold me! Stop acting like you don't know me
What'd I do so bad that it sent you away from me?
Not only sent you away, but made you stay away from me?

[Lord]
My child I'm here, as I've always been
It is you who went away and now are back again
[What did I say?] Follow your word, and be true
[What did you do?] Well, what I wanted to do
[What have you seen?] Darkness and hell at a glance
[What do you want?] All I want is another chance

Chorus

[Just because you went away, my doors are not locked
Wanna come back home? All you gotta do is knock]
You see I left home a boy, but returned as a man
Full grown, and I'm still not able to stand
[I gave you a hand] Well, but I was lookin' the wrong way
Figured out the plan, then I started to pray
And that prayer, took me from here—over there
Back to over here, now it got me like where
Do I belong, do I fit in?
Things on my mind, where do I begin?
It's easier to sin, but it hurts my heart
I'm really trying to win, so where do we start?
[Thou shalt not steal] But what if he stole from me?
[Thou shalt not kill] But what if he's tryin' to kill me?
[Thou shalt not take my name in vain
No matter how hard it rains, withstand the pain]

Chorus

I'm ready to meet him—our Father, who art in heaven
I'm not ashamed to ask for guidance at twenty-seven
No longer afraid to knock on your door
Not scared anymore to lose my life in the war
After what I just saw, I'm riding with the Lord
'Cause I really can't afford to lose my head by the sword
So now that I've seen what I need to see
Please take me where I need to be
[What have you learned?] It's better to tell the truth than to lie
[What have you learned?] To love my life until I die
[What have you learned?] Violence isn't always the key
[What have you learned?] You can't always believe what you see
[What have you learned?] It's better to forgive and forget
[What have you learned?] Give as you expect to get
[What have you learned?] That I can't go on without you
[What have you learned?] I must have been a fool to ever doubt you!

Chorus

"THE CONVO"
It's Dark & Hell Is Hot

You tell me that there's love here.
But to me it's blatant.
What's with all the blood here?
I'm dealing with Satan.
Plus with all the hating
It's hard to keep peace
Thou shall not steal, but I will to eat.
I tried doing good, but good's not too good for me.
Misunderstood. Why you chose the 'hood for me?
Me? I'm all right,
I just had to work hard at it.
Went to Grandma for the answer and she told me that God had it.
So now here I am. Confused and full of questions.
Am I born to lose or is this just a lesson?
And who it's going to choose when it gets turned around?
And will it be layin' in my own blood and on the ground?

[LORD]
My child, I've watched you grow up and I've been there
Even at those times you least suspected it I was there.
And look at what I've given you. A talent to rhyme.
I may not come when you call but I'm always on time.

Chorus
Somebody's knockin', should I let 'em in?
Lord we're just starting, but where will it end?
(repeat)

But when the funds are low the guns will blow.
Lookin' for that one that owe, make 'em run that dough.

[LORD]
No!
Put down the guns and write a new rhyme.
You'll get it all in due time. You'll do fine.
Just have faith 'cause you mine.
And when you shine it's gon' to be a sight to behold.
So don't fight to be old or lose sight when it's cold.
See that light down the road? It's going to guide you there
Two sets of footsteps, I was right beside you there.

[DMX]
But what about them times I only saw one?
Those were the times that I was under the gun...

[LORD]
It was then I carried you my son.
Led you to safety.
It just wasn't your time to face me

[DMX]
Ayo, a few of them times I thought you would erase me.
But all you did was embrace me.
Prepared me for the worst.
Offered me eternal light and scared me with the hearse.
And the curse turned to grace.
When the hurt turned to faith.
No more runnin' and slidin' in the dirt 'cause I'm safe.

Chorus

So if I'm your man, I'm in your hand.
What's your plan?
Never had a friend 'cause you couldn't trust your man.
Learned to stand before I crawled.
Things were twisted!
And if you showed me anything at all
Then I missed it.
Looked the wrong way, I've done some wrong things.
Kept a bad attitude, but that's what wrong brings.
And now you mean to tell me that after all this time,
It was You that kept the dog from going out of his mind?
It was You that breathed life into my lungs when I was born
And it was You that let me know what was right from what was wrong.
And it was You that let me do what I knew what could be done.
And it was You that gave me a good wife and a beautiful son.
And it's been You speaking to me inside my mind.
And it's been You who has forgiven time after time.
It was You who opened my eyes so I could see.
It was You that shined your light on me.

Chorus

"24 HOURS TO LIVE"
Mase featuring Black Rob, DMX, the LOX, and Puff Daddy, *Harlem World*

[DMX]
Twenty-four left until my death
So I'm gon' waste a lot of lives, but I'll cherish every breath
I know exactly where I'm goin', but I'ma send you there first
And with the shit that I'll be doin', I'ma send you there worse
I've been livin' with a curse, and now it's all about to end
But before I go, say hello to my little friend
But I gots to make it right, reconcile with my mother
Try to explain to my son, tell my girl I love her
C-4 up under the coat, snatch up my dog
Turn like three buildings on Wall Street into a fog
Out with a bang, you will remember my name
I wanted to live forever, but this wasn't fame

"GET AT ME DOG"
It's Dark & Hell Is Hot

Chorus
I'm right here, dog
Where my dogs at? (I'm right here, dog)
Where my dogs at? (I'm right here, dog)

What must I go through to show you shit is real?
And I ain't really never gave a fuck how niggas feel
Rob and I steal, not 'cause I want to 'cause I have to
And don't make me show you what the Mack do
If you don't know by now then you slippin'
I'm on some bullshit that's got me jackin' niggas flippin'
Let my man and them stay pretty but I'ma stay shitty
Cruddy. It's all for the money. Is you wit' me?
Get the bitches and I'll commit the crimes
And when it's on we transform like Optimus Prime
I'll form the head, roll out let's make it happen
If we ain't gonna get it wit' them we'll take it cappin'
Bustin' off, dustin' off on the softest niggas

324

Money with the biggest mouth, yo let's off this nigga
A novice nigga never made a sound
Breathe too fuckin' hard and you gettin' bust down

Chorus
[Sheek]
Y'all niggas wanna be killers? (get at me dog)
Y'all niggas wanna feel us? (get at me dog)
Y'all niggas want the real? (get at me dog)
(repeat)

Nowadays it ain't looking too good for certain niggas, I'm hurtin' niggas
What you doing? Robbin' niggas, jerkin' niggas
Stickin' niggas 'cause they deserved it; when money got murdered
They know he died slow 'cause they heard it
'Cause the nigga ain't blew up the spot a while
And the motherfucker ain't got shot in a while
It just takes a light up to fuck the night up
Blow everything in sight up, fuck around and I'll have your ass right up
You'll get mixed in some shit you wasn't able to stand
I got shit that'll disable a man with the wave of a hand
The days are longer and it seems like I'm facing time
I've got a lot of dreams but I'm not really chasing mine
I soak it all up like a simple fly
'Cause nowadays gettin' by is nothing more than an occasional meal and
    gettin' high
I live to die. That's where I'm headed
Let your man hold something now it's all about you can get it

Chorus

One in the back left your faggot ass face down
Lucky that you breathing but you dead from the waist down
What the fuck is on your mind? Talking that shit that you be talking
And I bet you wish you never got hit 'cause you'd be walking
But shit happens and fuck it, you done did your dirt
Niggas is wondering how the fuck you hid your skirt
Right under they eyes like a surprise to the guys
That one of their man was a bitch in disguise
Fuckin' with cats that order more hits and slaughter more kids
Let me holler at you young'n [hey yo!] Baltimore shit
YouknowwhatImean? I'm just robbin' to eat
And there's at least a thousand others like me mobbin' the street
When we starving we eat whatever's there

Come on you know the code in the street, whatever's fair
Bloodstains and chalk means your man couldn't walk
After the talk about him not being on the 11:33 to New York
Transforming ass niggas will get it quick
And yo, for real, that nigga K-Solo can suck my dick
And it's gon' take all these niggas in the rap game to barely move me,
'Cause when I blow up shit I'll have niggas fallin' like white bitches in a scary movie
[Aaah!] you know I don't know how to act
Get too close to niggas it's like "Protected by Viper, stand back"
What's this? I thought y'all niggas was killers, demented?
What the fuck y'all want me to do with this coward?
Finish him. Let's end it

"DAMIEN"

It's Dark & Hell Is Hot

Chorus
The Snake the rat, the cat, the dog,
how you gon' see them if you livin' in the fog?
(Repeat 2x)

Why is it every move I make turn out to be a bad one?
Where's my guardian angel
need one, wish I had one

[DAMIEN]
[I'm right here shorty and I'ma hold you down
You tryin' to fuck all these bitches I'ma show you how]
But who?
[My name is D like you but my friends call me Damien
and I'ma put you into somethin' about this game we in
You and me could take it there
and you'll be the hottest nigga ever livin']
That's a given?
[You'll see]
Hmmm that's what I've been wantin' all my life
Thinkin' 'bout my little man so I call my wife
Well your dada is about to make it happen
What you mean?

I'm about to make it rappin'!
Today I met this cat
He said his name was Damien
He thinks that we're a lot alike and wants to be my friend
Like Chucky?
Yeah, just like Chucky
Yeah Dada, looks like we're both lucky

Chorus

What up D
[DAMIEN]
[You a smooth nigga, I seen you
but nobody knew who pulled the trigger]
Yeah, you know it's always over dough
[You sure, I could've sworn it was over a ho]
Na, na that ain't my style
[Man you stay frontin' but you still my man
and I ain't goin' say nothin', got yo weed go 'head smoke it,
go 'head drink it, go 'head and fuck shorty
you know I can keep a secret
I'm about to have you drivin'
probably a Benz, but we gotta stay friends
Blood out, blood in]
Sounds good to me, fuck it, what I got to lose?
Hmm nothin' I can think of, any nigga would choose
Got me pushin' the whips, takin' trips across seas
Pockets stay laced, nigga I floss G's
For that nigga I would bleed, give him my right hand
Now that I think about it yo, that's my man

Chorus

[DAMIEN]
[You like how everything is goin'?
You like what I gave you?
You know if you was goin' down
I'd be the one to save you!
But yo I need a favor, these cat's across town hate me
Plus their behaviour hasn't been too good lately]
What!?! Anything for you dog
Where them niggas at?
[38th and Broadway]

327

Let me get the Gat
Run up on 'em strapped
Bust off caps on four niggas
Lay low for 'bout a month and kill two more niggas
Now I'm ready to chill but you still want me to kill
[Look at what I did for you dog, come on, keep it real]
Aight, fuck it, I'ma do it, who is it this time?
[Hey yo remember that kid Sean you used to be with in '89?]
Nah, that's my man
[I thought I was your man?]
But yo, that's my nigga
[Hey who's your biggest fan? Either do it or give me your right hand
That's what you said]
I see now ain't nothin' but trouble ahead

Chorus

"LOOK THRU MY EYES"
It's Dark & Hell Is Hot

Judge not, lest you be judged first . . .

Chorus
Look thru my eyes and see what I see
Do as I do, be what I be
Walk through my shoes and hurt your feet
Then know why I do dirt in the street

Burning in hell, but don't deserve to be
Got niggas I don't even know that wanna murder me
Just because they heard of me
And they know that the dark is for real
The bark is for real, when you see that spark it'll kill
Be pop pop, park it and chill. Take it over there walk wit' it
From Ohio to Cali to Baltimore back to New York wit' it
Come through flyin', up 1-2-9
Up to School Street 'cause I come through mine
Bark at my dogs, get at me nigga

[bark] [bark] [bark]
Get at me nigga!
What the deal is? Never forget what real is
The cats that used to say X is the best know he still is
Can't help feel this, putting goosebumps on your arms
Take it there if you want but I lose chumps with the bomb
It's the calm before the storm
Dr. Jekyll and Mr. Hyde and it's getting warm
Feel me, yo

Chorus

I can understand why y'all niggas is scared of me
And why the big dogs never wanted to play fair with me
'Cause I leave blood wherever I go, wherever I flow
Wherever I blow niggas who know I can go
Feel me, yo
What is it about the dark that gets niggas where they about to spark
About to bark?
Take it to the heart 'cause it's real like that
Give him chills, how do I make him feel like that?
Shit is real, what you don't know is gon' getcha
With the steel, what you don't know is gon' splitcha
I can blaze tracks, make niggas play racks and raise stacks
Payback's a bitch. Didn't you used to say that?
Play around in dirt you get mud
'Cause you know, I can either spread love or shed blood
And bloodshed turns the mud red and real sticky
Or I can hit you from the roof, make it a quicky, for real

Chorus

I bear my soul, niggas wouldn't dare, my role?
Gives a nigga a heart of gold but with a hole
Lost all control, my shoulders hold a lot of weight
Just like first I'm sold an eighth then told it's not an eighth
But then it's out of state, and it's too late for changes to be made
That's what I get for fucking with strangers in the shade
This is it, y'all niggas gots to give me a plate
For the same reason that fate chose to give me the weight
Take away hate, now I'm supposed to love the one that cursed me
The one that wouldn't give me a cup of water when I was thirsty
It was always him versus me, but now I got to teach him
Personal feelings put aside, 'cause now I got to reach him
What I'd like to do is turn my head, like I don't know him

But it seems like I've been called on to show him so I'ma show him
And if you've never met me, then you've no right to judge me
I've got a good heart but this heart can get ugly

Chorus

Feel the pain, feel the joy, of a man who was never a boy, for real

"A MINUTE FOR YOUR SON"
The Great Depression

You got a minute for your son, Father? I need to talk
I'm so tired of trying to run, Father. Let's take a walk
I'm so sorry for what I done, Father, it ain't my fault
But the devil's been on my back lately, he's like a hawk
You never give us more than we can handle, but it's getting hard
And I'm a strong individual, but I need you God
Lot of things that I used to, I don't wanna
Run the streets like I used to, I know I'm gonna
Speak the word for you one day
Up in there like, "Hallelujah!" on Sunday
I thank you Lord for the blessings that you gave me
And for my life with the blessings you have saved me
And for my wife you have carried me enough times—and that's the truth
Married me to rough times, throughout my youth
And through it all I saw that you was still with me
I was that one lost sheep and you was comin' to get me

Chorus
Lord you got me like . . . your love got me like . . .
Lord you got me like . . . your love got me like . . .
Lord you got me like . . . your love got me like . . .
Lord you got me like . . . your love got me like . . .

I look at life a little different now, since you hugged me
And I always loved my peoples, but now they love me
Thank you for the love, Lord, we praise ya
Jacob's descendants, from Africa to Asia
Bleeding the blood of Christ over our life
Wrong or right, just help us make it through the night and we'll

Shout your name in times of need
And times of joy, and when we bleed
And when we are overcome with greed
You ain't going to have to tell me twice, I'ma take heed
And because of what you've given me, I know you'll deliver me
And I won't drown no matter how deep the river be
You are the strength I never knew I had
Kept the heart good when they told me it was bad
All praises due to ya
That's why I had to dedicate something new to ya
Thank you, Father

Chorus

I never knew a love like, this before
Messing with the thug life, I missed it all
You opened the doors and, let me in
I'm down for the cause so, let's begin
Prayers that you give to me, I give to them
Same way you live in me, I live in them
Life is a blessing now
You got me smiling from inside of my heart, when inside it was dark
And it doesn't rain anymore, only sunshine
No pain anymore, I really love my
You washed away the tears with the fears
I'm happier than I've ever been in my life, the whole thirty years
You know that, one day I'll speak the word
You know that, when I do I will be heard
You know that, you gave me a permanent smile
And you know this Father because I'm your child

Chorus

"FAME"
And Then There Was X

Take it for what it's worth, my birth was a blessing
Sent to live and die, on earth as a lesson
We each have a star, all we have to do is find it

Once you do, everyone who sees it will be blinded
They'll tell you that you're bright, and say you have a future
When you turn your back, same cats'll try to shoot ya
Niggas ain't shit, I can live on both sides of the fence
Look at what you do, when you talk, see what you really meant
That's what I thought, them niggas was bluffing
They talk all day but say nothing
It gets so dark. The pain's so intense
Since this first rain it's like it's rained ever since
Never got paid for a rhyme but I flow
Never got a plate on time but I grow
Live your life, stay on the line but I go
Went from doing crime to being kind 'cause I know

Chorus
I'm gonna live forever, I'm never gon' die
Only thing I fear is that I'm never gon' fly
Carry my weight but I'm never gon' cry
Shit I tell y'all niggas straight 'cause I'm never gon' lie
(repeat)

What is about who I am that makes me unforgettable?
What it is about what I've done that makes it so incredible?
"Mo' money, mo' problems"—well the fame was worse
I reached out for love and what came back was thirst
Blessed with the curse, niggas don't hear me
Niggas don't hear me, y'all niggas don't hear me!
What'd I just say? "Niggas don't hear you!" See that?
You gots to feel me to catch what I'm sayin', believe that
But leave that alone
We gon' make a nigga wanna be at your home
Oh, you kinda quiet with the heat at your dome
If the dog got he's gonna bring back a bone
'Cause we got the chrome
This is what I live for, would die for
I'm the nigga with the high score, you try for
What you niggas wanna lie for? It changes nothing
I'm true for cats, it's some strangers bluffing

Chorus

Now if I take what he gave me and I use it right
In other words if I listen and use the light
Then what I say will remain here after I'm gone

332

Still here, on the strength of a song, I live on
No second-guessin' on what I stood for, I was good for
Stopping niggas from killing each other in the 'hood war
Coming through showing love, throwing love
Them cats not throwing up, you know wassup
Dark Man baby, that's my name
And I gots to be the realest nigga up in this game
'Cause ain't no shame, they don't make 'em like this no more
Real to the core, big heart but built for war
I stand for what I believe in
Even if what I believe in stops me from breathing
Relatives grieving but I ain't went nowhere
Listen to the song I'm right there

Chorus

"WHY WE DIE"
Busta Rhymes featuring DMX and Jay-Z, *Anarchy*

[DMX]
I see ghosts clearly, even though most don't hear me
They still wanna get near me, fear me, so I'm leery
Kinda eerie what I'm feelin', from the floor, to the ceiling
Straight through the roof, want the truth?
I kinda miss robbin' and stealin'
'Cause it kept a nigga hungry, only eating when I starved
I was ugly, so I robbed, no one loved me, shit was hard
Went to God once in a while when it got a little too hectic
He was the only one I knew that I respected
Didn't know why, didn't know what I was living was a lie
If I ain't shit then, why should I try?
See, plenty niggas die over dumb shit up in the 'hood
Real good heart, but up to no good
Thought I did what I could, but I guess it wasn't enough
The devil told me it would happen but I kept calling his bluff
When it rains it pours, now my pains are yours
As yours were once mine
Divine
Revolving doors

"PRAYER"
It's Dark & Hell Is Hot

I come to you hungry and tired
You give me food and let me sleep
I come to you weak
You give me strength and that's deep
You call me a sheep and lead me to green pastures
Only asking that I keep the focus in between the chapters
You give me the word and only ask that I interpret
And give me the eyes that I may recognize the serpent
You know I ain't perfect, but you'd like me to try
Unlike the devil who just wants me to lie till I die
Lord why is it that I go through so much pain?
All I saw was black. All I felt was rain
I come to you because it's you who knows
You showed me that everything was black because my eyes were closed
You gave me the light and let me bask in your glory
So it was only right that when you ask for this story
I put it together to do our dogs some good
Our dogs being brothers and sisters in the 'hood
Plenty of times you sent help my way but I hid
And I remember once you held me close but I slid
There was something that I just had to see
That you wanted me to see so I could be what you wanted me to be
And I think I've seen it, 'cause I don't feel the same
Matter of fact I know I've seen it, I can feel the change
And it's strange it's almost got me beating down your door
But I've never known love like this before
It's a wonderful feeling to get away from the pain
And up under the ceiling I get away from the rain
And the strain that I feel when I'm here is gone
I know real so I wipe away the tears with a song
And I almost lost faith when you took my man
Monty, Paso, and Jay's brother Dan
And I fear that what I'm saying won't be heard until I'm gone
But it's all good 'cause I really didn't expect to live long
So if it takes for me to suffer, for my brother to see the light?
Give me pain till I die!
But please Lord treat him right

"PRAYER II"
Flesh of My Flesh, Blood of My Blood

I thank you Lord for my birth, and everything that's followed
I thank you Lord for today, and I will pray for tomorrow
I thank you Lord for the love of my life and a friend
I made a promise—and I'm loving my wife till the end
I thank you Lord for your guidance, 'cause it's all that counts
And right here, right now? Lord, this is your house
I thank you Lord for a dream that came true to light
And I ask you to bless everybody in this room tonight
I don't always do the right thing, and I ask you to forgive me
'Cause I need you here with me
Without you in my life, it's empty
I think back how some people did me like violence was the remedy
And because I think of that now, I pray for my enemy
Not because of what I'll do, but because they don't know
There's something better after here but everybody won't go
So I ask you to forgive them, and we'll hope they see
And I thank you for the love that they've given to me
I will not abuse it, nor will I lead them astray
You see I love 'em like children that I see every day
And I pray . . . No, we pray together
If you get us through the bad weather, and we love you forever
Let your thought and my heart go hand in hand
I first thought "But to start?" But I stand a man
And for as long as I can, as long as you permit me
Please give me the strength I need to live
Bear with me
Amen

"PRAYER III"
And Then There Was X

Lord Jesus it is you who wakes me up every day
And I am forever grateful for your love
This is why I pray
You let me touch so many people, and it's all for the good

335

I influenced so many children, I never thought that I would
And I couldn't take credit for the love they get
Because it all comes from you Lord;
I'm just the one that's giving it
And when it seems like the pressure gets to be too much
I take time out and pray, and ask that you be my crutch
Lord I am not perfect by a long shot—I confess to you daily
But I work harder every day, and I hope that you hear me
In my heart I mean well, but if you'll help me to grow
Then what I have in my heart, will begin to show
And when I get going, I'm not looking back for nothing
'Cause I will know where I'm headed, and I'm so tired of the suffering
I stand before you, a weakened version of your reflection
Begging for direction, for my soul needs resurrection
I don't deserve what you've given me, but you never took it from me
Because I am grateful, and I use it, and I do not worship money
If what you want from me is to bring your children to you
My regret is only having one life to do it, instead of two
Amen

"PRAYER IV"
The Great Depression

Father God I am just learning how to pray, so bear with me
First I thank you for the life of everyone that's here with me
Then I thank you for the love you give me, why?
I don't know; I don't deserve it, and it hurts inside
Many nights I cried, and called your name out loud
But didn't call you when I was doing good, I was too proud
And still you gave me love, I wasn't used to that
Most of the people that gave me love, they ended up taking it back
That's something new to me, so I'm asking you for time to adjust
Let me make it there, I will be one you can trust
What I stand for, I put my life on, I DO!
I guess what I'm asking is—show me how to stand for you
And I will rap for you, sing for you, preach for you, teach for you
Reach for you—I will love you like you love me, unconditionally
And I will always be prepared, for whatever the mission will be
Give the nutrition to me, and I'll properly digest it

And when I give it back, I'll show you word well invested
And whenever I go, before I go, let me give
Thanks to you Lord, my birth, for every day that I've lived
You gave me a love most of my life I didn't know was there
In the name of Jesus, I give you my life 'cause you care

Notes

1. "Slippin'," *Flesh of My Flesh, Blood of My Blood*, 1998
2. "Coming From," *Flesh of My Flesh, Blood of My Blood*, 1998
3. Ibid.
4. "Dogs for Life," *Flesh of My Flesh, Blood of My Blood*, 1998
5. "I Can See Clearly Now," Johnny Nash
6. Unreleased
7. "Let Me Fly," *It's Dark & Hell Is Hot*, 1998
8. "Silver Shadow," Atlantic Starr
9. Unreleased
10. "Sesame Street," unreleased
11. "Heat," *Flesh of My Flesh, Blood of My Blood*, 1998
12. Unreleased
13. "Breakin' it Down," unreleased
14. "Coming From"
15. "Spellbound," unreleased
16. "What These Bitches Want," *And Then There Was X*, 1999, rerecorded
17. Unreleased
18. "Yonkers AKA Y-O," unreleased
19. "Can't Keep My Hands to Myself," Fat Larry's Band
20. "Once upon a Time," unreleased
21. Ibid.
22. "The Future," *Live on Lenox*, Dame Grease, 2000, rerecorded
23. "Dogs for Life"
24. "Coming for Ya," *And Then There Was X*, 1999
25. "Born Loser," 12" single, 1992
26. "Fuckin' wit' D," *It's Dark & Hell Is Hot*, 1998
27. "Niggas Can't Touch Me Kid," unreleased
28. "I Can Feel It," *It's Dark & Hell Is Hot*, 1998
29. "Let Me Fly"

30. "Prayer," *It's Dark & Hell Is Hot*, 1998

31. "Ruff Ryders Anthem," *It's Dark & Hell Is Hot*, 1998

32. "Make a Move," *And Then There Was X*, 1999

33. "Let Me Fly"

34. "Scenario 2000," *Ruff Ryders First Lady*, Eve, 1999, rerecorded

35. "Who's Next," *The Professional, Pt. 2*, DJ Clue, 2000, rerecorded

36. Ibid.

37. Unreleased

38. "Time to Build," *The Natural*, Mic Geronimo, 1995

39. Unreleased

40. "Dogs for Life"

41. "Let Me Fly"

42. "Coming From"

43. "Ready to Meet Him," *Flesh of My Flesh, Blood of My Blood*, 1998

44. Unreleased

45. "The Convo," *It's Dark & Hell Is Hot*, 1998

46. "I Can Feel It," *It's Dark & Hell Is Hot*, 1998

47. "Coming From"

48. "24 Hrs. To Live," *Harlem World*, Mase, 1997

49. Ibid.

50. "Get at Me Dog," 12" single, 1998

51. "Get at Me Dog," *It's Dark & Hell Is Hot*, 1998

52. "Damien," *It's Dark & Hell Is Hot*, 1998

53. "Look Thru My Eyes," *It's Dark & Hell Is Hot*, 1998

54. "Slippin'"

55. "Coming From"

56. "A Minute for Your Son," *The Great Depression*, 2001

57. "Fame," *And Then There Was X*, 1999

58. "A Minute for Your Son"

59. "Why We Die," *Anarchy*, Busta Rhymes, 2000

60. "Coming From"

61. Ibid.

Acknowledgments

THIS PROJECT BEGAN MORE THAN FOUR YEARS AGO WHEN I was the U.S. editor of *Trace*, a small British-based hip-hop and fashion magazine. It was the spring of 1998 and I was eager to get an interview with this new MC who had just dropped a single called "Get at Me Dog" that almost overnight had gotten every hip-hop head in New York City growling and barking and chanting "Where my dogs at?" But Gabrielle Peluso, DMX's publicist at Def Jam Records, regretfully told me that the artist had already built a reputation for not doing interviews. She could do me a favor if I really wanted to meet him, but she needed to let me know, as a friend, that "he doesn't like journalists." That only made me more interested and a few days later I was sitting in a Manhattan recording studio waiting for the Dog.

Producer Grease was there that night working on tracks for what would become X's first album, as was Darrin and Waah from Ruff Ryders. But it wasn't until four hours after my scheduled interview time that I got to meet the man who, over the next few years, would take me on a journey that would change both of our lives.

"Excuse me, dog. But I gotta watch *The Simpsons*," X said to me rushing into the studio's back room. More than a little embarrassed, Gaby kept apologizing for the time I had spent waiting, but it didn't bother me. There was more than enough atmosphere to take in, and, well, if the dude wants to watch a TV show, I thought, then I'll catch him during the commercials.

Muting the television during every break, DMX and I began to talk about his music, and surprisingly our thirty-minute stop-and-start interview turned into a three-and-a-half-hour conversation.

"You know I'm just starting to realize that I may have done some bad things, but I'm not a bad person," he told me that night.

Over the next two years, I would interview DMX three more times, each for cover stories for *The Source*, where I had become music editor. Every time we spoke, both he and those around him would be shocked about how "deep" our conversations would get and how well the two of us communicated. "Damn. You mean he actually talked about that with you?" It was then that we jointly decided to write this book.

DMX made a commitment to me to tell an honest story, and in return, I promised to treat his life history with the kind of respect and literary integrity that I believed it deserved. This was not going to be your typical celebrity biography. This was going to be the story of a man and a boy, the history of a family and a neighborhood, the portrait of the people and communities that X so passionately represented in his music.

In July of 2000, I joined him in Toronto, Canada on the set of *Exit Wounds* and, by the time we were finished, had rolled with X for the making of a movie, an album, a world tour, and the better part of two years worth of Earl Simmons's life's travels. There were trips to Philadelphia to see his father and trips upstate on vacation. Car rides, plane rides, and hazardous trips in the vehicles he calls "quads." There were times I spent with him and his family at home, evenings I spent with him and his crew in clubs and pool halls and restaurants, and the many late nights we chilled in fancy hotel suites just talking the night away.

Then there were the times he sent me out on my own to talk to (and sometimes search out) the people in his life he knew held meaning but for reasons sometimes purposeful, sometimes not, he had lost contact with. That's when I went back to Yonkers and first met his mother, uncles, brothers, sisters, and former teachers and counselors. I paid a visit to the group homes and institutions where he spent so much time to find former friends, schoolmates, and running buddies.

We knew we were done, not when there were no more stories to tell, but when the faith and trust that had grown between artist and biographer told us it was time.

There are many people to thank:

Arnett Simmons, for her courage to tell me the history of herself and her son. Her daughters, Bonita, who helped bring clarity to the memories of a childhood, and Shayla, who had the strength to remember those things she didn't want to. Robert, or "Uncle Pinky" for being similarly honest about the family's life in the early seventies and his sister Vern whose vivid memories of her favorite nephew were invaluable.

My first contact in Yonkers was Earl's uncle Collins or "Collie." Many days and nights he hosted my travels through the city, introducing me to friends and other members of X's extended family. He told me so much about their teenage years together that without his help much of my research into that era would not have been possible. His brothers Buzzy and Buckeye and friend Big Al were also helpful.

In Yonkers, manager Jack MacNasty was a profound resource for this story and being able to reunite him with his former artist was a powerful moment. Superior was good enough to let me view some of his old video footage of X he has stashed away that gave me images to match the words. Kason's mind is still as sharp as his legendary DJ skills, Big Jack (Grandpa) took me through Ravine and co-signed many of X's stories with the same passion. Hip's memory of two of the times X was almost killed were vital as was Bill Blass and his partner Cloud's memory of those legendary battles at School 12 and the Center.

Mrs. Gains still runs the Nepperhan Community Center with as much devotion to the kids as ever and she and her staff gave me a lot of insight. Miss Santos had a wealth of information about Earl's time at Children's Village as did Miss Moore and Aron, a former student. Officer Nizich was gracious enough to give me a tour of the juvenile units of Suffolk County Correctional Facility and thanks is due to the officers at the Yonkers Courthouse and City Jail for their candid conversation.

Being on the road with X demands a lot not only from him, but also from those around him responsible for making it happen. Many thanks to Kenneth Butler, who facilitated many of my first moments with X, Ali Samii, a friend to X and a personal assistant, Jap, Maurice, Skip (thanks for reading that early draft), Bo, and DJ LS-One.

Security has to roll with X even harder than I did and their help and support over the past two years was much appreciated. Ben, Mark (thanks for the conversation), Patrick (thanks for the pictures), Clay, Davin, and all the other local security guards in L.A. and elsewhere who held the man down.

Back at the office, Jazz Young has perhaps worked with X longer than anyone. Thank you for your memories and insight. Thank you Mel, Simone, Nas, Daniella, and Sheena. Thanks also to Faatimah Draughn, who made it fun to call the office, and Tashera's other sisters Shabazza and Sadiyah.

Thanks again to Gabrielle Peluso at Def Jam for setting up that first interview, Kevin Liles for his thoughts, Irv Gotti for his stories of the hungry days, Randy Acker, Jana Fleishman, and Lyor Cohen.

Many thanks also to Angelo Ellerbee, Brandon Himmel, and the staff at Double XXposure.

My conversations with producer Grease about X as an artist and musician showed me why their work together is so powerful. Thanks to Big Stan, whose eyes and ears were always open over the years, for not forgetting anything; PK for bringing me back to the Powerhouse days, Swizz, Loose, Ron G, Drag-On, and Eve.

Many thanks are due to Tiny from Ruff Ryders for letting me know how true ruff ryders roll, and of course brothers, Darrin and Waah Dean and their sister Chivon.

Agent Manie Baron bought this project for HarperCollins, and even though he didn't see it through publication, his help getting it started was crucial. Thanks also to my agent Loretta Barrett, Nick Mullendore, X's agent Marie Brown, lawyer James Walker, and Matt Middleton.

Thanks to attorney Murray Richman, who gave me a primer one afternoon about the New York criminal justice system and X's battles with the law, Londell McMillan, Cheryl Sharp, and Bonnie Berry.

Thanks to editor Josh Behar for sticking with and supporting a great project, Dee Dee DeBartlo, Dave Brown, Dawn DiCenso, April Benavides, Atticus Gannaway, lawyer Kyran Cassidy, and the rest of the staff at HarperCollins.

Many thanks to photographer Jonathan Mannion for giving us access to his archive of X material, and his assistant Alexis for pulling it all together. Thanks also to lensman Nitin Vadukul for coming through in such short notice.

Much respect is due to the folks who personally gave me support and friendship during this project: friend and writer Scott Poulson-Bryant, who's been an inspiration to me since I started my career (do you know your *Hi-Fi Q?*); Sean Sharp, my closest partner for more than a decade; Matthew Nelson; Daniel Soriano (who keeps pushing me onward and upward); Carlito Rodriguez; Riggs Morales; Kenneth Clark; Bobby Donaldson; Karu Daniels; and Norma Augen-blick. Thanks to my extended family: Carol Addison, Richard and Beth Luciano; my brother Daniel, his wife, Christine, and their three boys. And special thanks to brother-in-law and photographer-on-the-spot, Ennis Addison, whose focus on making a difference is truly inspiring.

Shout to *The Source* gang who were there when all this first went down: Selwyn Hinds (who assigned me that first X cover, or at least asked me to save the day), Dave Mays, David Curcurrito, kris ex, Michael Gonzales, Amy Linden, Akiba Solomon, and Frank Williams.

Thanks also to the North Bergen Public Library and New York's Writer's Room for giving me hours and hours of quiet space to work in.

Earl's father, Joe Barker, told me what he could, and for that I am grateful. This book would not have been as thorough without the help of his son, Joseph Jr. Thanks also to his wife and their other children, Patti and Jessie.

There are three people above all who helped make this project a success. First, Ray Copeland, who as manager and uncle to X was a crucial reason why I gained access to the worlds of Earl Simmons. His support throughout is truly appreciated. Tashera Simmons, Earl's wife, best friend, and so many other things, whose selfless devotion to her family is a remarkable thing to witness. Tashera, this story is also yours. And, Earl himself, whose courage and willingness to let me into his life was a remarkable achievement. You often said if we had met when we were kids, we probably would have become great friends. Well, I'm glad it happened now and it's been an honor to do this work with you.

. . . . .

Finally, I dedicate this book to my late grandmother, Lena E. Hartley, who continues to give me all the strength that I have ever asked for; my parents, Richard and Patricia Hartley Fontaine, who each in their respective ways have supported my life and my writing in more ways than they know; and to my wife, Stephanie, simply the best and most loving woman this world could have ever given me.

—SMOKEY D. FONTAINE
July 2002